THE LOEB CLASSICAL LIBRARY

FOUNDED BY JAMES LOEB 1911

EDITED BY

JEFFREY HENDERSON

AESCHYLUS

III

LCL 505

AESCHYLUS

FRAGMENTS

EDITED AND TRANSLATED BY
ALAN H. SOMMERSTEIN

HARVARD UNIVERSITY PRESS
CAMBRIDGE, MASSACHUSETTS
LONDON, ENGLAND
2008

Library of Congress Control Number 2008931944

ISBN 978-0674-99629-8

*Composed in ZephGreek and ZephText by
Technologies 'N Typography, Merrimac, Massachusetts.
Printed on acid-free paper and bound by
Edwards Brothers, Ann Arbor, Michigan*

CONTENTS

PREFACE

The Loeb edition of Aeschylus by Herbert Weir Smyth is
now more than eighty years old, and its translation is
couched in a pastiche version of the English of several centuries earlier. It was augmented in 1957 by the addition of
an invaluable appendix by Hugh Lloyd-Jones, updating
the Fragments section in the light of papyrus discoveries,
but no changes were made to the original portion of the
work. Aeschylus has long been overdue for a Loeb edition
that would provide a text based on up-to-date information
and a translation intelligible to the present-day reader.
This, following in the footsteps of the admirable Loeb
editions of the other great Greek dramatists by Geoffrey
Arnott (Menander), Jeffrey Henderson (Aristophanes),
David Kovacs (Euripides) and Hugh Lloyd-Jones (Sophocles), I have endeavoured to provide, together with annotation which, while remaining within the space limitations
necessitated by the format of the series, is somewhat more
generous than has hitherto been usual. I am deeply grateful to Jeffrey Henderson for giving me the opportunity to
do so; I wish also to thank all who have assisted me with information or advice, including copies of published or un-
published work which I might otherwise have overlooked
or found hard to trace. I am grateful to the School of Hu-
manities, University of Nottingham, for two semesters of

research leave in 2003 and 2006, but for which this project would have taken far longer to complete. I am happy to recall and acknowledge my debt to my teachers, especially Martin Lowry with whom I first read Aeschylus; to my Nottingham colleagues—I cannot imagine a more pleasant human environment in which to work—among whom particular mention is due to Patrick Finglass and to Isabelle Torrance, now of the University of Notre Dame, Indiana; and not least to my students, many of whom have contributed, directly or indirectly, valuable ideas to this edition, often without knowing it and sometimes, very likely, without my being consciously aware of it.

I have not in general been able to refer to studies which appeared, or came to my notice, later than the summer of 2007.

Alan H. Sommerstein
Nottingham, October 2007

INTRODUCTION

Following the practice of Weir Smyth in the first Loeb edition, and of Lloyd-Jones in the Loeb Sophocles (vol. iii [1996]), I have included only fragments containing at least one complete line, or two connected half-lines; I have, however, been somewhat more hospitable to papyrus fragments, so long as they preserve enough to provide a reasonable clue to the subject-matter of a passage.

The bibliographical information presented here on fragmentary plays is normally confined to "recent studies", i.e. those published since the appearance of *TrGF* iii in 1985.

The table of sigla given in the previous volumes is not reproduced, since in this volume, except in the case of papyrus fragments (where readings of the papyrus text are denoted by Π), sigla normally refer to mss. of the text in which a fragment is quoted.

When a fragment is given a second numerical designation in parentheses, e.g. "23b (= 23a)", the bracketed numbering is that of *TrGF*.

I very much regret that the richly annotated Spanish translation of the *Fragmentos y Testimonios* by J. M. Lucas de Dios (Madrid, 2008) reached me too late for me to do more than draw attention to it here.

ABBREVIATIONS

AJA	*American Journal of Archaeology*
AJP	*American Journal of Philology*
BCH	*Bulletin de Correspondance Hellénique*
BICS	*Bulletin of the Institute of Classical Studies, University of London*
CA	*Classical Antiquity*
CGITA	*Cahiers du Groupe Interdisciplinaire du Théâtre Antique*
CJ	*Classical Journal*
CP	*Classical Philology*
CQ	*Classical Quarterly*
CR	*Classical Review*
D-K	H. Diels (rev. W. Kranz), *Die Fragmente der Vorsokratiker* (Berlin, 1951–2)
FGrH	F. Jacoby and others, *Die Fragmente der griechischen Historiker* (Leiden, 1923–)
Gantz	T. R. Gantz, *Early Greek Myth* (Baltimore, 1993)
GRBS	*Greek, Roman and Byzantine Studies*
HSCP	*Harvard Studies in Classical Philology*
IG	*Inscriptiones Graecae*
K-A	R. Kassel and C. Austin, *Poetae Comici Graeci* (Berlin, 1983–)

KPS	R. Krumeich, N. Pechstein and B. Seidensticker, *Das griechische Satyrspiel* (Darmstadt, 1999)
JHS	*Journal of Hellenic Studies*
LIMC	*Lexicon Iconographicum Mythologiae Classicae* (Zürich, 1981–97)
MH	*Museum Helveticum*
PCPS	*Proceedings of the Cambridge Philological Society*
PMG	D. L. Page, *Poetae Melici Graeci* (Oxford, 1962)
Podlecki	A. J. Podlecki, "Aischylos satyrikos", in G. W. M. Harrison ed. *Satyr Drama: Tragedy at Play* (Swansea, 2005) 1–19
Prag	A. J. N. W. Prag, *The Oresteia: Iconographic and Narrative Traditions* (Warminster, 1985)
QUCC	*Quaderni Urbinati di Cultura Classica*
REG	*Revue des Études Grecques*
RhM	*Rheinisches Museum für Philologie*
SIFC	*Studi Italiani di Filologia Classica*
Sommerstein *AT*	A. H. Sommerstein, *Aeschylean Tragedy* (Bari, 1996)
TAPA	*Transactions of the American Philological Association*
Taplin, *Stagecraft*	O. P. Taplin, *The Stagecraft of Aeschylus* (Oxford, 1977)
trag. adesp.	*tragica adespota* (anonymous tragic fragments)

ABBREVIATIONS

TrGF	*Tragicorum Graecorum Fragmenta:* vol. iii, *Aeschylus* ed. S.L. Radt (Göttingen, 1985). vol. iv, *Sophocles* ed. S. L. Radt (2nd ed., Göttingen, 1999)
West, *Studies*	M. L. West, *Studies in Aeschylus* (Stuttgart, 1990)
YCS	*Yale Classical Studies*
ZPE	*Zeitschrift für Papyrologie und Epigraphik*

The surviving plays of the Aeschylean corpus are abbreviated as *Pers., Seven, Supp., Prom., Ag., Cho.* and *Eum.*; the poet's name may be abbreviated as "Aesch."

ATTRIBUTED FRAGMENTS

ATTRIBUTED FRAGMENTS

ΑΘΑΜΑΣ

Athamas, son of Aeolus, was a central figure in several myths, mostly concerned with the actions and fate of his wives and children. These were the subject of several tragedies, including three by Sophocles and three by Euripides. We do not know what part of Athamas' story was dealt with in Aeschylus' play; our only clue is provided by two fragments (frr. 1, 2a) which show that there was mention of a child (probably one of a pair) being thrown into a cauldron. This will refer to one or the other of Athamas' two children by his second wife Ino, Learchus and Melicertes. According to pseudo-Apollodorus (3.4.3, cf. 1.9.2) Athamas and Ino were driven mad by Hera for having agreed to care for the child Dionysus (whose mother Semele was Ino's sister): Athamas shot Learchus with an arrow, under the delusion that he was a deer, while Ino threw Melicertes into a boiling cauldron and leaped into the sea, taking the cauldron with her. In another version, preserved in the ancient introduction (Hypothesis) to Pindar's Isthmians, it was Learchus, after he had been killed, whom Ino put in the cauldron (presumably in the hope of restoring him to life—compare the story of Medea and the daughters of

1

τὸν μὲν τρίπους ἐδέξατ᾽ οἰκεῖος λέβης
αἰεὶ φυλάσσων τὴν ὑπὲρ πυρὸς στάσιν

Athenaeus 2.37e

2

ATHAMAS

Pelias), and it was only later that she was driven mad and leaped into the sea with Melicertes; but this was clearly not the version Aeschylus gave, since τὸν μὲν in fr. 1 shows that the boy who was boiled was mentioned before the one who was shot. In any case, the account appears to be a retrospective summary rather than a full narrative, and Aeschylus' play will therefore have been about something that befell Athamas after his loss of Ino and her children. The story about Athamas that was dramatized most often was that of the near-sacrifice of Phrixus, his son by Nephele, who eventually escaped with his sister Helle on a golden ram (Helle falling off into what became known as the Hellespont, Phrixus safely reaching Colchis). This story usually begins with a plot against the sons of Nephele by their stepmother Ino, but in some accounts (reported by a scholiast to Pindar, Pythian 4.288 [162]), the stepmother is differently named, and the mythographer Pherecydes (fr. 98 Fowler), a contemporary of Aeschylus, named her as Themisto—who is virtually always Athamas' last wife, after Nephele and Ino. Possibly therefore Aeschylus' play dealt with the Phrixus story but placed it after (and not, like most later accounts, before) the Learchus-Melicertes story.

1

One of them was swallowed up by a three-legged household cauldron, which always kept its place over the fire.

Referring to the fate of Melicertes or, less likely, Learchus (see above).

2

χαλκέοισιν ἐξαυστῆρσι(ν) †χειρούμενοι†

Etymologicum Genuinum s.v. ἐξαυστήρ

ἐξαυστῆρσι(ν) Dindorf: ἐξαυστῆρες codd.   χειρούμενοι
B: ὀρχούμενοι χειρούμενοι A: ἐξαιρούμενοι Dindorf

ΑΙΓΥΠΤΙΟΙ

2

Taking it out[1] with bronze flesh-hooks.

[1] Adopting Dindorf's emendation. It can hardly be the child's corpse that is being fished out of the pot; more likely the reference is to pieces of sacrificial meat.

EGYPTIANS

This was either the first or the second play of the Danaid trilogy (see introduction to Suppliants); *only a single word of its text survives.*

AITNAIAI

According to the Life of Aeschylus *(§9), this play was produced, during one of Aeschylus' visits to Sicily, at (or at least in honour of) the new city of Aetna, which was founded by Hieron of Syracuse in 476/5* BC. *Fragments of what is probably a hypothesis of the play are preserved in Oxyrhynchus Papyrus 2257; they reveal that, most abnormally, it had many changes of scene, the setting being successively Aetna (perhaps the mountain rather than the city), Xuthia (a district near Leontini), Aetna again, Leontini, Syracuse, and another unidentifiable locality— all of them places within Hieron's dominions. References to the play by Macrobius (*Saturnalia *5.19.16–31) and Stephanus of Byzantium (496.7–13) suggest strongly, though they do not conclusively prove, that the play told the story of a Sicilian nymph called Thaleia, daughter of Hephaestus (fr. 7), who was made pregnant by Zeus and then swallowed up by the earth—some say by command of the jealous Hera, others by the act of Zeus to protect her from Hera's wrath. The chorus of women of Aetna (or maybe rather of mountain nymphs, sisters of Thaleia?) may perhaps have been wandering across Sicily in search of her. In due time her twin offspring emerged from*

WOMEN OF AETNA
(*or* NYMPHS OF MOUNT ETNA?)

below ground and were named the Palici (see fr. 6); they became gods, worshipped (originally by the indigenous Sicels) at a lake in south-eastern Sicily (now the Lago Naftia). The catalogue of Aeschylus' plays found in some medieval manuscripts lists both a "genuine" and a "spurious" Women of Aetna; these designations are not found elsewhere, and it has been suggested that some time after the play was produced in Sicily, Aeschylus—or possibly his son Euphorion—revised it for production at Athens, and that both the original and the revised text survived at least into Hellenistic times.

On the question whether the "Dike play" (frr. 281a, 281b, perhaps 451n) was identical with Women of Aetna, *see introductory note to that play.*

Recent studies: C. Dougherty, "Linguistic colonialism in Aeschylus' *Aetnaeae*", *GRBS* 22 (1991) 119–132; C. Corbato, "Le 'Etnee' di Eschilo", in B. Gentili ed. *Catania antica* (Pisa, 1996) 61–72; G. Basta-Donzelli, "Katane-Aitna tra Pindaro ed Eschilo", *ibid.* 73–95; A. Ippolito, "De Aeschyli deperdita fabula quae Aitnaiai inscribitur", *Latinitas* 45 (1997) 3–12; l. Poli-Palladini, "Some reflections on Aeschylus' 'Aetnae(ae)', *RhM* 144 (2001) 287–325.

6

A. τί δῆτ᾽ ἐπ᾽ αὐτοῖς ὄνομα θήσονται βροτοί;
B. σεμνοὺς Παλικοὺς Ζεὺς ἐφίεται καλεῖν.
A. ἦ καὶ Παλικῶν εὐλόγως μενεῖ φάτις;
B. πάλιν γὰρ ἵκουσ᾽ ἐκ σκότου τόδ᾽ εἰς φάος.

Macrobius, *Saturnalia* 5.19.24

2 Ζεὺς ἐφίεται Camerarius: ζευσεφνεται P, ζευφευεται N
4 ἵκουσ᾽ Camerarius: ηκουσ codd.   σκότου Hermann (σκότους
Camerarius): στουσ codd.

ΑΜΥΜΩΝΗ

*This was the satyr-drama of the Danaid tetralogy. The
story behind it is told, with some variations, by several
later mythographers, notably pseudo-Apollodorus (2.1.4)
and Hyginus (Fabulae 169a). Amymone, one of the daughters of Danaus, was sent into the Argive countryside to
fetch water, and there attracted the attention of a satyr (accounts differ as to how this happened) who attempted to
rape her. She called for help to Poseidon, who appeared at
once, put the satyr to flight, and then himself lay with
Amymone; afterwards he created for her the spring of
Lerna by striking the ground with his trident. In the play
there must of course have been a whole chorus of satyrs,
and they can have been driven off (if at all) only at the end
of the drama; a series of vase-paintings from the late fifth
and early fourth centuries (see for example KPS, pl. 18a,*

6

A. So what name will mortals give them?

B. Zeus ordains that they be called the holy Palici.[1]

A. And will the name of Palici be appropriate and permanent?

B. Yes, for they have *come back* from the darkness to this realm of light.

[1] Etymologized as "Back-comers" (from πάλιν and ἵκειν).

AMYMONE

18b) suggest that at one stage—as we might expect— Amymone was besieged lustfully by the whole band, but that eventually Poseidon pacified them and the play ended with them joining in celebration of his union with Amymone. Echoes of the preceding tragic trilogy are evident, as Amymone, like her sisters, is placed by her father in a dangerous situation, is threatened with and resists forcible violation by an arrogant, shameless band of males, and is finally joined in an apparently willing union with an honourable suitor who becomes a benefactor of Argos; it may also be significant that in Suppliants *(1023–9) the Danaids are made to praise the rivers of Argos as givers of both vegetal and human fertility.*

Recent studies: A. Wessels and R. Krumeich in KPS 91–97; P. Yziquel, *CGITA* 14 (2001) 1–22, esp. 13–19; Podlecki 8–9.

13

σοὶ μὲν γαμεῖσθαι μόρσιμον, γαμεῖν δ᾽ ἐμοί

Ammonius, *On Differences between Related Words* 120; pseudo-Herodian, *On Incorrect Vocabulary* 3; *Etymologicum Gudianum* s.v. γῆμαι (310.21 de Stefani); Bachmann, *Anecdota* 2.375.8–10; Symeon, *Synagoge* 168

14

κἄγωγε τὰς σὰς βακκάρεις τε καὶ μύρα

Athenaeus 15.690c

ΑΡΓΕΙΑΙ

Fragment 17 shows that this play dealt with the aftermath of the expedition of the Seven against Thebes. It probably formed part of the same trilogy as Eleusinians; *it has been placed by some scholars before* Eleusinians, *by others after. Fragment 17, from a lyric lamenting Capaneus, tends to suggest that his body (or what remained of it), and those of his colleagues, were now available to be lamented over; if so, our play will have followed* Eleusinians *and presented the final return of Adrastus to Argos with the bodies of the Seven, Theseus having persuaded the Theban authorities to surrender them for burial. However, Plutarch (*Theseus 29.5*) seems to say that in* Eleusinians *Theseus gave Adrastus permission to have the Seven buried at Eleusis; in that case, a play set at Argos would most likely have preceded* Eleusinians *and dealt with the arrival at Argos of*

13

It is your fate to be wedded[1] and mine to wed.

Evidently spoken to Amymone, either by Silenus or by Poseidon.

[1] Cf. *Suppliants* 1047–51 "Whatever is *fated*, you know, that will happen . . . and this outcome, *marriage*, would be shared with many women before you."

14

And I <   >[1] your powders and perfumes.

Since Amymone would hardly have powdered and perfumed herself when going to fetch water, this is probably Silenus (or the chorus-leader, if the two were not one and the same) commenting on the fragrance of Poseidon, god of the aristocratic pursuit of horsemanship, here evidently presented as a luxurious symposiast.

[1] The verb will have had to be understood from the preceding line (spoken by someone else, very likely as part of a stichomythia).

WOMEN OF ARGOS

the news of the failure of Adrastus' original expedition, with the leaders being mourned in their absence. Epigoni *was probably the third play of the trilogy.*

The play is titled Ἀργεῖοι (Men of Argos) *in the medieval catalogue of Aeschylus' plays; the authors who quote the surviving fragments are divided between* Ἀργεῖοι *and* Ἀργεῖαι. *The latter is the* lectio *difficilior, and a chorus of women is appropriate for a play containing a substantial amount of lyric lamentation. Similar issues arise in connection with the plays here presented as* Lemnian Women *and* Women of Salamis *(qq.v.)*

16

καὶ παλτὰ κἀγκύλητα καὶ χλῆδον βελῶν

Harpocration χ8

παλτὰ κἀγκύλητα Scaliger: πολτα κἀν κύληταν A: ποτὰ κάν
κύληγαν B.   βελῶν M. Schmidt: βαλών codd.

17

Καπανεύς †μοι καταλείπεται†
λοιποῖς ἃ κεραυνὸς ἄρθρων
ἐνηλυσίων ἀπέλειπεν

Etymologicum Genuinum, Etymologicum Symeonis, Etymo-
logicum Magnum s.v. ἐνηλύσια; Photius ε921

2 λοιποῖς *Etymologica*: λοιπὸν Photius   ἃ κεραυνὸς
Welcker: ἀκέραυνος vel sim. Codd.   ἄρθρων M. Schmidt:
ἀρόρων codd.   3 ἐνηλυσίων Stanley (the lemma in all
sources is ἐνηλύσια): ἐπηλυσίων vel sim. codd.   ἀπέλειπεν
Pauw: ἀπέλιπεν codd.

16

And hand-held and thonged spears, and a heap of weapons[1]

[1] Presumably referring to the abandoned Argive arms heaped together by the victorious Thebans on the battlefield.

17

Capaneus is left to me[1] (?)
with the remnants of his lightning-stricken limbs
which the thunderbolt left behind.[2]

[1] The first-person singular pronoun may, as often, be used collectively by the chorus of itself, but it is also possible that the singer is Euadne, the wife of Capaneus, whose implausible appearance at Eleusis (to commit suttee on her husband's pyre) in Euripides' *Suppliant Women* is best accounted for if she had been a prominent individual mourner at Argos, her home city, in Aeschylus' play.   [2] In the attack on Thebes, Capaneus was killed by a thunderbolt from Zeus; see note on *Seven* 445.

ATTRIBUTED FRAGMENTS

ΑΡΓΩ ἢ ΚΩΠΑΣΤΑΙ

This play was obviously about the Argonautic expedition, but all we can say about it for certain is that mention was made of the marvellous beam of the ship which had the power of speech (frr. 20, 20a) and of the helmsman (T)iphys (fr. 21). Since the latter died before reaching Colchis (Apollonius Rhodius 2.851–860), it is a reasonable supposition that the play dealt with the early stages of the expedition, perhaps even with its very beginning (with Iolcus as its scene).

Since only five known Aeschylean plays had an Argonautic connection, one of which (Phineus) is known to have been produced together with plays on other subjects, it is likely that the remaining four—The Argo, Lemnian Women, Hypsipyle and Cabeiri—formed a tetralogy. The Argo has usually been put down as one of the three tragedies in this production, most likely the first. However, it then becomes very difficult to account for its alternative title.

This second title is found only in the medieval catalogue of plays, where it appears as Κωπαστής[1] (The Oarsman). This is an impossible title for a tragedy, and the emendation Κωπασταί is unavoidable. Even then, "oarsmen" is a

14

THE ARGO *or* OARSMEN

surprising description of a chorus presumably consisting of the noble heroes who manned the Argo, *and the title would fit much better a chorus of satyrs who, as often happens, are engaged in an unfamiliar, often menial occupation.[2] This would also make good sense of the context in which Philo quotes fr. 20: he says that the* Argo, *"being endowed with soul and reason, would not allow slaves to step aboard her". Very possibly the satyrs (who are slaves of Dionysus), attracted by the prospect of winning the Golden Fleece, volunteered to crew the* Argo *for Jason (perhaps not much to his liking) and were prevented from doing so by the ship herself (probably the speaking beam complained, cf. fr. 20).*

Recent studies: B. Deforge, "Eschyle et la légende des Argonautes", *REG* 100 (1987) 30–44 (esp. 33–36); D. Holwerda, "Zur Interpretation und Emendation zweier Aischylos-Fragmente", in H. Hofmann and A. M. Harder ed. *Fragmenta Dramatica* (Göttingen, 1991) 1–7, at 1–3; A. Wessels and R. Krumeich in KPS 204–5.

[1] So M: κωπευστής V: Κωπευσταί Welcker: Κωπασταί Hippenstiel.   [2] As in Euripides' *Cyclops* (where they are shepherds); on this common satyric theme see further R. A. S. Seaford, *Euripides: Cyclops* (Oxford, 1984) 33–36.

15

ATTRIBUTED FRAGMENTS

20

ἀνέστεν' Ἀργοῦς ἱερὸν αὐδᾶεν ξύλον

Philo, *That Every Virtuous Man is Free* 143 (not specifying the play)

ἀνέστεν' Holwerda: ἔνεστιν MPAQT: δὴ ἔνεστιν H (AN > ΔH): γ' ἐστὶν G: ἐν F: in most mss. ποῦ precedes, but AQT rightly accent ποῦ and take this as part of the introductory sentence (ὅθεν καὶ ὁ Αἰσχύλος ἐπ' αὐτῆς εἶπέ ποῦ·)   αὐδᾶεν Cobet (αὐδῆεν Hartung): δαπὲν (sscr. ο) M: αὔδασε (-σαι G) cett.

ΑΤΑΛΑΝΤΗ

ΒΑΚΧΑΙ

20

The holy speaking beam of the *Argo* groaned aloud[1]

[1] sc. when a slave stepped on board (Holwerda); that Philo's context requires the line to have approximately this meaning was seen by Radt (*TrGF* iii 135).

ATALANTA

A play of this name is listed in the medieval catalogue, but it is nowhere else quoted or referred to, and we have no way of telling which of the various stories about Atalanta it presented; it is perhaps most likely, though, that the play had to do with her participation in the Calydonian Boar Hunt, a famous heroic episode not otherwise known to have formed the subject of any complete play of Aeschylus (though compare Libation-Bearers *602–612, on the death of Meleager).*

BACCHAE

This play is known only from its inclusion in the medieval catalogue of plays and from a single citation by Stobaeus (see below), and it may have been identical with one of the better-attested Dionysiac plays such as Bassarids, Wool-carders *or* Pentheus *(qq.v.) The one surviving fragment would suit any play about the punishment of an enemy of Dionysus.*

22

τό τοι κακὸν ποδῶκες ἔρχεται βροτοῖς
καὶ τἀμπλάκημα τῷ περῶντι τὴν θέμιν

Stobaeus 1.3.26–27; Theophilus of Antioch, *To Autolycus* 2.37
(Theophilus does not name the play)

ΒΑΣΣΑΡΙΔΕΣ

*This was the second play of the Thracian or Lycurgus
tetralogy, following* Edonians *and preceding* Youths *and
the satyr-drama* Lycurgus. *It is known from the* Catasterisms *of pseudo-Eratosthenes (§24; see West, Studies 33–
36) that the play dealt with the death of Orpheus at the
hands of Thracian women, who in this version, unusually,
are devotees of Dionysus, called Bassarids. "Orpheus," we
are told, "after going down to Hades in quest of his wife
and seeing what things were like there, ceased to honour
Dionysus, by whom he had been glorified, and regarded
the Sun (whom he also called Apollo) as the greatest of the
gods; he would rise before daybreak and await the sunrise
on the [Thracian] mountain called Pangaeum, so as to be
the first to see the Sun. Dionysus was angry at this and sent
against him the Bassarids (as the tragic poet Aeschylus
says), who tore him in pieces and scattered his limbs far
and wide; but the Muses collected them together and buried him at the place called Leibethra [in Macedonia]." It
has been persuasively argued that Aeschylus' story reflects
a rivalry between the Pythagorean sect (whose most vener-*

18

22

Evil, you see, comes swiftly upon mortals: the offence
comes home to him who breaks the bounds of right.

BASSARIDS

*ated deity was Apollo) and Dionysiac mystery-cults, which
both claimed Orpheus as their prophet, and that the Dio-
nysus-Apollo conflict provided the overarching theme of
the whole trilogy, ending (in Youths) with the firm establishment in Thrace of cults of both gods. Like Edonians
(q.v.), this play clearly served in part as a model for Euripides' Bacchae.*

The play is sometimes cited as Βασσαρίδες *and sometimes as* Βασσάραι: *the manuscripts of pseudo-Eratosthenes are divided between the two forms. In Edonians (fr.
59) Aeschylus uses the word* βασσάρα *in reference to a
garment, so it is perhaps more likely that he called the
Thracian women by the longer name.*

Recent studies: West, Studies 26–50, esp. 32–46; F. Jouan, "Dio-
nysos chez Eschyle", Kernos 5 (1992) 71–86, esp. 74–75; M. Di
Marco, "Dioniso ed Orfeo nelle Bassaridi di Eschilo", in
A. Masaracchia ed. Orfeo e l'orfismo (Rome, 1993) 101–153;
C. Marcaccini, "Considerazioni sulla morte di Orfeo in Thracia",
Prometheus 21 (1995) 241–252; R. A. S. Seaford, "Mystic light in
Aeschylus' Bassarai", CQ 55 (2005) 602–6.

23 (= 23.1 + *trag. adesp*. 144)

ὁ ταῦρος δ' ἔοικεν κυρίξειν· τίν' ἄκραν,
τίν' ἀκτάν, τίν' ὕλαν δράμω; ποῖ πορευθῶ;

Hephaestion, *Handbook of Metre* 13.8 (line 1; ascribed to this play by Choeroboscus *ad loc*. [p. 249.4 Consbruch]); Dionysius of Halicarnassus, *On Composition* 17 (line 2); combined by R. Kannicht, *Hermes* 85 (1957) 285–291.

1 κυρίξειν Turnebus: κηρύξειν Heph.^A: κυρίζειν Heph.^I: κυρίζει Choer.^U: κερίζειν Choer.^K   τίν' ἄκραν Kannicht (who preferred, however, to treat the phrase as merely a corrupt doublet of τίν' ἀκτάν): τίν' ἀρχὰν codd.

23a (= 23.2 + 341)

φθάσαντος δ' ἐπ' ἔργοις προπηδήσεται †νιν†
ὁ κισσεὺς ἀπόλλων, ὁ Βακχεύς, ὁ μάντις

Hephaestion *loc. cit*. (line 1, following on directly from fr. 23.1); Macrobius, *Saturnalia* 1.18.6 (line 2); combined by West, *Studies* 46.

1 νιν codd.: νῦν West   2 Βακχεύς, ὁ μάντις Nauck: BAXIOCOMANTIC F: BAKCIOCOMANTIC BVZ: KABAIO-COMANTIC NDP: BA (only) R: βακχειόμαντις Ellis

23

The bull[1] seems about to charge me! What peak,
what shore, what wood can I flee to? Where can I go?[2]

Doubtless Orpheus, driven mad by Dionysus.

[1] Cf. Euripides, *Bacchae* 618–622 (Pentheus tries to tie up a bull, thinking he has captured the priest who is in fact Dionysus), 920–2 (Pentheus, looking at the priest, sees him as a bull). [2] The metre is, appropriately, bacchiac (based on the unit ∪– –).

23a

Though he has got a start, the ivy-crowned destroyer,[1]
the Bacchic god, the seer, will now(?) leap forth upon
him for his crimes[2]

[1] Punning on a popular etymology of Ἀπόλλων, as Cassandra does in *Agamemnon* 1080–2: Dionysus, whom Orpheus has rejected, is in this sense more truly his "Apollon" than the god he now worships who actually bears that name. [2] The metre is again bacchiac, and this fragment, whose first line is quoted by Hephaestion directly after the first line of fr. 23, was almost certainly part of the same lyric sequence, probably sung by the chorus after Orpheus has fled from the scene. Evidently, as in Euripides' *Bacchae*, the chorus are a group of bacchants distinct from those who actually kill the central figure; this moment in the play will correspond to *Bacchae* 977–1023.

23b (= 23a)

Παγγαίου γὰρ ἀργυρήλατοι
πρῶνες τότ᾽ ἀστράψουσι πευκᾶεν σέλας

Scholia (cod. V) to [Euripides], *Rhesus* 922

1–2 ἀργυρήλατοι πρῶνες Rabe: ἀργυρήλατον πρῶν᾽ ες
cod.   2 τότ᾽ ἀστράψουσι West (τότ᾽ already Croenert): τὸ
τῆς ἀστραπῆς cod.

24

σκάρφει παλαιῷ κἀπιβωμίῳ ψόλῳ

Scholia to Nicander, *Theriaca* 288

ΓΛΑΥΚΟΣ

This was the title of two Aeschylean plays about two persons of the same name, Glaucus the Sea-god *and* Glaucus of Potniae, *which are dealt with separately below. Some of the surviving fragments are quoted with a full play-title, others simply from* Glaucus; *most of the latter can be confidently assigned to one play or the other on the basis of their content or of what is said about them by the quoting author, but there is one (fr. 25a) about which it has generally not been thought possible to reach a firm decision. In this volume I have followed Radt in printing it separately without assigning it to either of the two plays, but I have elsewhere argued (in the article cited below, and more*

GLAUCUS

23b

For the silvered peaks of Pangaeum[1] will flash like light-
ning with the gleam of pine-torches.

[1] The region of Mount Pangaeum was noted for its gold and
silver mines (cf. Herodotus 7.112; [Euripides], *Rhesus* 921, 970).

24

With old wood-chips and soot from the altar.[1]

[1] Perhaps ingredients for some concoction to be used in a
ritual.

GLAUCUS

briefly in the Introduction to Persians *[vol. i]) that it comes
from* Glaucus of Potniae, *which was produced together
with* Persians, *and that its reference to Himera in Sicily
indicates that the play contained a prophecy, probably
by Poseidon, of the victory gained there in 480—on the
same day as the battle of Salamis, or so it was believed
(Herodotus 7.166)—by Gelon of Syracuse over the Carthaginians.*

Recent studies: A. H. Sommerstein, "La tetralogia di Eschilo sulla
guerra persiana", forthcoming in *Dioniso* n.s. 7 (2008) (English
version forthcoming in J. Davidson and D. Rosenbloom ed. *Greek
Drama IV* [London]).

25a

καλοῖσι λουτροῖς ἐκλελουμένος δέμας
εἰς ὑψίκρημνον Ἱμέραν ἀφικόμην

Scholia to Pindar, *Pythian* 1 [79] 153.

1 ἐκλελουμένος Heyne: ἐκλέλουμαι codd.   2 εἰς codd.:
εἶθ' Burzacchini   Ἱμέραν Heyne: Ἱμέραν δ' codd.

ΓΛΑΥΚΟΣ ΠΟΝΤΙΟΣ

*The Glaucus of this play was a fisherman of Anthedon, on
the Boeotian shore of the Euripus facing Euboea. Having
caught and landed a fish, he threw it on some grass; it ate
the grass and came back to life. Glaucus then ate the grass
himself, leaped into the sea and became a sea-god with prophetic powers. See Pausanias 9.22.7; Ovid,* Metamorphoses *13.917–965; and the scholia to Euripides,* Orestes *364
and to Lycophron,* Alexandra *754. It is not clear how the
story was given dramatic shape; since Glaucus was a character after his transformation (fr. 29), it probably had a
seashore setting. In the papyrus fragment 25e a countryman, probably an oxherd, seems to be reporting the first
appearance of the new god in the waters of the Euripus;*

GLAUCUS THE SEA-GOD

25a

Having thoroughly washed myself in its fair streams,[1]
I came to Himera on its high cliffs.

[1] i.e. those of the river Himeras.

GLAUCUS THE SEA-GOD

according to Plato (Republic *611c-d*) *he was almost unrecognizable because his body had been battered by the wave and covered with stones, seaweed and shellfish (cf. fr. 34). Glaucus himself will have come on stage in a later scene, and his appearance will presumably have answered to this description. This grotesquerie, the theme of revivification and immortality, and the apparent absence of any tragically sinister plot-features, have suggested to many that this was a satyr-play, and this would be confirmed by the appearance of the untragic word* θηρίον *in fr. 26 if we could be sure that its text was sound.*

Recent study: A. Wessels and R. Krumeich in KPS 125–130; Podlecki 12.

25d

[*remains of one line*]

XOPOΣ (?)

2 φοιτ[.... (?)]δειπ .[
   ἐνιςπ[...]ων τιςς[

BOYKOΛOΣ (?)

   ςτῆςον[..]. [.]μαπρο[
5 οὐ γὰ[ρ μύ]ωπες οὐδ[
   ἀνδρ[ῶν γε]ραιῶν ..[

XOPOΣ

[*remains of four lines*]
11   ]ουθ' ἱππ[
    [*remains of one line*]

Oxyrhynchus Papyrus 2255 fr. 12 column II (left side of text) +
fr. 13 (right side).

4 ςτῆσ[ον τὸ] ῥ[ῆ]μα Snell   5, 6 suppl. Snell

GLAUCUS THE SEA-GOD

25d

On this scanty papyrus fragment, it is possible to read four to six letters from the beginning of each of five consecutive lines, and one to six letters from the middle of about eleven lines; change of speaker is marked twice, and at line 7 the speaker label "Chorus" appears. The other speaker may well be the oxherd who is the speaker in fr. 25e. From the chorus's first utterance the only certain word is Tell *(3), but from the other speaker's reply it is evident that they are expressing scepticism about the reliability of his story. The skeleton of his reply appears to be* Stop what you're saying! *(4) . . . For the* [eyes?] *of old men are not short-sighted nor . . . (5–6). In the next few lines, spoken by the chorus, no word can be made out, but in line 11 we find* nor *followed by some word connected with horses. It may be added that in the left margin, opposite line 5, stands a note explaining the name* Euripus *(fr. 25c), which presumably appeared in the (lost) preceding column.*

25e

ΒΟΤΚΟΛΟΣ

....]αυτα μωρο[

.....]τιν' ἢ θύελ[λαν

......]. παύρουϲ[

....] μὲν ἴϲθι ϲ[

5 τούτ]ων δ' ἔτ' ἐϲτὶ π[ι]ϲτιϲ ὀμμά[των ϲαφής

οὐκ ἀ]μβλυώϲϲων οὐδὲ μὰψ αὔ[τωϲ βλέπων

ἤθρη]ϲα δεῖμα καὶ περιϲπε..[

ἴϲθ'] ὡϲ ἄγραυλόϲ τ' εἰμὶ κἀπιχ[ώριος,

ἀεὶ θ]αμίζων τῇδε Χαλκίδο[ϲ πέραν

10 Μεϲϲ]απίου τ' ἄφυλλον ὑψηλὸ[ν λέπαϲ

....]ναπι ... βουϲὶ φορ[βάϲιν

ἔνθ]εν κατεῖδον θαῦμα .[

Εὐβοΐδα καμπὴν ἀμφὶ Κηναίου Διὸϲ

ἀκτὴν κατ' αὐτὸν τύμβον ἀθλίου Λίχα

15 κάμπτο]νθ' ἅπερ τέθριππον [

Oxyrhynchus Papyrus 2159; Strabo 10.1.9 (lines 13–14)

2 e.g. [ζάλην] τιν' (Görschen) or [τυφῶ] τιν' (Radt) 4 e.g.
[ἐμὸν] μὲν ἴϲθι σ[ῶμα (Siegmann) γηρᾶϲαν χρόνῳ] (Sommerstein) 5 [τούτ]ων Sommerstein, π[ί]ϲτιϲ Lobel, ὀμμά[των
ϲαφής] Cantarella 6 [οὐκ] Diggle, αὔ[τωϲ βλέπων] Siegmann 7 [ἤθρη]ϲα Siegmann 8 [ἴϲθ'] Sommerstein
([οἶϲθ'] Page), κἀπιχώριοϲ Siegmann, Cantarella 9 [ἀεὶ
θ]αμίζων Cantarella, Χαλκίδο[ϲ πέραν] Lloyd-Jones
10 suppl. Fraenkel 11 φορ[βάϲιν] Görschen 12 [ἔνθ]εν
Görschen 13]ιδα — κηνα[Π 14]ν κατ —
τυμβον αθ[Π αὐτὸν Strabo[nxq]: αὐτὴν Π Strabo[BCD]
15 [κάμπτο]νθ' ἅπερ Diggle:]ντ' απερ Π

25e

OXHERD

. . . fool(ish) [. . .]
. . . a [gust/whirlwind (?)] or a squall [. . .]
. . . a few [. . .]
I tell you that while my [body has aged with the years,]
I still have [reliable] evidence from my eyes for [this]: I
was [not] dim-sighted, nor [looking] vainly [at emptiness,]
when I [beheld] something fearful and . . . [. . . Know] that
I am a countryman, a native of this region, [who always]
frequents [the parts facing] Chalcis[1] hereabouts and the
lofty, leafless [crags] of [Mess]apium[2] [. . .] . . . for my
gra[zing] cattle. From [there[3]] I saw something astonish-
ing, [a . . . round]ing the extremity[4] of Euboea like a four-
horse chariot, off the shore sacred to Zeus Cenaeus, right
by the tomb of the unfortunate Lichas[5] [. . .

---

[1] Cf. *Agamemnon* 190 (referring to Aulis).   [2] See on *Agamemnon* 293.   [3] Probably from the heights of Messapium;
he would need to be in an elevated position to see all the way to
Cape Cenaeum, at the extreme western tip of Euboea, some 60
km away.   [4] lit. "turning-post", as if the long, narrow island
of Euboea were the spine of a race-track.   [5] The herald of
Heracles, whom the hero in his agony threw over the cliffs after
putting on the poisoned robe which Lichas had brought him from
his wife Deianeira; see Sophocles, *Trachinian Maidens* 772–782.
The mountain and the cape, and a village between them, still bear
Lichas' name today.

26

ἀνθρωποειδὲς θηρίον †ὕδατι συζῶν†

Phrynichus, *Praeparatio Sophistica* p. 6.1 de Borries; Photius, *Lexicon* α1981 (ἐπὶ τοῦ Γλαύκου (τοῦ) ἀναφανέντος ἐκ τῆς θαλάσσης· Αἰσχύλος)

ὕδατι συζῶν codd.: συζῶν ἁλί Heimsoeth

27

δαῦλος δ' ὑπήνη καὶ γενειάδος πυθμήν

Etymologicum Genuinum and *Etymologicum Magnum* s.v. Δαυλίς (Αἰσχύλος); *Et.Gen.* s.v. δαῦλος (παρ' Αἰσχύλῳ); Eustathius on *Iliad* 2.520 (Αἰσχύλος); cf. Pausanias 10.4.7 Αἰσχύλον τὰ Γλαύκου τοῦ Ἀνθηδονίου γένεια ὑπήνην ὠνομακέναι δαῦλον

δ' Eustathius: om. cett.

28

ὁ τὴν ἀείζων ἄφθιτον πόαν φαγών

Anecdota Bekkeri 1.347.20; Photius, *Lexicon* α409

29

ΓΛΑΥΚΟΣ

καὶ γεύομαί πως τῆς ἀειζώου πόας

Anecdota Bekkeri 1.347.25; Photius, *Lexicon* α409 (both Αἰσχύλος); cf. Athenaeus 15.679a τῆς ἀειζώου βοτάνης, ἧς ὁ Ἀνθηδόνιος ἐκεῖνος δαίμων ἐμφορηθεὶς ἀθάνατος †πάλιν ἥτις† γέγονε.[1]

26

A beast that looks like a man, living in the water

27

His moustache, and the bottom of his beard, were shaggy

Both these lines are very probably from the oxherd's narrative.

28

He who ate the grass that gives undying, eternal life

29

GLAUCUS

And I somehow tasted the grass that gives everlasting life.

---

[1] Scholiasts on Lycophron (*Alexandra* 754) and on Aelius Aristeides (*Oration* 3.301 [p.248 Frommel]) also speak of the grass that Glaucus ate as ἀείζωος in the unusual sense of "conferring [rather than 'possessing'] eternal life".

31

κἄπειτ᾽ Ἀθήνας Διάδας παρεκπερῶν

Life of Aratus 1 p. 77.5–6 Maass = p. 7.8 Martin

Διάδας παρεκπερῶν (παρὲκ περῶν) Scaliger: δαΐδας παρ᾽ ἐκ περσῶν cod.

ΓΛΑΥΚΟΣ ΠΟΤΝΙΕΥΣ

Glaucus of Potniae (a town about 2 km south of Thebes) was famous for having been devoured by his own mares during the chariot-race at the funeral games for Pelias. Our sources give various explanations of how this came to happen, which are not necessarily incompatible. The fourth-century scholar Asclepiades, in his Tales Told in Tragedy (Τραγῳδούμενα: FGrH 12 F 1), said that Glaucus had reared the mares on human flesh, to make them fiercer in war, and that they turned on him when they ran short of this food; his source was almost certainly Aeschylus' drama, since no other major tragic dramatist made this story the subject of a play. Virgil, however (Georgics 3.266–8), in a passage on the power of sexual desire in horses and other animals, ascribes the madness of Glaucus' mares to the influence of Venus/Aphrodite, and his commentator Servius (ad loc.) says this was because he had neglected her worship and/or because, in order to increase the mares' speed, he had not allowed them to mate. In the fragments of the play we can probably detect Glaucus de-

GLAUCUS OF POTNIAE

31

And then, going on past Athenae Diades[1] . . .

Probably again from the oxherd's narrative.

[1] A settlement on Euboea, believed to be an Athenian foundation, overlooking the Euripus a short distance east of Cape Cenaeum.

GLAUCUS OF POTNIAE

parting for the games (cf. fr. 36.5–6), perhaps after an attempt to dissuade him (fr. 37 may be his reply to this); the catastrophe will have been narrated in a messenger-speech (frr. 38 and 39, and parts of fr. 36b), apparently to Glaucus' wife (fr. 36b.2.II.9 γύναι lady), and fr. 36b.7 may possibly contain an affirmation of the power of Aphrodite.

Glaucus of Potniae *was produced together with* Persians *in 472 (see Introduction to* Persians, *where the possibility is discussed that it may have included a prophecy of the defeat of the Carthaginians at Himera in 480). In this connection it is striking that Glaucus, like Xerxes, is being punished in part for violating the order of nature (Xerxes turned sea into land; Glaucus is turning grass-eating animals into flesh-eaters and denying them the right to breed).*

The papyrus fragments, though preserved and published separately (as Oxyrhynchus Papyrus 2160 *and* PSI 1210), *are all parts of the same copy. Except for fr. 36 and fr. 36b.7 (see below), none presents enough coherent text to be worth printing here.*

36

ΓΛΑΥΚΟΣ (?)

νίκ]ης ἑλὼν ἵπποις[ι]ν .. [

ΧΟΡΟΣ (?)

οὗτ]ῳ γένοιτο· καί σ᾽ ἐπευχ . [.] . [
εὐε]ξίας ἕκατι πρωτο ... [.] . [
τῇδ᾽] ἐν κελεύθῳ ξύμβολο[

5   εὐοδίαν μὲν ὁμοῦ
πρῶτον ἀπὸ στόματος χέομεν
[remains of one further line]

PSI 1210 fr. 1; scholia to Aristophanes, *Frogs* 1528 (lines 5–6)

1 suppl. Goossens   2 suppl. Cantarella   3 suppl.
Vitelli   4 [τῇδ᾽] Sommerstein; at end e.g. ξύμβολο[ν
κεδνὸν λαβεῖν].   5 ὁμοῦ Π: om. Σ Ar.   6]ωτο[Π

---

[1] This song (during which Glaucus presumably leaves the
scene) is imitated by Aristophanes in the send-off given to Dionysus and Aeschylus by the chorus at the end of *Frogs* (1528–33),
when they have been asked to "escort [Aeschylus] on his way,
hymning his praises with his own lyrics and melodies" (1525–7).

*Nothing can be made of fr. 36a except the word δνόφος dark-
ness (1). Fragment 36b.1 possibly narrates a dream (of Glaucus'
wife?) about a chariot-race (ἔδοξε γὰρ for he seemed, 1; ἔχων
ϲτεφ[ανον wearing a garl[and], 2; ἵππους horses or ἱππεὺϲ horseman, 3); 36b2.I contains lyrics or anapaests, perhaps commenting
on the dream (μελάθρων of the house, 9; φάϲματα visions, 10;
κατὰ νοῦν as is desired, 11); in 36b2.II we are probably into the
messenger-speech (ὀδ[ά]ξ with their teeth, 2; ἕλκει[drag, 4; κἀγώ*

34

36
GLAUCUS (?)

...] having taken [the prize of victo]ry with my horses ... [
...]

CHORUS (?)

[S]o may it be; and we pray (?) that you may [...] because
of your excellence (?) first in ... [... get a good] omen on
[this] journey.
[*Singing*]
First of all we pour from our lips,
all together, our wishes for a good journey[1] ...

turning-post(s), *11*; καὶ λοίϲθι[and the last [lap], *12*; νίκης ἀρέϲ
[θαι κῦδος (?) to gain [the glory(?)] of victory, *13*; ἀνδρός of the
man, *14*). *It seems as though, as in the fictitious Pythian chariot-
race described in Sophocles'* Electra *(680–763), the race went well
for the central figure until nearly the end—*ὀδάξ *may refer e.g. to
the mares taking the bit between their teeth. In 36b.3 the disaster
seems to be happening (*ὀδάξ *with their teeth, 3;* χαλινο . *the bit,
4;* φέρει *carries, 5;* πλήξας *striking, 6;* προ[ϲ]δέδορκ . *look(s) at, 7;*
ἀγῶνος *of the contest, 8;* ακεῖϲθα[ι] *to heal, 9;* θυτ[η]ρι *to the sac-
rificer, 11; line 12 is plausibly restored by Deichgräber as referring
to an offering and/or prayer* [τοῖϲ πρ]οϲτατηρ[ίο]ιϲιν, ὡ[ϲ] νό[μος,
θεοῖϲ] *to* [the] *protecting gods, a*[s] *is cus*[tomary]. *Perhaps the
chariot was first overturned (together with, or after, a number of
others? compare fr. 38 and Sophocles,* Electra *724–730), and only
then did the mares attack their driver; 36b.4 contains likely traces
of this in* [γν]άθοιϲ λα[βεῖν] *to ta*[ke] *in their* [j]aws *(3) and*
[ἱπ]πηλάτην *charioteer (4).*

35

36b.7

ἀλλ᾽ οὔτιc ἐν [χέ]ρcοιcι κω . [
ἀλλ᾽ ἐν θαλά[c]cῃ δεινὸc α . [
οἷον τὸ χρῆμα τοῦτ᾽ ἐ[. .] . . [
ὅπωc ὄρειοc τῶν ἰθα[γενῶν
5 πόθεν γὰρ [
φῦcαι γὰρ εἰκ[οc
κἄμοιγ᾽ ἐναν[
[remains of two lines]

Oxyrhynchus Papyrus 2160, fr. 7

1, 4 suppl. Siegmann, Cantarella; at end perh. [λέων]
6 suppl. Siegmann

37

ἀγὼν γὰρ ἄνδρας οὐ μένει λελειμμένους

Scholia to Plato, Cratylus 421d

36b.7

This fragment reads like dialogue rather than continuous speech, but no changes of speaker are marked in the papyrus.

But no [. . .] on dry land . . . [. . .]
But in the sea [. . .] is fearsome [. . .][1]
What a thing [is] this [that has appeared (?) . . .]
like an indigenous (?) mountain [lion (??)]
For whence [. . .] ?
For it is natural (?) that [. . .] should beget [. . .]
And for myself . . . [. . .

[1] Cf. Sophocles fr. 941.9–11, describing Aphrodite's power over creatures of sea, land and air; Euripides, *Hippolytus* 1272–82; *Homeric Hymn to Aphrodite* 2–5; Lucretius 1.3–4.

The remaining papyrus fragments tell us little more. In 36b.8 we can read εἰ δ' ἐϲθλὸν *and if it is (?) good (3),* [τ]έλειον *final or perfect (4),* ξύνμαρτυ[*with witnesses or testify (6),* ἔϲτιν γὰρ ἡμ[ῖν] *for we have (7); from line 10 the lines are indented, and here a choral song probably began, seemingly a hymn to Hermes, in which the legible words are* ναίειϲ *you dwell (15),* πιθανὰϲ *persuasive,* Ζηνὸϲ ἄγγελε *O messenger of Zeus(17). In 36b.9 the only words that survive are* ποντίαϲ ἁλόϲ *(of) the salt waters of the sea in the last line (6).*

37

For a contest does not wait for men who arrive late

Probably Glaucus, rejecting an attempt (by his wife?) to dissuade him from going to the games

38

ΑΓΓΕΛΟΣ

ἐφ᾽ ἅρματος γὰρ ἅρμα καὶ νεκρῷ νεκρός,
ἵπποι δ᾽ ἐφ᾽ ἵπποις ἦσαν ἐμπεφυρμένοι

Aristophanes, *Frogs* 1403 (line 1 only) with scholia; Scholia to
Euripides, *Phoenician Maidens* 1194

2 ἐμπεφυρμένοι Valckenaer: ἐμπεφυγμένοι Rf: ἐκπεφυγμέ-
νοι MAB.

39

ΑΓΓΕΛΟΣ

εἷλκον δ᾽ ἄνω λυκηδόν, ὥστε διπλόοι
λύκοι νέβρον φέρουσιν ἀμφὶ μασχάλαις

Scholia (T) to *Iliad* 13.198 (Αἰσχύλος περὶ Γλαύκου); Scholia
(BCE³E⁴) *ibid.* (εἷλκον—λυκηδόν: Αἰσχύλος); Eustathius on *Iliad* 13.198 (εἷλκον—φέρουσι: Αἰσχύλος)

1 δ᾽ Pauw: om. codd.

ΔΑΝΑΙΔΕΣ

38

MESSENGER

For chariot on chariot, corpse upon corpse, horses on horses, were piled in confusion.

39

MESSENGER

They dragged him up in the manner of wolves, the way a pair of wolves carry off a fawn by the shoulders.

DANAIDS

This was the third play of the Danaid tetralogy. Its action began on the morning after the Danaids' murder of their bridegrooms (fr. 43); how it may then have developed is discussed in the introduction to Suppliants. *For the possibility that* Suppliants 977–9 *was transferred to that place from* Danaids *by a later producer, see discussion* ad loc.

43

κἄπειτα δ' εἶσι λαμπρὸν ἡλίου φάος,
ἐγὼ δ' ἐγείρω πρευμενὴς τοὺς νυμφίους
νόμοισι θέλγων σὺν κόροις τε καὶ κόραις

Scholia to Pindar, *Pythian* 3. [19] 32

1–2 εἶσι Kalliergis, ἐγώ δ' ἐγείρω Bothe: εἰσὶ . . . ἕως ἐγείρω
codd.: εὖτε . . . ἕως ["dawn"] ἐγείρη, Wilamowitz
2 πρευμενὴς Heath: προυμέν . . Β: προυμ(μ)ενεῖς cett.
3 θέλγων Bothe: θέντων codd.

44

ΑΦΡΟΔΙΤΗ

ἐρᾷ μὲν ἁγνὸς οὐρανὸς τρῶσαι χθόνα,
ἔρως δὲ γαῖαν λαμβάνει γάμου τυχεῖν·
ὄμβρος δ' ἀπ' εὐνάεντος οὐρανοῦ πεσὼν
ἔκυσε γαῖαν, ἡ δὲ τίκτεται βροτοῖς
5 μήλων τε βοσκὰς καὶ βίον Δημήτριον
δένδρων τ' ὀπώραν· ἐκ νοτίζοντος γάμου
τέλειός ἐστι· τῶν δ' ἐγὼ παραίτιος.

Athenaeus 13.600b; Eustathius on *Iliad* 14.201 (lines 1–5;
Eustathius, following an error made by Athenaeus' epitomator,
ascribes the passage to Aeschylus of Alexandria)

3 εὐνάεντος AthenaeusA, sscr. in AthenaeusCE: εὐνάοντος
AthenaeusCE, Eustathius   6 τ' ὀπώραν Diels: τις ὥρα δ'
Athenaeus.

DANAIDS

43

And then will come the brilliant light of the sun, and I will graciously awake the bridal couples, enchanting them with song with a choir of youths and maidens.[1]

Presumably from the prologue of the play, spoken by someone unaware of the plot to murder the sons of Aegyptus.

[1] For the custom of singing a "waking song" (διεγερτικόν) outside the bridal chamber on the morning after a wedding, cf. Theocritus 18.56–57 with scholia.

44

APHRODITE

The holy Heaven passionately desires to penetrate the Earth, and passionate desire takes hold of Earth for union with Heaven. Rain falls from the brimming fountains of Heaven and makes Earth conceive, and she brings forth for mortals grazing for their flocks, cereals to sustain their life, and the fruit of trees: by the wedlock of the rain she comes to her fulfilment.[1] Of this, I am in part the cause.

[1] τέλειος "final, perfect, fulfilled" was often used in reference to marriage, and according to Pollux (3.38) the word could actually mean "married". Hera as goddess of marriage was Ἥρα τελεία (*Eumenides* 214, Aesch. fr. 383), and sacrifices made by, or on behalf of, maidens before their marriage were called προτέλεια (or, in *Eumenides* 835, θύη πρὸ ... γαμηλίου τέλους).

ΔΙΚΤΥΟΥΛΚΟΙ

We owe our knowledge of this play almost entirely to a series of papyrus fragments, which confirmed the guess of Gottfried Hermann that the play was set on the island of Seriphos (mentioned in fr. 47b.1) and dealt with the arrival there of Danaë and the infant Perseus, whom Danaë's father Acrisius had set adrift on the sea in a wooden chest, and the kind reception given them by Dictys, the brother of the local king Polydectes. The fragments show plainly that the play was a satyr-drama, and it is tempting to associate it with two other plays about Perseus, Phorcides and Polydectes; however, no fourth play suggests itself to complete a tetralogy.

The first major fragment (46a) comes from the prologue: a fisherman has apparently netted a large object offshore, and seeks help in bringing it to land. The fragment ends with a call for all and sundry to come and help, which will have brought the satyrs onstage. There will then have been a long scene, from which the play took its name, during which the chest is hauled on shore; fr. 46c gives us a snatch of this. Finally the chest will have been landed; Dictys (who seems to have been present from the start) must have gone away for some reason, and the satyrs open

NET-HAULERS

the chest and find Danaë and Perseus in it. Their intense erotic interest in Danaë, which dominates fr. 47a, will undoubtedly, as is usual, have come to nothing, and Dictys will eventually have rescued her.

To the thirty-sixth line of fr. 47a is prefixed the letter theta, a "stichometric" mark indicating that this was the 800th line of the play; but we are clearly then still some way from the end of the action, so it seems likely that this satyr-drama was about as long as most of Aeschylus' surviving tragedies—in marked contrast to a later satyr-drama such as Euripides' Cyclops, which at 709 lines is less than half the length of an average Euripidean tragedy.

Recent studies: M. Guardo, "Note critico-testuali ai Δικτυουλκοί (fr. 47a R.)", *Giornale Filologico Ferrarese* 12 (1989) 17–18; M. R. Halleran, "The speaker(s) of Aeschylus, Diktyoulkoi fr. 47a Radt (= P.Oxy. 2161) 821–32", *ZPE* 79 (1989) 267–9; Sommerstein *AT* 330–3; S. E. Goins, "The date of Aeschylus' Perseus tetralogy", *RhM* 140 (1997) 193–210; A. Wessels and R. Krumeich in KPS 107–124; W. B. Henry and R. Nünlist, "Aeschylus, Dictyulci (fr. 47a Radt) und Isthmiastae (fr. 78 a-d)", *ZPE* 129 (2000) 13–16, at 13–14; Podlecki 9–11.

46a

ΔΙΚΤΥΣ

ξυνῆκ[ας   ;

ΑΛΙΕΤΣ

ξυνῆκα … [φύλαccέ μοι.

ΔΙΚΤΥΣ

τί cοι φυλάccω [;

ΑΛΙΕΤΣ

εἴ που θαλάccηc [

ΔΙΚΤΥΣ

5 ἄσημα· λεῖοc πόν[τοc

ΑΛΙΕΤΣ

δέρκου νυν εἰc κευ[θμῶνα

ΔΙΚΤΥΣ

καὶ δὴ δέδορκα τῷδε ˙ [
ἔα·
τί φῶ τόδ' εἶναι; πότερα ˙ [
φάλλαιναν, ἢ ζύγαιναν, ἢ κη[
10 ἄναξ Πόcειδον Ζεῦ τ' ἐνά[λιε
[δ]ῶρον θαλάccηc πέμπετ[

PSI 1209.

2 [φύλασσέ μοι] Steffen   9 κῆ[τος βλέπω] Page after Lobel   10 ἐνα[λι', οἷον τόδε] Page   11 πέμπετ' [ἐλπίδος πέρα] Page

46a

DICTYS
Do [you] understand [. . .   ?

FISHERMAN[1]
I understand . . . [. . . Keep an eye on   . . .   for me.]

DICTYS
What am I to keep an eye on for you [. . .   ?

FISHERMAN
If [you can see . . .] anywhere in the sea.

DICTYS
No sign of anything: a smooth se[a . . .

FISHERMAN
Well, look into [that] hollow [. . .

DICTYS
Ah, now I see in this . . . [. . .
Hey, what can I say this is? Am [I looking at a . . . ,] a whale,
a shark or some se[a-monster?] Lord Poseidon, and Zeus
of the sal[t water,[2] what a] gift of the sea [this is that] you

---

[1] This character has also been identified as Silenus, but it would be unusual for him to be on the scene independently of the chorus.   [2] It is slightly easier to make continuous sense of lines 10–11 if we assume—as the particle τ' would naturally suggest—that Ζεὺς ἐνάλιος and Poseidon are two different gods (so that we can read πέμπετ' "you (pl.) are sending", or maybe πέμπετον "you two are sending", in the next line) rather than two names for the same god as Proclus (*On Plato's Cratylus* 148) claims (without reference to Aeschylus).

.. σοι θαλάϲϲηϲ δίκτυον δ[
[π]εφυκί[ω]ται δ᾽ ὥϲτε μ᾽ ἀγνο . [
⟩⟨] ἔναιμον η ...... εν[
15   ] . ε. ων νηϲαῖοϲ ... [
     ] ἐϲτι. τοὔργον οὐ χωρεῖ πρόϲω.
     β]οὴν ἵϲτημι τοῖϲδ᾽ ἰύγμαϲιν.
     ]πάντεϲ γεωργοὶ δεῦτε κἀμπελοϲκάφοι
       ]ε ποιμήν τ᾽ εἴ τίϲ ἐϲτ᾽ [ἐ]γχώριοϲ
20   ]οι τε καὶ μα[ριλ]ευτῶν ἔθνοϲ
         ]ἐναντιωτάτηϲ

12 τί ϲοι Körte   δ[ῶρον ϲτέγει] Schadewaldt
13 ἀγνοί[αν ἔχειν] Goossens: ἀγνοε[ῖν πάνυ] Gerhard
14 [ἆρ᾽ ἔϲτ᾽] ἔναιμον; Lloyd-Jones   ἤ τι χρῆμ᾽ (Kamerbeek)
ἐν [λάρνακι] Lloyd-Jones   15 (beginning) [πέμπει] Lloyd-
Jones, then γέρων Norsa & Vitelli   17 [καὶ δὴ β]οὴν Norsa &
Vitelli   18 (beginning) [εἶα δή] Diggle   19 [καὶ πόλοϲ
βούτηϲ τ]ε Norsa & Vitelli   20 μαριλευτῶν Snell

46c

[remains of three lines]
ὦ τ]ῆϲδ[ε] χώραϲ ποντ[ίαϲ
5 π]άντεϲ τ᾽ ἀγρῶϲται κα[ὶ
βοηδρομεῖτε κ[.]ν[
ϲ]ε[ι]ρᾶϲ δὲ μὴ μεθῆ[ϲθε
[remains of one line]

Oxyrhynchus Papyrus 2256 fr. 72

4 [ὦ τ]ῆϲδε Mette   ποντ[ίαϲ ἐνοικέται] Mette
7 [ϲ]ε[ι]ραϲ Lobel

are sending [. . .] [*To the fisherman*] [What] g[ift] of the sea
is your net [concealing?] It's so covered in seaweed that I
have no i[dea. Is it] a creature with blood, or [has] the Old
Man of the Islands[3] [sent us something] in [a chest? . . .] is [
. . .][4] We're not getting anywhere with the job. [Look,] I'm
raising a call for help with these cries. [Hey there!] Come
here, all you farmers and vine-diggers, [and] any [goatherd
or oxherd] or shepherd there is in these parts, and [. . .]s
and you tribe of charcoal-burners! [. . .] most adverse [. . .

*Fragment 46b, also from PSI 1209, is too scanty to offer any con-
tinuous sense, but it must come from a stage of the play when
Dictys had already left the scene, since he is referred to in the third
person (Δίκτυνο[c], 2), and the speaker (Silenus?) appears to regard him as a πολέμιο[enemy (4). Other words that can be read
are ἄλγοc pain (1), ὄμμα [eye(s) (5), ποταίν[ιον (?) fresh (6),
[ο]ὐ καλῶc not well (7), and [πρ]έcβυc old man (9).*

3 Lloyd-Jones (537 n.1) suggests that this may have been an alternative title for the ἄλιος γέρων, the Old Man of the Sea (*Odyssey* 4.384, 13.96, etc.).   4 Probably about this point Dictys
and the fisherman make a vain attempt to haul in the chest, before
Dictys decides that further assistance is needed.

46c

You [inhabitants] of this sea-girt land, and all you rustics
and [. . .], come to our aid . . . [. . .] And don't let go of the
[r]o[p]e!

*The satyrs have evidently been trying to haul in the chest without
success, and Silenus (?) calls for yet further assistance, at the same
time warning the satyrs not to allow themselves to be distracted.*

47a¹

ΣΙΛΗΝΟΣ

765   ].‚ [‚]αν καὶ θεοὺς μαρτύρομαι
      ]‚ παντὶ κηρύccω cτρατῷ
      ]πάντ’ ἅπαc̣τ̣’ ἀποφθαρῇc
      ]κ̣ο̣υ̣ca πρόξενόν θ’ ἅμα
      ]‚‚ ου με καὶ προπράκτορα
770   ]‚ ε μαῖαν ὡς γεραcμίαν
      ]‚‚ ἠπίοιc προcφθέγμαcιν
      ] ‚‚‚ ὅ̣ρ̣κο̣c ἐν χρόνῳ μενεῖ.

ΔΑΝΑΗ

      ]‚ μ̣ε̣ καὶ γενέθλιοι θεοί
      ]‚‚ α̣c τά̣cδε μοι πόνων τιθεὶc

¹ Readings of the papyrus which differ from those reported by
Radt are those of Henry & Nünlist.

Oxyrhynchus Papyrus 2161 (part of same copy as *PSI* 1209);
ὄβριχα (line 809), in the corrupt form ὄβρια, is cited from this
play by Aelian *On the Nature of Animals* 7.47, Aelius Dionysus *Attic Words* o2, and Photius s.v.; θῶcθαι (line 818) is cited from this
play by Hesychius θ1024.

767 Henry & Nünlist note that μὴ must have stood in the lost part
of the line
768 [δεῦρ’] Siegmann, then [ἤ]κουσα e.g. Henry & Nünlist
769 [δ]έχου Fraenkel
770–1 e.g. [καὶ μὴν ὁ παῖς] γε μαῖαν ὡς γερασμίαν [σαίνει
προσαυδ]ῶν ἠπίοις προσφθέγμασιν Page
774 [καὶ Ζεῦ τελε]ντὰς Siegmann

47a

SILENUS

[. . .] I call [. . .] . . . and the gods to witness
[. . .] I proclaim to the whole host[1]
[. . . that] you may [not] be utterly destroyed by starvation.
[. . .] now you have [c]ome [here, . . . acce]pt me as at once
your [very kindly] official host[2] and your protector. [And
look, the baby is greeting me fondly] as if I were his honoured nurse, [and address]ing me with tender sounds. [
. . .] . . . my oath will stand firm through time.

DANAË

[O . . .] . . . and ancestral gods, [and Zeus] who has given
me this [en]d to my travails, [are] you [really now] going to

---

[1] This may refer (i) to the satyrs, (ii) to the people of Seriphos,
or (iii) to the theatre audience.   [2] πρόξενος, properly a citizen of one state made responsible for assuring the well-being of
visitors from, and generally maintaining good relations with, a
particular other state. It is not clear (cf. previous note) whether
Silenus is offering to protect Danaë vis-à-vis the satyrs, the
Seriphians, or both.

775
]οιϲδε κνωδάλοιϲ με δώϲετε

] … γοιϲι λυμανθήϲομαι

αἰ]χμάλωτοϲ ουϲ᾽ οἴϲω κακά

]. αι γουν· ἀγχονην ἄρ᾽ ἅψομαι

]αϲ τεμοῦϲα κωλυτήριον

780
]ωϲ μὴ ποντίϲῃ τιϲ αὖ πάλιν

]τηϲ ἢ πατήρ· δέδοικα γὰρ.

]πεμπ᾽ ἀρωγόν, εἰ δοκεῖ, τινα·

cὺ γὰρ μετ]εῖχεϲ αἰτίαϲ τῆϲ μείζονοϲ,

τὴν ζημία]ν δὲ πᾶϲαν ἐξέτειϲ᾽ ἐγώ.

785
]εὖ ϲ᾽ ἔλεξα. πάντ᾽ ἔχει[ϲ] λόγον.

ΣΙΛΗΝΟΣ

ἰδο]ύ, γελᾷ μου προϲορῶν

].. ὁ μικκὸϲ λιπαρὸν

τὸ μ]ιλτ[ό]πρεπτον φαλακρὸν

]ειε[.]παπαϲ τιϲ ἀρεϲ-

790
]ωϲ[.]. ποικιλονω-

].

] … λαιϲμοι

775 [ἦ δῆτα τ]οῖϲδε Siegmann: [εἰ δὴ τοι]οῖϲδε Kamerbeek:
perh. [ἦ νῦν τοι]οῖϲδε   776 [ἔργοιϲι κο]ὺ λόγοιϲι Ferrari
779 [δυϲπραξί]αϲ Siegmann   780 [ἄκεϲμ᾽, ὅπ]ωϲ Snell
782 [Ζεῦ, τῶνδε] πέμπ᾽ Mette   783–4 suppl. Lobel
785 εὖ ϲ᾽ Lobel: ευϲ Πpc: ευτ Πac.   786 suppl. Kamerbeek
787 [οὖτ]οϲ Siegmann   788 suppl. Siegmann
789–790 ἀρέϲ-[κει] Fraenkel
790–1 "some case of ποικιλόνωτοϲ" Lobel
792 [προ]ϲγελᾷϲ μοι Cantarella

deliver me over to beasts like these? I will be treated outrageously [in deed, and not in wo]rd [alone! . . .] I shall endure suffering as a [ca]ptive [. . .] . . . at any rate. I know, I will fasten a noose to effect a drastic [cure] that will put an end to my [afflictions, s]o that I may not be left to drown all over again by some [. . .] . . . or by my father—for I am fearful of that. [Zeus,] send me someone to aid me [in this plight,] if such be your will; [for you] had the greater [share of] responsibility for it, but I've had to pay the entire [penalty. . . .] I have spoken well of you. You have heard everything.

SILENUS[3]

[Loo]k, [this] little one is laughing
as he looks at my sleek
smooth dome,[4] picked out in red . . .

Lines 789–792 are very poorly preserved; we can perceive a daddy
is pleasing *(789), with* multi-coloured back *(790), possibly* you
[smi]le at me *(792), after which there is a stage-direction for
Silenus to make a clucking sound (793).*

[. . .] you are looking at [your fat]her.
How fond the little chick is of willies!

Of the next three lines, again, little remains, but looking *(796) and*
he delights *(798) are plausible restorations.*

---

[3]This passage is lyric.   [4] φαλακρὸν could mean either "bald head" or *"glans penis"* (= φαλλὸν ἄκρον); the former interpretation is supported by Sophocles fr. 171 (the smiling baby Dionysus caressing Silenus' nose and then moving his hand *up* towards Silenus' φαλακρόν), the latter by Aristophanes, *Clouds* 538–9 (a stage phallus ἐρυθρὸν ἐξ ἄκρου), and the ambiguity was probably designed.

$(\pi o]\pi\pi\underline{v}\underline{c}\mu\acute{o}c)$

$]\underline{\tau}\underline{\rho}\iota$ δέρκη·

795   ὡc] ποσθοφιλὴc ὁ νεοccόc.

$]\underline{\epsilon}\underline{\rho}\kappa\acute{o}\mu\epsilon\nu o c$

$]\underline{c}\iota o\nu$

$]\upsilon\tau\alpha\iota$

εἰ μή cε χαίρω . [

800   ὄλοιτο Δίκτυc κ$\underline{\rho}$[

τᾱcδέ μ' ἄγραc μ[

XOPOΣ

στρ. ὦ φίντων, ἴθι δε[ῦρο.

    $(\pi o\pi\pi v\sigma\mu\acute{o}c)$

    θάρcει δή· τί κινύρη;

805 δεῦρ' εἰc παῖδαc ἴωμεν ὡc $\underline{\tau}\acute{\alpha}$[χιcτα·

    ἴξῃ παιδοτρόφουc ἐμά[c,

    ὦ φίλοc, χέραc εὐμενεῖc,

    τέρψῃ δ' ἴκτιcι κα[ὶ] $\underline{\nu}$εβ$\underline{\rho}\underline{o}$[ῖc

    ὑcτρίχων τ' ὀβρίχοι$\underline{c}$[ι,]

810 κοιμάcῃ δὲ τρί$\underline{\tau}$οc ξὺν

    ματρὶ [καὶ π]ατρὶ τῷδε.

793 suppl. Siegmann, Cantarella (cf. 803)
794 [πα]τρὶ Diggle
795 suppl. Fraenkel   ποσθοφιλὴϲ Lobel: ποϲθοϲφιλεϲ Π
796 [δ]ερκόμενοϲ Siegmann   798 [γάν]υται Cantarella
799 π[ροϲορῶν] Siegmann   802 suppl. Lobel
805 suppl. Fraenkel   807 εὐμενεῖϲ Setti: ευμενηϲ Π
811 suppl. Lobel

. . . if I don't take pleasure in [looking at] you.
A curse on Dictys . . . [who tried
to deprive (??)] me of this prey!

CHORUS

[*to the baby Perseus*]
Come he[re], diddums!
[*They make clucking noises*]
Don't be frightened! Why are you whimpering?
Come here, let's join the boys ri[ght away:]
you'll come, my dear, to my kindly
child-rearing hands,
you'll take delight in martens, fawns,
and young porcupines,
and you'll make a third in bed
with your mother [and] your father here.

ἀντ. ὁ πάππα[ϲ δ]ὲ παρέξει
τῷ μικκῷ τὰ γελ[οῖ]α
καὶ τροφὰς ἀνόϲους, ὅπωϲ π[
815 ἀλδὼν αὐτὸϲ ε .... [.] ... [
χαλᾷ νεβροφόνο[υ] ποδ[ὸϲ
μάρπτων θῆραϲ ἄνευ δ[
θῶσθαι ματρὶ παρέξειϲ
κ]ηδεϲτῶν τρόπον οἷϲιν
820 ἔ]ν̣τροφοϲ πελατεύϲειϲ.

ἀλλ'] εἶα, φίλοι, ϲτείχωμεν, ὅπωϲ
γά]μον ὁρμαίνωμεν, ἐπεὶ τέλεοϲ
κ̣αιρὸϲ ἄναυδοϲ τάδ' ἐπαινεῖ.—
καὶ τήνδ' [ἐ]ϲορῶ νύμφην ἤδη
825 πάνυ βουλομένην τῆϲ ἡμετέραϲ
φιλότητοϲ ἄδ̣ην κορέϲαϲθαι.—
καὶ θαῦμ' οὐδέν· πολὺϲ ἦν αὐτῃ
χρόνοϲ, ὃν χήρα κατὰ ναῦν ὕφαλοϲ

812, 813 suppl. Lobel   814 π[οτ' ἰσχὺν] Page
815 ἐν οὐρ[ε]σιν Siegmann
816 νεβροφόνο[υ] Lloyd-Jones, ποδ[ός] Lobel
817 δ[ορὸς] Lobel   820 [ἔ]ντροφος Harrison:]ντροποϲ Π.
821, 822 suppl. Lobel   825 πάνυ Lobel: καιπανυ Π

54

And daddy will provide
his little one with fun
and a healthy upbringing, so that [eventually,] after
       growing
[to full strength,] you can yourself [in the mountains],
with the hoof[5] of your fawn-slaying foot,
chase down the wild creatures, and without a s[pear][6]
provide fare for your mother to feast on,
in the same way as do your stepbrothers,
among whom you will be reared as a dependant.

But hey, friends, let's go, in order[7]
to get on quickly with the wedding, because the time
is ripe and silently approves this.
[*A second voice*]
And I can see that the bride here is already
very eager to take her full fill
of our loving.[8]
[*The first voice*]
And no wonder: she has had a long
time during which she was in a distressed state of
       celibacy
on board ship, below the waterline. Now, anyway,

[5] The idea is apparently that the child will acquire some of the
equine characteristics of his adoptive father. See H. Lloyd-Jones,
CR 37 (1987) 144.   [6] i.e. killing them with your bare hands.
[7] The metre has changed to "marching" anapaests. The chorus
cannot actually "go", since the play can hardly have ended here;
perhaps they merely march round the orchestra.   [8] The satyrs are apparently assuming (cf. also 830) that Danaë, though
"married" to Silenus, will be sexually available to all of them.

τείρετο· νῦν δ' οὖν
830 ἐ]ϲορῶϲ' ἤβην τὴν ἡμετέραν
...]ει γάνυται νυμφίῳ οἷον
...]ϲιν λαμπραῖϲ τῆϲ Ἀ[φ]ροδίτηϲ

831 [γαθ]εῖ Kamerbeek: [χαίρ]ει Henry & Nünlist   [ο]ιον
Πˢˢᶜʳ: ηδη (from 824) Π   832 [χαρί]σιν Diggle   after
832 e.g. [ἔξει στίλβοντα σύνευνον] Diggle

ΕΛΕΤΣΙΝΙΟΙ

Our information about this play comes mainly from a reference to it in Plutarch's Life of Theseus *(29.4–5), which shows that it dealt with the same events as Euripides'* Suppliants—*the recovery by Theseus, at the request of Adrastus, of the bodies of the Seven against Thebes, which the Theban authorities were refusing to release for burial. In Euripides, Theseus secures possession of the bodies by defeating the Thebans in battle; in Aeschylus, according to Plutarch (compare also Isocrates,* Panathenaicus *168–171), he did so by a negotiated agreement, and afterwards*

53a
ὤργα τὸ πρᾶγμα· διεμύδαιν' ἤδη νέκυς

Didymus on [Demosthenes] 13.32 (col. XIV 12–15 Diels-Schubart) (Αἰσχύ[λ]ος ἐπὶ τῶν πρὸ τῆς Καδμείας νεκρῶν τ[ῶ]ν πρὸς τὴν ταφὴν ἑτοίμως ἐχόντων)

seeing our youthful vigour,
she [rejoic]es and delights—such a bridegroom
[she will have for a bedfellow, radiant]
with the brilliant [charm]s of Aphrodite!

Frr. 47b and 47c, both from Oxyrhynchus Papyrus 2255 *(fragments 21 and 20), have often been assigned to* Net-Haulers *because fr. 47b contains the word* Σέριφον Seriphus *(line 1) and fr. 47c probably stood close to it in the papyrus. Other words that can be read are: in fr. 47b,* δεδορκ . . look(s) *(line 3) and* παῖδα καὶ γέρ[οντ child and old m[an] *(line 4); in fr. 47c,* χρωμ[colour *(line 2).*

ELEUSINIANS

gave Adrastus permission to have the bodies buried at Eleusis.[1] *The play may have formed a trilogy with* Women of Argos *and* Epigoni *(qq.v.)*

[1] Where "the tombs of the Seven" existed in Pausanias' time (Pausanias 1.39.2) and doubtless in Aeschylus' time too. Euripides also speaks of tombs being built at Eleusis (*Suppliants* 935–8), but these appear to be cenotaphs, since while he has the Seven *cremated* at Eleusis, their ashes are then taken back to Argos (*Suppliants* 1185–8).

53a
The matter was urgent; the corpse was already putrefying.

ΕΠΙΓΟΝΟΙ

The story of the Epigoni—the sons of the Seven against Thebes, who succeeded where their fathers had failed, capturing and destroying the city—was the subject of one of the poems in the Epic Cycle. The only clue to Aeschylus' treatment of the story is the reference in fr. 55 to the pouring of libations in connection with a wedding; but whose wedding can it have been? One of the Epigoni was Alcmeon, son of Amphiaraus and Eriphyle, and Sophocles' Epigoni (whether or not it was the same play as his Eriphyle) was centred on the story of Alcmeon's killing of his mother in revenge for her treachery against Amphiaraus in sending him to his death at Thebes; and a tantalizing fragment of the Eriphyle *of Stesichorus (SLG 148 col. ii) seems to speak of Eriphyle making a journey to*

55

λοιβὰς Διὸς μὲν πρῶτον ὡραίου γάμου
Ἥρας τε

* * * * *

τὴν δευτέραν γε κρᾶσιν ἥρωσιν νέμω

* * * * *

τρίτον Διὸς σωτῆρος εὐκταίαν λίβα

Scholia to Pindar, *Isthmian* 6.[7]10; Arsenius 10.77a (lines 1–3)

3 γε B: τε D: om. Arsenius: δὲ Schütz

EPIGONI

arrange a marriage between her son and "the daughter of arrogant Anaxander" (a figure not known from any other source). One could envisage a drama that included the celebration of Alcmeon's marriage (or perhaps betrothal) and culminated in the matricide, all against the background of the attack upon Thebes, and probably involving Adrastus (who was Eriphyle's brother); but there may well be other possibilities of which we know nothing. The play would fit into a trilogic sequence with Women of Argos *and* Eleusinians *(qq.v.), in both of which Adrastus will also have appeared; Euripides too, at the end of* Suppliants, *makes a close connection between the recovery and burial of the bodies of the Seven and the war of revenge by their sons.*

55

First [I make] the libation of Zeus and Hera, for a marriage in good season.

* * * * *

The second share of the mixed wine I allot to the Heroes.

* * * * *

Thirdly, a libation and prayer to Zeus the Saviour.[1]

[1] This was the usual sequence of libations after a meal, except that the first was normally to Olympian Zeus alone; here, in the context of marriage, his consort Hera is appropriately added.

ΗΔΩΝΟΙ

This was the first play of the tetralogy known as the
Lycurgeia *(Aristophanes,* Women at the Thesmophoria
135) and probably, except for the satyr-drama Lycurgus,
*the only one in which Lycurgus, king of the Edonians (a
Thracian people living near the river Strymon), actually
appeared. It told the story of his attempt to suppress the
worship of Dionysus in his kingdom, along more or less the
same lines as [Apollodorus,]* Library *3.5.1. At the start of
the play Dionysus had just arrived in Thrace with his
male and female followers. Lycurgus had both him and
the women bacchants arrested, but they miraculously escaped, and Dionysus then drove Lycurgus mad, so that
he killed his own son Dryas with an axe, believing that
he was cutting a vine-branch. Lycurgus may well in the
end, as in [Apollodorus] and as in Sophocles,* Antigone
*955–965, have been imprisoned perpetually in a rocky
chamber on Mount Pangaeum. It has been attractively
conjectured that Orpheus, who was the central figure of*
The following play *(Bassarids, q.v.), also figured in this
one, before his apostasy, as a devotee (maybe a priest) of*

EDONIANS

Dionysus, imprisoned with his master by Lycurgus (cf. fr. 60); West, Studies 29–30, has suggested that Orpheus "warned Lycurgus of the unwisdom of theomachy", but that his warnings were ignored. This play was extensively imitated by Euripides when he wrote about the fate of another enemy of Dionysus in The Bacchae, and the Roman poet Naevius in his Lucurgos seems to have followed it closely.

The apparent presence of a stage-building (fr. 58) suggests that this was a late play of Aeschylus, and West, Studies 48–50, has argued that there is other evidence corroborating this. If so, Aeschylus will have been following in the footsteps of Polyphrasmon, son of his old rival Phrynichus, who produced a Lycurgeia in 467.

Recent studies: West, *Studies* 26–32, 48–50; F. Jouan, "Dionysos chez Eschyle", *Kernos* 5 (1992) 71–86, esp. 73–74; M. Di Marco, "Dioniso ed Orfeo nelle *Bassaridi* di Eschilo", in A. Masaracchia ed. *Orfeo e l'orfismo* (Rome, 1993) 101–153; P. Mureddu, "Le 'lunghe gambe' di Dioniso (Aesch. fr. 62 R.)", *Eikasmos* 5 (1994) 81–88; *ead.*, "Note dionisiache: osservazioni sulle 'Baccanti' di Euripide e sugli 'Edoni' di Eschilo", *Lexis* 18 (2000) 117–125.

57

σεμνὰ Κοτυτοῦς δ' ὄργι' ἔχοντες

* * * * *

ὁ μὲν ἐν χερσὶν
βόμβυκας ἔχων, τόρνου κάματον,
δακτυλόθικτον πίμπλησι μέλος,
5 μανίας ἐπαγωγὸν ὁμοκλήν,
ὁ δὲ χαλκοδέτοις κοτύλαις ὀτοβεῖ

* * * * *

ψαλμὸς δ' ἀλαλάζει·
ταυρόφθογγοι δ' ὑπομυκῶνταί
ποθεν ἐξ ἀφανοῦς φοβεροὶ μῖμοι,
10 ἠχὼ τυπάνου δ', ὥσθ' ὑπογαίου
βροντῆς, φέρεται βαρυταρβής

Strabo 10.3.16; Athenaeus 11.479b (line 6); scholia (bT), and
Eustathius, on *Iliad* 23.34 (line 6); Hesychius τ255 Schmidt (ταυρόφθογγοι, line 8)

1 Κοτυτοῦς Nauck: κόπτους C, κόπτουσ' D h: Κότυς cett.
δ' ὄργι' Mette: ὄρ(ε)ια δ' ὄργαν' codd.   ἔχοντες cett.: ἔχον-
τας D h i n o p Bᵖᶜ kᵖᶜ: ἔχοντα kᵃᶜ x   4 -θικτον Jacobs:
-δεικτον codd.   perh. δακτυλοθίκτου . . . μέλους?
9 φοβεροὶ E: φοβέριοι (φομ- Bᵖᶜ C k) cett.   10 ἠχὼ τυπάνου δ' F. W. Schmidt: τυμπανοῦ δ' ἠχώ (k n o: εἰχών Bᵖᶜ l x:
εἰκών cett.) codd.

57

And, practising the holy ecstatic rites of Cotyto[1] . . .

* * * * *

One man holds in his hands
a pair of pipes, fashioned on the lathe,
and plays out a fingered melody,[2]
a loud cry that brings on frenzy,
while another crashes the bronze cymbals

* * * * *

. . . and the twang of strings resounds;
and terrifying imitators of the voice of bulls[3]
bellow in response from somewhere out of sight,
and the fearful deep sound of the drum
carries to the ear like thunder beneath the earth.[4]

*Anapaestic lines, chanted probably by the chorus of Thracian
men, describing the worshippers of Dionysus newly arrived in
their country.*

[1] A Thracian goddess. The meaning is that Dionysiac cult
practices (or at least those about to be mentioned) are essentially
similar to practices that were already familiar to Thracians as part
of the worship of Cotyto.   [2] Or, reading $\delta\alpha\kappa\tau\upsilon\lambda o\theta i\kappa\tau o\upsilon$ . . .
$\mu\acute{\epsilon}\lambda o\upsilon\varsigma$, "fills it with fingered melody".   [3] i.e. bullroarers
($\dot{\rho}\acute{o}\mu\beta o\iota$), which can be heard over great distances. They are mentioned in Euripides, *Helen* 1362–3, in connection with orgias-
tic worship of Dionysus and the Great Mother.   [4] Ancient
Greeks thought of thunder as reverberating beneath the earth as
well as in the sky. Cf. *Prom.* 993–4; Sophocles, *Oedipus at Colonus*
1606; Aristophanes, *Birds* 1745.

ATTRIBUTED FRAGMENTS

58

ἐνθουσιᾷ δὴ δῶμα, βακχεύει στέγη

"Longinus", *On the Sublime* 15.6 (παρὰ ... Αἰσχύλῳ ... τὰ τοῦ Λυκούργου βασίλεια κατὰ τὴν ἐπιφάνειαν τοῦ Διονύσου θεοφορεῖται)

59

ὅστις χιτῶνας βασσάρας τε Λυδίας
ἔχει ποδήρεις

Photius, *Lexicon* β85; *Etymologicum Genuinum* s.v. βασσάραι

60

τίς ποτ᾽ ἔσθ᾽ ὁ μουσόμαντις, <–∪> ἄλλος
   ἁβροβάτης,
ὃν σθένει <   >;

Scholia to Aristophanes, *Birds* 276; Suda μ1301 (line 1)

1 ἔσθ᾽ Pauw (cf. Ar. *Birds* 276): ἐστὶν Γ: ἔσται cett. Suda lacuna before ἄλλος posited by Sommerstein (e.g. <γύννις>): after ἁμαλὸς (*sic*: cf. below) by M. Schmidt   ἄλλος V: ἄλαλος cett. Suda: ἁμαλὸς Hermann   ἁβροβάτης Hermann, Friebel (cf. Ar. loc. cit. ὀρειβάτης): ἀβρατοῦς V: ἀβρατεὺς cett. Suda 2 ὃν σθένει taken as the start of a second line by Mette

58

Truly the house is possessed—the building is in bacchic frenzy!

According to "Longinus" a reaction to "the epiphany of Dionysus", evidently after his imprisonment in the palace; compare Euripides, Bacchae *576–603.*

59

One who wears Lydian tunics and fox-skin mantles down to his feet.

A pejorative description of Dionysus, doubtless by Lycurgus.

60

Who on earth is this musical prophet, another ‹effeminate(?)› who walks with delicate tread, whom ‹   › by force?

Evidently Lycurgus again, probably about Orpheus.

61

ΛΥΚΟΥΡΓΟΣ

ποδαπὸς ὁ γύννις; τίς πάτρα; τίς ἡ στολή;

* * * * *

τί φής; τί σιγᾷς;

Aristophanes, *Women at the Thesmophoria* 136, 144 (κατ᾽
Αἰσχύλον ἐκ τῆς Λυκουργείας), with scholia on 135; some other
material in the Aristophanic passage (136–145) probably comes
from this play too, but its extent cannot be precisely defined

62

μακροσκελὴς μέν· ἆρα μὴ χλούνης τις ἦν;

Scholia (*B), and Eustathius, on *Iliad* 9.539

---

1 For this interpretation of the obscure word χλούνης, compare *Adespota Iambica* fr. 51 West, and see P. Mureddu, *Eikasmos*
5 (1994) 81–88. The point of the joke is that street robbers have to
be fast runners to get away from their enraged victims.

61

LYCURGUS

[to Dionysus][1]

Whence comes this epicene? What is its country, what its garb?

* * * * *

What do you say? Why are you silent?[2]

[1] The Aristophanic scholiast states that "he [i.e. Lycurgus] says [this] in *The Edonians* to Dionysus after his arrest".   [2] In Aristophanes' *Women at the Thesmophoria* these questions are part of a long series addressed by Euripides' (brother?-)in-law to the effeminate tragic poet Agathon; he describes himself as speaking "in the manner of Aeschylus, from the *Lycurgeia*". I translate the whole speech here, italicizing the words that seem to me most likely to come unaltered from Aeschylus (only the first question is explicitly attested as his by the scholiast): "*Whence comes this epicene? What is its country, what its garb*? What confusion of lifestyles is this? What has a bass to say to a *saffron gown*, or a lyre to a hair-net? What's an oil-flask doing with a breast-band? How incongruous! *And what partnership can there be between* a mirror *and a sword*? *And as for yourself, boy, are you being brought up as a man*? Then where's your prick? Where's your cloak? Where are your Laconian shoes? Or as a woman, then? Then where are your tits? *What do you say? Why are you silent*? Or shall I find you out by your song, seeing that you don't want to tell me yourself?"

62

He's certainly got long legs! He wasn't once a clothes-snatcher, was he?[1]

Lycurgus, sneeringly, about Dionysus.

ATTRIBUTED FRAGMENTS

ΗΛΙΑΔΕΣ

Pliny the Elder (Natural History 37.31–32) names Aeschylus among a number of poets who told of how, when Phaëthon perished by the thunderbolt of Zeus, his sisters were turned into poplar trees and shed tears of amber by

DAUGHTERS OF THE SUN

the river Eridanus.[1] *Since Phaëthon was a son of the Sun-god Helios, this evidence alone would leave little doubt that* Daughters of the Sun *presented, as later did Euripides'* Phaëthon, *the story of how he met his death when attempting to drive his father's chariot through the sky; and this assumption is confirmed by fr. 71 (on which see footnote). The fragments do not enable us to define the plot more closely than this.*

[1] This river was very vaguely located by early Greeks. Herodotus (3.115) criticized poets who spoke of the Eridanus as flowing into "the sea to the north . . . on the far side of Europe". By the time of Euripides (*Hippolytus* 737–741) the Eridanus was envisaged as flowing into the Adriatic, and perhaps already identified with the Po; and fr. 71 seems to be consistent with this view. Pliny's statement that Aeschylus located the river in Iberia and identified it with the Rhodanus (Rhône) may be explained by supposing that Aeschylus believed the Po and the Rhône to be joined together, far inland (an idea later exploited by Apollonius Rhodius, *Argonautica* 4.627–8), and that, like several other fifth- and fourth-century writers, he thought of "Iberia" as beginning at the Rhône rather than at the Pyrenees (cf. Herodorus fr. 2 Fowler [Iberian tribes extending as far as the Rhône]; Scylax, *Periplous* 3 [a mixed population of Iberians and Ligurians between the Pyrenees and the Rhône]; Thucydides 6.2.2 [the Sicans displaced by Ligurians from the river Sicanus in Iberia]; and probably Herodotus 1.163.1 ["Tyrrhenia, Iberia and Tartessus" apparently representing the whole European shore from the Tiber to Cadiz]).

68

Ῥῖπαι μὲν δὴ πατρὸς Ἡελίου

Scholia to Sophocles, *Oedipus at Colonus* 1248

perh. e.g. πατρὸς Ἡελίου <δυσμαί>?

69

ἔνθ᾽

ἐπὶ δυσμαῖσιν ἐμοῦ
πατρὸς Ἡφαιστοτυκὲς
δέπας, ἐν τῷ διαβάλλων
5 πολὺν οἰδματόεντα
†φέρει δρόμου† πόρον εὕδει,
μελανίππου προφυγὼν
ἱερᾶς νυκτὸς ἀμολγόν

Athenaeus 11.469f

2 δυσμαῖσιν ἐμοῦ Sommerstein: δυσμαῖς ἴσον cod.
3 -τυκὲς Hermann: -τευχὲς cod.   4 διαβάλλων ed. pr.:
διαβάλλει cod.   6 φέρει δρόμου cod.: metre requires ∪ ∪ –
(–)   εὕδει Bothe, cf. Mimnermus fr. 12.8 West: οὐδ᾽ εἰς ed. pr.:
ουθεις cod.

---

1 For the Sun's golden cup or bowl, in which he travelled from
the west to the east during the night, cf. fr. 74; *Titanomachy* fr. 10
West; Mimnermus fr. 12 West; Stesichorus *PMG* 185; Panyassis,

68

Rhipae,[1] the ‹setting-place(?)› of our father the Sun.

Anapaests, no doubt chanted by the chorus; perhaps the opening words of the play.

[1] The location of the fabulous "Rhipaean mountains". It is usually taken to be in the far north, but it could hardly then have a connection with Helios, and the Sophocles scholiast who quotes this fragment positively asserts that Rhipae was in the far *west* ($\pi\rho\grave{o}\varsigma\ \tau\hat{\eta}\ \delta\acute{v}\sigma\epsilon\iota$). Neither the passage on which he is commenting (*Oedipus at Colonus* 1248, where a location in the far north is guaranteed by the context), nor a passage of Alcman which he cites (*PMG* 90), offer any support to this view, so it is reasonable to suppose that the Aeschylus passage once did, and that it has been truncated in transmission.

69

Where
at my father's setting
is the cup fashioned by Hephaestus,[1]
in which he crosses
the wide, swelling waters
‹of Ocean (?)[2]›, asleep,
escaping the darkness
of holy Night with her black horses.

From a choral ode.

Heracleia fr. 12 West; Peisander, *Heracleia* fr. 5 West; Pherecydes fr. 18a Fowler.   [2] This is approximately what sense and context require, and $o\hat{\iota}\delta\mu\alpha\tau\acute{o}\epsilon\nu\tau'\ \dot{'}\Omega\kappa\epsilon\alpha\nuo\hat{v}$ (or $o\hat{\iota}\delta\mu\alpha\tau\acute{o}\epsilon\nu\tau o\varsigma\ \pi o\tau\alpha\mu o\hat{v}$) would be reconcilable with the (ionic) metre, but it would then be very hard to explain how $\phi\acute{e}\rho\epsilon\iota\ \delta\rho\acute{o}\mu o\upsilon$ came to stand in the transmitted text.

70

Ζεύς ἐστιν αἰθήρ, Ζεὺς δὲ γῆ, Ζεὺς δ' οὐρανός,
Ζεύς τοι τά πάντα χὤ τι τῶνδ' ὑπέρτερον

Clement of Alexandria, *Stromateis* 5.4.114.4; Eusebius, *Praeparatio Evangelica* 13.13.41 (neither names the play); Philodemus, *On Piety* p.22.5–10 Gomperz (paraphrase)

2 χὤ τι (χώ, τι) Grotius, τῶνδ' Sylburg: χ' ὦτι τῶν δέ τοι Clement: χωρεῖ τῶδε Eusebius.

71

Ἀδριαναί τε γυναῖκες τρόπον ἔξουσι γόων

Anecdota Bekkeri 1.346.10

72

†ὅρα σε† κρήνης ἀφθονεστέραν λίβα

Etymologicum Genuinum s.v. ἀφθονέστατον; Athenaeus 10.424d (ἀφθ. λίβα); Photius, *Lexicon* a3349 (ἀφθονεστέραν); Eustathius on *Iliad* 9.203 (ἀφθονέστερον) (the last two do not name the play)

ὅρα σε *Et. Gen.*: perh. <ἐν>ῶρσε (cf. *Iliad* 6.499)   ἀφθονεστέραν Photius: ἀφθονεστερα (variously accented) *Et. Gen.*: ἀφθονέστερον Athenaeus, Eustathius

λίβα Athenaeus: λιβασιλ *Et. Gen.*A (interpreted by Reitzenstein as λιβὰς Ἡλ<ιάσιν>): om. *Et. Gen.*B

70

Zeus is the aether, Zeus is earth, Zeus is heaven—yes, Zeus is everything,[1] and whatever there may be beyond that.

[1] Or "the universe".

71

And the women of Adria[1] shall have this manner of lamentation.[2]

From a choral ode?

[1] The former seaport (now well inland), near the mouth of the Po, which still bears this name (from which that of the Adriatic Sea is derived) and/or the surrounding region. The later Greek belief was that the people of this region (men and women alike) continued to show their grief for Phaëthon by wearing black (Polybius 2.16.13; Plutarch, *Moralia* 557d–e).   [2] The metre is again ionic (cf. fr. 69).

72

He/it stirred up in them/you/us (?) a flow more abundant than a fountain.[1]

[1] The "flow" is surely that of the tears of Phaëthon's sisters (or perhaps of the whole local population, cf. fr. 71).

ATTRIBUTED FRAGMENTS

ΗΡΑΚΛΕΙΔΑΙ

CHILDREN OF HERACLES

All that can be said with confidence about this play is that it dealt in some way with the fate of Heracles' children after the end of his earthly life, and that he himself made an appearance in it, probably as a god (frr. 73b, 75a); perhaps his family had not previously known of his apotheosis. It is not unlikely that Aeschylus, like Euripides in his play of the same name, presented the story, of which Athenians were always proud, of how Athens had defended Heracles' children against their father's old persecutor Eurystheus; but there is simply no actual evidence either for or against this supposition.

Recent studies: T. C. W. Stinton, "The apotheosis of Heracles from the pyre", in L. Rodley ed. *Papers given at a Colloquium on Greek Drama in honour of R. P. Winnington-Ingram* (London, 1986) 1–15, at p.6 = Stinton, *Collected Papers on Greek Tragedy* (Oxford, 1990) 493–507, at pp. 500–1; A. H. Sommerstein, "Ἀμφιμήτωρ", *CQ* 37 (1987) 498–500; P. Holt, "Heracles' apotheosis in lost Greek literature and art", *L'Antiquité Classique* 61 (1992) 38–59; J. Wilkins, *Euripides: Heraclidae* (Oxford, 1993) xviii–xix; C. Hahnemann, "Mount Oita revisited: Sophocles' *Trachiniai* in light of the evidence of Aeschylus' *Herakleidai*", *ZPE* 126 (1999) 67–73.

73b

[*remains of one line*]
πυρὰ]ν γὰρ αὐτότευκ[τον] ηνεν[
Οἴτη]c ἐν ὑψηλοῖcι θα[μν]ούχοι[c
    ]. δε παῖδεc οἵδε μ᾽ [ἀ]μφιμή[τορεc
5   ]ν ἄρδην καυcίμοιc ἐνδ[
    ]τα καὶ λοπῶντα φαρμάκου [

"Papyrus du Fayoum" 2 ed. G. Lefebvre, *Bulletin de la société royale d'archéologie d'Alexandrie* 14 (1912) 192; Hesychius α4065 (ἀμφιμήτορες· . . . Αἰσχύλος Ἡρακλείδαις).

2 [πυρὰ]ν Srebrny   αὐτότευκ[τον] Snell   ἦν ἐν[ταῦθ᾽ ἰδεῖν] Lloyd-Jones   3 suppl. Srebrny, who suggested [τόποις] at the end.   4 [εἰς τή]νδε Lloyd-Jones   5 [ἤνεγκο]ν Lloyd-Jones   ἐν δ[ένδρεσιν] Lloyd-Jones   6 [οἰδοῦν]τα Nisbet: [φλέγον]τα Radt: perh. [ἀλγοῦν]τα or [πονοῦν]τα   φαρμάκου [μένει] Latte

73b

[There in view] was a [pyr]e which they themselves had built,[1] on the br[u]sh-cover[ed] heights of [Oet]a. [On thi]s these children of mine, who had two mothers,[2] [carryi]ng me aloft, placed me among the [wood] for the fire, [in agony,] my skin peeling [from the effect] of the poison.

Heracles, apparently addressing a third party (the Athenian king Demophon??), but in the presence of his children, recalls how he was taken to be burned alive, after being poisoned by the robe sent him by Deianeira.

[1] Cf. Sophocles, *Trachinian Maidens* 1195–7, 1213.
[2] The usual story was that the children of Heracles who remained together as a group after his passing all had Deianeira as their mother. Either Aeschylus included among their number one or more of Heracles' many children by other women, or, as I suggested in *CQ* 37 (1987) 498–500, the children's second "mother" is Iole, who had been about to supplant Deianeira as Heracles' consort.

ATTRIBUTED FRAGMENTS

74

ἐκεῖθεν ὅρμενος
ὀρθόκερως βοῦς ἤλασεν
ἀπ' ἐσχάτων γαίας Ὠκεανὸν περάσας
ἐν δέπᾳ χρυσηλάτῳ
5 βοτῆράς τ' ἀδίκους κτείνας
δεσπόταν τε †τριύτατον†
τρία δόρη πάλλοντα χερσίν,
τρία δ' ἴτας σάκη προτείνων,
τρεῖς δ' ἐπισσείων λόφους
10 ἔστειχ' ἶσος Ἄρει βίαν

Scholia (M) to Aelius Aristeides, *Oration* 3.167 ed. Wilamowitz (*Kleine Schriften* i [1935] 14–15)

5 κτείνας Radt: κτεῖναι cod.   6 δεσπόταν Weil: δεσπο-
τῶν cod.   τριύτατον cod.: τρίπτυχον Weil: τρίζυγα τὸν
Kiessling: perh. τρίζυγον[1]   7 χερσίν Weil: χεροῖν cod.
8 δ' ἴτας (δ' ἴτης) Hercher, van Herwerden, σάκη Wilamowitz:
διὰ τῆς σάκου cod.   9 δ' ἐπισσείων λόφους Wilamowitz:
δέ τις ειπλοφους cod.   10 Ἄρει Wilamowitz: αρη cod.

[1] The corruption would be due to a conflation of this reading
with a variant τρίζυγα.

75

οὐ γάρ τι μεῖζον ἄλλο τοῦδε πείσομαι

Stobaeus 4.54.2

78

74

Starting from there,[1]
he[2] drove away the straight-horned cattle
from the most remote place on earth,[3] after crossing the
        Ocean
in a golden cup[4]
and killing the wicked herders[5]
and their threefold master,
who brandished three spears in his hands,
and boldly holding three shields before him
and shaking three crests on his heads
advanced, the equal of Ares in his might.

From a choral song looking back on Heracles' heroic career.

[1] Probably from Tartessus in south-western Spain (cf. Stesichorus *PMG* 184, 185).   [2] Heracles, who was performing his
tenth Labour.   [3] The island of Erytheia (to be imagined as
somewhere out in the Atlantic), where the triple-bodied monster
Geryon lived.   [4] The cup of Helios (see on fr. 69), which
Heracles borrowed for this purpose.   [5] These must be the
herdsman Eurytion and the dog Orthos (e.g. Hesiod, *Theogony*
293; [Apollodorus], *Library* 2.5.10).

75

For I shall never suffer anything else greater than this.

.

75a

κἀξηονήθην, κοὐδὲν ἦν προσωτέρω

Photius, *Lexicon* ε1245; *Etymologicum Genuinum, Etymologicum Symeonis, Etymologicum Magnum* s.v. ἐξηονήθην (citing that word only, without attribution to Aeschylus)

κἀξηονήθην Tsantsanoglou (cf. the *Etymologica*): κἀξαιονήθην Photius[ac] (-ξοιο- Photius[pc])

ΘΑΛΑΜΟΠΟΙΟΙ

Of this play we know nothing for sure except that it existed and, as fr. 78 shows, was indeed concerned with the building of a chamber or chambers—very likely, in view of the usual connotations of θάλαμος in tragedy, for one or more bridal couples. The apparent presence of a chorus employed on a building project has led to its being widely, though not universally, accepted that this was a satyrdrama.

It has, however, been twice independently suggested in recent years that fr. 451l Radt (Oxyrhynchus Papyrus 2254) may come from Chamber-Makers. The fragment is almost certainly from a satyr-drama, as the reference to these beasts (line 15) indicates; it makes mention of a θάλαμος (line 22) and of a wife (line 26); and the reference to someone or something Teucrian (line 25), and what seems to be an address to Priam (line 12), make it likely that the play was set in Troy. Mette had already proposed that the fragment might come from a satyr-drama linked to the Achilles trilogy (Myrmidons, Nereids, Phrygians),

75a

And I was drenched, and after that there was nothing more.

This can hardly refer to anything but the dousing of Heracles' pyre by water-nymphs under the direction of Athena;[1] we can reasonably guess that when he woke up he was on Olympus, with the ravages of the poison healed.

[1] This story, which appears to be distinctively Attic (though a Boeotian variant of it appears in Herodotus 7.198.2), is evidenced by a series of vase-paintings, the earliest from about 460 BC, discussed by C. A. Faraone, *JHS* 117 (1997) 43–46.

CHAMBER-MAKERS

and Chamber-Makers *could well be that play; the fragment is accordingly treated here as belonging to* Chamber-Makers, *and renumbered 78a. Since only one chamber appears to be in question, the play probably centred on a single rather than a multiple wedding. Di Marco thought of Paris and Helen, but there is perhaps more to be said for Hector and Andromache:[1] Hector, unlike Paris or Helen, was an important figure in the Achilles trilogy, offstage at first but later (as a corpse) onstage, and Aeschylus seems to have gone out of his way in* Phrygians *to mention Hector's marriage (fr. 267).*

Recent studies: M. Di Marco, "P. Oxy. 2254: dai Thalamopoioi di Eschilo?", *QUCC* 45 (1993) 49–56; Sommerstein *AT* 348.

[1] The wedding of Hector and Andromache, and the great public rejoicing that accompanied it, are the subject of an unusually well-preserved poem by Sappho (fr. 44).

78

ἀλλ' ὁ μέν τις Λέσβιον φατνώματι
κῦμ' ἐν τριγώνοις ἐκπεραινέτω ῥυθμοῖς

Pollux, *Onomasticon* 7.122

78a (451l)

*Remains (3–10 letters per line) of 27 lines; intelligible
words and phrases are*]. μαχον·[*(?)-fighting (4),* τῆϲ
ἀληθ[*of the truth (?) (7),*]ῶν φῦλον *the tribe of . . . (9),*
Π]ρίαμε *Priam (12),* μ]ακεδνὸϲ *tall (13),* θῆρες οἵδ[ε *these
beasts (15),* ἄκοντες *unwillingly (16),* κ]ρεοβότους *meat-
eating (17),* δρᾶν τε κα[ὶ *to do and . . . (18),*]ọπτέροισιν
(?)-winged (19), βίοτον *life or livelihood (20),* θάλαμον
chamber (22), εὐτολ[μ *bold(ly) (23),* Τευκρίδ[*Teucrian
(i.e. Trojan) (25), and* πλατιδ.[*wife (26).*

ΘΕΩΡΟΙ Η ΙΣΘΜΙΑΣΤΑΙ

*Our knowledge of this play is almost entirely dependent on
the fragments preserved as* Oxyrhynchus Papyrus 2162.
*Their arrangement is now fairly firmly established, except
for one narrow strip (fr. 78b). The scene is before the temple of Poseidon at the Isthmus of Corinth, the occasion that
of a celebration of the Isthmian Games. The "story so far"
appears to be that Dionysus has been training the satyrs
for a dancing performance at a great festival (33, 71–74),
but that they have run away from him, decided to become
athletes instead, and been taken under the wing of another
character, who has been identified as Sisyphus or Theseus*

78

But let one of you complete a Lesbian wave-moulding,[1]
with its triangular pattern, on the coffered ceiling.

[1] The "Lesbian cyma(tium)"—now usually called *cyma reversa*—was a moulding typical of the Ionic order. It was usually ornamented with the "leaf-and-dart" pattern, in the simpler forms of which the "leaf" is a pendent shape rather like a heraldic shield, i.e. a triangle with bulging curved sides and its apex at the bottom. See D. S. Robertson, *Greek and Roman Architecture*[2] (Cambridge, 1943) 37–38 with figs. 16a and 41.

THE SACRED DELEGATION
or AT THE ISTHMIAN GAMES

(rival claimants to the title of founder of the Games), as Daedalus, and as Hephaestus. In the papyrus, we first see the satyrs receiving likenesses of themselves (possibly in the form of masks), at which they marvel (1–17); they are about to fix them on the front of the temple (18–22) when Dionysus enters and upbraids, mocks and threatens them for their disloyalty to him (23–78). They remain defiant (79–84). Someone then presents the satyrs with some "new toys" made with adze and anvil, which they are reluctant to accept (85ff); this may be their new protector returning, bringing athletic equipment (e.g. javelins) for the games, but it is more probably Dionysus, displaying shackles which he will make them wear if they remain disobedient to him (see Taplin, Stagecraft 421–2). In the end the satyrs will certainly have been reconciled to Dionysus, but we cannot tell how this may have come about. The play must

78c (78a + 78c)[1]

(?)

(78a.1)   ὁρῶντεc εἰκού[c] οὐ κατ᾽ ἀνθρώπουc[∪–·
         ὄπη δ᾽ ἂν ἔ[ρ]δηc, πάντα cοι τάδ᾽ εὐcεβῆ.

ΧΟΡΟΣ

ἦ κάρτ᾽ ὀφείλω τῶνδέ cοι· πρόφρων γὰρ εἶ.

[1] I present the main fragments of *POxy* 2162 in a single sequence, as first proposed by Bruno Snell (*Hermes* 84 [1956] 1–11)
and now confirmed by the re-examination of the papyrus by
Henry and Nünlist. The line numbering of *TrGF* is added in
brackets. Fragment 78b, from the same papyrus, contains remains (2–7 letters) of twelve lines, but only one word, [o]ὐδαμῶc
"not at all" (line 4), can be read with any confidence.

Oxyrhynchus Papyrus 2162 fr. 1(a) col. I + fr. 2(a) col. I + fr. 1(a)
col. II + fr. 2(a) col. II + fr. 2(b) (ends of lines 84–87)

have been a late one, since the temple of Poseidon was visible on stage (18).

Recent studies: A. Melero, "Οὐκ ἄνευ Θησέως: a propósito de los Teoros de Esquilo", in C. Codoñer et al. ed. *Homenaje M.C. Giner* (Salamanca, 1988) 121–8; M. Di Marco, "Sul finale dei Theoroi di Eschilo (fr. 78c, 37ss. R.)", *Eikasmos* 3 (1992) 93–104; A. Melero, "Notas a los Teoros de Esquilo", in J. A. López Férez ed. *De Homero a Libanio* (Madrid, 1995) 57–71; Sommerstein *AT* 333–5; A. Wessels and R. Krumeich in KPS 131–148; W. B. Henry and R. Nünlist, "Aeschylus, Dictyulci (fr. 47a Radt) und Isthmiastae (fr. 78 a-d)", *ZPE* 129 (2000) 13–16, at 14–16; R. Krumeich, "Die Weihgeschenke der Satyrn in Aischylos' Theoroi oder Isthmiastai", *Philologus* 144 (2000) 176–192; W. B. Henry, "Aeschylus, Isthmiastae 77–89 Snell", *ZPE* 134 (2001) 12; Podlecki 13–14; C. Marconi, "I *Theoroi* di Eschilo e le antefisse sileniche siceliote", *Sicilia Antiqua* 2 (2005) 75–93.

$$78c \ (78a + 78c)$$
$$(?)[1]$$

. . . seeing likenesses of more than human [. . .] . However you act, it will all be within the bounds of piety.[2]

CHORUS
I am very much indebted to you for this; you are being kind. [*The other character departs*.]

---

[1] This is the end of a speech by the satyrs' new (would-be) protector.   [2] i.e. it will not be sacrilegious if the satyrs decide, for example, as in fact they do, to nail the images to the temple.

ἄκουε δὴ πᾶϲ· cῖγα δ' ειθελειδ . [.] .

5 ἄθρηϲον, εἰ . [..] .. [

εἴδωλον εἶναι τοῦδ' ἐμῇ μορφῇ πλέον

τὸ Δαιδάλου μ[ί]μημα· φωνῆϲ δεῖ μόνον.

ταδ[..] . ει ..

ὅρα . [.].(.)ρ[

10 χώρει μάλα.
(78a.10)

— εὐκταῖα κόϲμον ταῦτ[α] τῷ θεῷ φέρω

καλλίγραπτον εὐχάν.

— τῇ μητρὶ τἠμῇ πράγματ' ἂν παραϲχέθοι·

ἰδοῦϲα γάρ νιν ἂν ϲαφῶϲ

15 τρέποιτ' ἂν αἰάζοιτό θ', ὡϲ

δοκοῦϲ' ἔμ' εἶναι, τὸν ἐξ-

έθρέψεν· οὕτωϲ ἐμφερὴϲ ὅδ' ἐϲτίν.

εἶα δή, ϲκοπεῖτε δῶμα ποντίου ϲειϲίχθο[νοϲ

κἀπιπαϲϲάλευ' ἕκαϲτοϲ τῆϲ κ[α]λῆϲ μορφῆϲ . [

20 ἄγγελον, κήρυκ̣' [ἄ]ναυδον, ἐμπόρων κωλύτορ[α,
(78a.20)

ὅ[ϲ] γ' ἐπιϲχήϲει κελεύθου τοὺϲ ξένο[υϲ] φο[β‿∪‑.

χαῖρ', ἄναξ· χαῖρ', ὦ Πόϲειδον, ἐπίτροπο[ϲ θ']

ὑφ[ίϲταϲο.

5 εἴ π[ου] δο[κεῖ] Kamerbeek 6 τοῦδ' Fraenkel: τουτ' Π
15 αἰάζοιτό Page: αξιαζοιτο Π 19 τ[ύπον] Setti, τ[ορὸν]
Fraenkel. 20 ἐμπόρων Fraenkel, Dodds: εμπορον Π.
21 ὅ[s] γ' Cantarella φό[βον βλέπων] Untersteiner:
φο[βουμένουϲ] Cantarella 22 suppl. Mette

Now listen, everyone, and . . . [. . .] in silence!
Look and see whether [you] th[ink] at [all]
that Daedalus' models[3] are a closer image of my form
than this is. All it needs is a voice!
[*Remains of two lines, including* this *and* see.]
Come on now!
[*A single voice*]
I bring these votives to the god to adorn his house –
fine paintings to fulfil a vow!
[*The full chorus*]
It would cause my mother some problems!
If she saw it, I'm quite sure
she'd turn about and cry out in horror, because
she'd think it was me, the child
that she brought up! That's how like me it is!

Ho there![4] Set your eyes on the house of the Sea-god,
    the Earth-shaker,
and each of you nail up there an [image] of your fair
    form
as a messenger, a voiceless herald, a restrainer of
    travellers,
which will make visito[rs] halt in their path [by the]
    fea[rsome look in its eyes].
Hail, lord! Hail, Poseidon, [and] unde[rtake to be our]
    guardian!

[3] The master-craftsman Daedalus was able to make living, moving, talking sculptures. Cf. Euripides, *Hecuba* 836–840; Euripides fr. 372; Cratinus fr. 75; Plato, *Euthyphro* 11b-c, *Meno* 97d.

[4] The speaker may now be the chorus-leader (or Silenus, if the two roles were distinct).

ΔΙΟΝΥΣΟΣ

ἔμελλον εὑρήcειν ποθ' ὑμᾶc, ὦγαθο[ί.
οὐ τοῦτ' ἐρῶ c· "οὐ δῆλοc ἦcθ' ὁδοιπο[ρῶν"·

25   αὐ[τὴ] κέλευθοc ταῦτά μοι προcεν[
          ]ορῶντα τούcδε πληc[ι]οcφ[
       ]. αυτα καὶ cαφῶc ἡγεῖτό μο[ι
          ]. τα . δω[.]μη . [.]δῳ πατ[
       ὁρῶν μύουρα καὶ βραχέα τὰ . [....]α,

30   ὡc ἐξέτριβεc Ἰcθμιαcτικὴν [....]ν,
(78a.30)
       κοὐκ ἠμέληcαc, ἀλλ' ἐγυμνάζ[ου κα]λῶc.
       εἰ δ' οὖν ἐcῴζου τὴν πάλαι παρο[ιμία]ν,

24 ουτουτερωc (Π) so divided by Lloyd-Jones
25 προcεμ[πεδοῖ] Diggle
26 (beginning) [cτίβουc θ'] ὁρῶντα Winnington-Ingram (θ'
could be dispensed with)
27 [ἐδίδαcκε] ταῦτα Winnington-Ingram (ταῦτα already Setti)
28 (beginning) [ἔγνων] e.g. Mette
29 φ[αλλί]α Maas, but Henry & Nünlist find this inconsistent
with the traces
30 [πάλη]ν Tovar
31, 32, suppl. Lobel

THE SACRED DELEGATION

*[The CHORUS are about to approach the temple when DIO-
NYSUS enters.]*

DIONYSUS

Ah, I was bound to find you some time, my good fellows! I
won't say of you that you travelled[5] incognito: your journey
it[self] con[firmed] this for me . . . seeing these [tracks (?)]
. . . [. . . informed (?) me of t]his and gave me clear guid-
ance. [I knew (?) . . .], when I saw your [phalli] short like a
mouse's tail,[6] that you were polishing up your Isthmian
[wrestling], and that you hadn't neglected it but were in
good training.[7] Well, if you'd stayed faithful to the old

---

[5] From ὁδοιπορῶν and κέλευθος we can gather that the satyrs' previous lodgings had been some distance from the Isthmus
(perhaps in Corinth city, but quite possibly further afield, e.g.
Phleius—home town of the first great satyr-dramatist, Pratinas—
or even Athens) and that they had then absconded.   [6] The
reference is to the practice, regular among ancient Greek athletes, of tying up the penis in a curled shape (just "like a mouse's
tail") by a string tied round the foreskin and then round the waist
(often, but wrongly, called "infibulation"). See D. Sansone, *Greek
Athletics and the Genesis of Sport* (Berkeley, 1988) 119–122 and
figs. 20, 22, 23. For the satyrs to come on stage in this condition
would make a striking contrast with their accustomed state of hy-
per-erection.   [7] There is probably a *double entendre* in this
sentence: πάλη and derivatives, (ἐκ)τρίβειν, γυμνάζομαι, and
references to the Isthmus, were all capable of being understood in
sexual senses (see J. J. Henderson, *The Maculate Muse* [New Ha-
ven, 1975] 137–8, 169, 176; Palaestra, Gymnasium and Isthmias
were all names of real or fictitious *hetairai*)—which might suggest
an alternative explanation for the state of the satyrs' phalli!

τοὔρχημα μᾶλλον εἰκὸс ἦν сε . [.....]ειν·
сὺ δ' ἰсθμιάζειс καὶ τρόπουс και[νοὺс μ]αθὼν
35 βραχίο[ν' ἀ]сκεῖс, χρήματα φθείρων ἐμὰ
(78a.36) κτεα[   ]ε ταῦτ' ἐπηράνω πόνων.
(78c.1)   ] ἔνορκόν ἐстί со[ι] κα[κῶс] φρονεῖν,
      ] κακῶс ὄλοιο καὶ τ . ε ...... ε.

ΣΙΛΗΝΟΣ (?)

]... χρηι сοι προста . [...] .... ν ἔπη
40   ] . [ ]ονοντωσῆ . [
δ]ουλον ἢ τρίδουλ[
ἄν]αξ, δικαι[. ( )] . [ ]θενα[...]μ[..] ..
]ῳ τε κοί[τ]ωι καὶ κακαῖс δ[υс]αυλίαιс
]ει παλαίοντ' οὐδὲν οἰκτίρε[ιс ἐμ]έ
45   ] . δετ[.] . [ ]αс πολυπ[ό]νου[......] ..
(78c.10) φ]εύγων[...] .. [ ]α τονδ' [.] . [   ] .

ΔΙΟΝΥΣΟΣ

π]οτερα παθὼν τι δε[ινὸν
ο]ὐ πολλὰ δράсαс ω[

34, 35 suppl. Lobel   33 σ' ἐπ[ισκοπ]εῖν Snell: σε
τ[ημελ]εῖν Kamerbeek   36 κτέα[να τιθείς γ]ε Kamerbeek
37 (beginning) [ἀλλ' εἴ γ'] Snell   κα[κῶс] Snell   38 (beginning) [ἐμοί,] Mette   39–46 regarded as trochaic tetrameters
by Reinhardt (39–48 by Radt)   39 [πότερ]ά με χρή сοι
πρὸς τάδ' [ἔνν]έπειν ἔπη; e.g. Henry & Nünlist   42 [ἄν]αξ
Kamerbeek   43 (beginning) [κακ]ῷ Cantarella, [σπαρν]ῷ
Diggle   44 suppl. Nünlist   45 [ἐγ]ὼ δὲ τ[α]ύ[τ]ας Snell
πολυπ[ό]νου[с] Nünlist   46 suppl. Cantarella   47 suppl.
Fraenkel   48 [κο]ὐ Snell   ὡ[ν δίκην δώσεις τάχα] Reinhardt

proverb,[8] you'd have more likely been [practis]ing dancing; but you're learning a new way of life, that of Isthmian
athletes, exercising your arms and injuring this property of
mine[9] by putting it into the hands of the person who's help-
ing you in your efforts. [Well, if] you're absolutely committed to being[10] ho[stile to me], then a curse upon you[11] and
. . . .

SILENUS (?)[12]

[What kind] of words should I [sp]eak in reply to what you
have said? [*One line unintelligible.*] [. . .] a slave or thrice a
slave [. . . , lo]rd, just(ly) [. . . with scant]y bedding and
poor lodging [. . . you] take no pity on [m]e when I am
wrestling[13] [. . .] And I [. . .] t[h]e[s]e laborious [. . .
f]leeing [. . .] this [. . .]

DIONYSUS

[I]s it after suffering something te[rrible that you are ap-
pealing to me (?) or is it n]ot, rather, after *doing* a great
deal f[or which you will soon pay the penalty?]

---

[8] As Lobel saw, the proverb referred to is ἔρδοι τις ἦν
ἕκαστος εἰδείη τέχνην "a man should stick to the trade he knows"
(quoted by Aristophanes, *Wasps* 1431, and Cicero, *To Atticus*
5.10.3 and *Tusculan Disputations* 1.41).   [9] i.e. their own bodies.
[10] lit. "it is a matter of oath for you to be", i.e. you are sworn to be.
[11] lit. "may you perish miserably".   [12] Calculations of where
the beginnings of lines would stand in the papyrus suggest that
this speech, and possibly also Dionysus' reply, were in trochaic
tetrameters rather than iambic trimeters.   [13] Silenus may
possibly, with typical effrontery, be claiming Dionysus' sympathy
in the hardships he is suffering as a result of running away from
Dionysus!

ΧΟΡΟΣ (?)

]ια θαρϲῶν λεξ[

50
(78c.14)

]ωι ἱερῷ μεν[

[remains of two lines, after which eight lines are missing; then remains of three more lines]

64
(78a.64)

ΔΙΟΝΥΣΟΣ

ϲάκει καλύψαϲ[...]εν[

65

ϲπείρειϲ δὲ μῦθον τόνδε . [

καὶ ῥηματίζειϲ εἰϲ ἔμ' ἐκτρ .. [

ὡϲ οὐδέν εἰμι τὴν ϲιδηρῖτι[ν

γύννιϲ δ' ἄναλκιϲ οὐδενειμ . [

καὶ νῦν τάδ' ἄλλα καὶ ποταίν[ι'

70
(78a.70)

ἔχθιϲτα πάντων τῶ[ν

πλύνειϲ τ' ἔμ' αὐτὸν [

(78a.72)

ἐφ' ἣν ἀγείρω πλῆ[θος

(78c.37)

κοὐδεὶϲ παλαιῶν οὐδὲ τῶν νεωτέρων

ἑκὼν ἄπεϲτι τῶνδε διϲτοίχω[ν χορῶν·

75

ϲὺ δ' ἰϲθμιάζειϲ καὶ πίτυος ἐϲτ[εμμένοϲ

50 [ἐν τ]ῷ Setti   μεν[ῶ] Snell, μεν[οῦμεν] Kamerbeek
66 ἐκτρόπ[ουϲ λόγουϲ] Kamerbeek: ἐκτρέπ[ων κότον] Lloyd-
Jones   67 (end) [μάχην] Kamerbeek, cf. Pindar, *Nemean*
5.19   68 οὐδ' ἔνειμ' ἐ[ν ἄρϲεϲιν] Lloyd-Jones: οὐδέν εἰμ'
(Cantarella) ἐν ἀνδράϲιν Reinhardt   69 ποταίν[ι'
ἐγκαλεῖϲ] Fraenkel   70 τῶ[ν] Cantarella, then [πάροιθε
δυϲφρόνων] Kamerbeek: perh. e.g. τῶ[ν ὀνειδῶν τῶν πάλαι]
71 e.g. [καὶ χορείαν τὴν ἐμὴν] (Kamerbeek) or [τήν τ' ἐμὴν
πανήγυριν] (Reinhardt)   72 πλ[ῆθοϲ] (sic: η was first read
by Henry & Nünlist) Kamerbeek   74, 75 suppl. Lobel

From what follows we can read speak (?) with confidence *(line 49) and* remain [in] the sanctuary *(line 50), then no more until line 64, when Dionysus is speaking again.*

DIONYSUS

[. . .] covering [yourself] with a shield[14] [. . .] and you disseminate this story [. . .] and utter against me [words that are] out of [order (?)], that I am no good at [fighting (?)] with iron, but am a cowardly, effeminate being and do not belong [among males (?)]. And now you [make] these further, fresh [allegations (?)], more hateful than any of [your previous insults (?)], and you vilify[15] me myself [and the choral festival (?)] for which I am assembling a multitude [. . .] and none of the old people or of the young willingly stays away from these double-file[16] [dances]. But you are playing the Isthmian athlete and gar[landing] yourselves

---

14 Kamerbeek attractively suggested that the satyrs had been intending not only to wrestle but also to compete in the foot-race in armour (ὁπλιτοδρομία).

15 lit. "soak" (like a garment being washed); cf. the English phrase "take to the cleaners" (= criticize severely).

16 This seems to indicate that in Aeschylus' time the normal formation of a satyric chorus was in two rows (with six performers in each). According to Pollux (4.108–9), the *tragic* chorus (in the later fifth century, when it had fifteen members) normally performed in three rows of five; it is a plausible, but far from secure, inference that both types of chorus (which were composed of the same performers) changed from two to three rows at the same time as they changed their numbers.

(78c.40)   κλάδοιϲι κιϲϲοῦ δ᾽ οὐδ[α]μοῦ τιμη[
ταῦτ᾽ οὖν δακρύϲειϲ οὐ καπνῷ [
παρόντα δ᾽ ἐγγὺϲ οὐχ ὁρᾷϲ τα[

ΧΟΡΟΣ

ἀλλ᾽ οὔποτ᾽ ἔξειμ᾽ ϵ[
80   τοῦ ἱεροῦ· καὶ τί μοι
ταῦτ᾽ ἀπειλεῖϲ ἔχ[ων;]
Ἴϲθμιον αντϵ[
Ποϲειδᾶνοϲο[
ϲὺ δ᾽ ἄλλοιϲ ταῦτ[α π]εμπε [

76 κλάδοιϲι Lobel: καλλοιϲι Π   τιμὴ[ν νέμειϲ] Lobel
77 [δεδηγμένοϲ] Kamerbeek, Maas
78 τὰ [δεϲμά ϲοι] Reinhardt
79 ἑ[κὼν] Cantarella: ἑ[γὼ] Mette
81 suppl. Kamerbeek
82–83 ἀντϵ[(ι)ϲκαλῶ] Ποϲειδᾶν᾽, ὃ[ϲ οἰκτιρει·] Kamerbeek
84 suppl. Snell, who ends the line with [δῶρα]

with pine branches,[17] and not paying the ivy[18] its due honour at all. For this you'll shed tears, and it won't be [because you're stung by (?)] smoke! Don't you see [your bonds (?)] here, close by?[19]

CHORUS

No, I will never [willingly (?)] depart
from the sanctuary! Why, pray,
do you ke[ep] threatening me like this?
In response [I summon (?)]
Poseidon of the Isthmus, who [will have mercy on me
       (?)]

[17] The Isthmian temple of Poseidon was surrounded by a pine grove (Strabo 8.6.22, Pausanias 2.1.7), and victorious athletes there were originally crowned with a pine wreath, later replaced by a celery wreath in imitation of the Nemean games (see Plutarch, *Moralia* 675d-677b; by Plutarch's time the wreath was of pine once more).

[18] Typically used for Dionysiac wreaths; cf. e.g. Euripides, *Bacchae* 81, 105, 177.

[19] If Dionysus is indeed here referring to the objects soon to be offered to the chorus as "novel toys", the fact that (so far as we know) neither he nor the chorus has made any previous mention of them in the 55 lines he has been on stage makes it likely that they are not in his own hands but are being carried by attendants, who hitherto have been positioned unobtrusively but now step forward.

ΔΙΟΝΥΣΟΣ (?)

85
(78c.50)

ἐπεὶ [τ]ὰ καινὰ ταῦτα μα[νθά]νειν φιλεῖ[ς],
ἐγὼ [φέ]ρω σοι νεοχμὰ . [...] ἀθύρματα,
ἀπὸ [σκε]πάρνου κἄκμ[ονος ν]εόκτ[ιτα.]
τουτ[ὶ τὸ] πρῶτόν ἐςτί σοι τ[ῶ]ν παιγ[νίω]ν.

ΧΟΡΟΣ

ἐμοὶ μὲν οὐχί· τῶν φίλων νεῖμόν τινι.

ΔΙΟΝΥΣΟΣ (?)

90

μὴ ἄπειπε μηδ' ὄρνιθος οὕνεκ', ὦγαθε—

ΧΟΡΟΣ

τί δὴ γανοῦςθαι τοῦτο; καὶ τί χρήςομαι;

ΔΙΟΝΥΣΟΣ (?)

ἥνπερ μεθεῖλ[ες τὴ]ν τέχνην, ταύτῃ πρεπ[ει—

ΧΟΡΟΣ

τί δρᾶν; τί ποιεῖν; [τοὐ]πίπλουν μ' οὐχ ἀνδάν[ει].

ΔΙΟΝΥΣΟΣ (?)

ξυνιςθμιάζειν [.....] ἐμμελέςτατον.

85 ἐπεὶ [τ]ὰ Barigazzi   μα[νθά]νειν φιλεῖ[ς] Setti
86 [φέ]ρω Lobel:]ρω (or]ροω) Πᵖᶜ:]ροι Πᵃᶜ   [δεῦρ'] Kamerbeek, [ταῦτ'] Snell (traces of the first letter were first reported by
Henry)   87 suppl. Lobel
88 τουτ[ὶ τὸ] Fraenkel, Siegmann   τ[ῶ]ν παιγ[νίω]ν Siegmann
92 μεθεῖλ[ες τὴ]ν Lobel   πρέπ[ει] Kamerbeek   93 so
read and supplemented by Henry (μ' οὐ[χ] ἀνδάν[ει] [sic] already
Kamerbeek)   94 [ἐστὶν] Cantarella: [γ' οἶον] Radt

DIONYSUS[20] (?)

Since you are set on lea[rn]ing these new ways, I [br]ing
you [here (?)] some novel toys, [f]reshly fa[shioned] on the
[ad]ze and the anv[il]. [*Presenting one of the "toys"*] This
here is the first of the play[thing]s for you.

CHORUS

Not for me! Give it to one of my friends.

DIONYSUS (?)

Don't refuse, my good fellow, just because of an evil omen,
to—

CHORUS

To get what pleasure out of this? And what use will I make
of it?

DIONYSUS (?)

It is appropriate to the new trade you have taken up—

---

[20] It remains disputed whether the character who takes part in
this dialogue is Dionysus (so e.g. Diggle) or the satyrs' new patron
(so e.g. Lloyd-Jones, Wessels & Krumeich). I prefer Dionysus,
partly for the reasons given by Taplin *Stagecraft* 421–2, and also
because (i) line 77 is unquestionably a threat of punishment (cf.
81), which one would expect to be followed up when the satyrs remain recalcitrant, and (ii) [τ]ὰ καινὰ ταῦτα (85) is not how one
would expect a supporter of athletes to describe athletics, but
rather recalls Dionysus' disparaging words at 32–35. In this case,
of course, Dionysus' words about his "gifts" will be ironic throughout.

ΧΟΡΟΣ

95   φερω[   ] ἐμβήcεται.

ΔΙΟΝΥΣΟΣ (?)

(78c.60)   ἐπιϲ[   ]βάδην ἐλ[ᾶ]ιϲ.

ΧΟΡΟΣ

..]ει[   ] . [.]φέρων σφυρά.

[remains of one further line]

95 φέρω[ν τάδ' οὐδεὶς] Barigazzi, then [εἰς ἀγῶν'] Snell
96 ἐλ[ᾶ]ις Cantarella   97 perh. e.g. [ἐν ξύλ]ω[ι] φέρων?

79

καὶ μὴν παλαιῶν τῶνδέ σοι σκωπευμάτων

Athenaeus 14.629f; cf. Hesychius σ1218

CHORUS

For doing what? For what activity? I don't like [this] equipment!

DIONYSUS

For joining in the Isthmian Games—[it's] just the right thing.

CHORUS

[Nobody (?)] is going to enter [the contest (?)] wearin[g these (?)]

DIONYSUS' reply ends you'll advance at a steady pace *(96), and the* CHORUS *may then express scepticism about their ability to do so* with my ankles [in gyves (?)] *(97).*

79

And also, of these old look-out dances[1] of yours . . .

[1] Referring to a dance which included the turning of the head from side to side, and the raising of hand to eyebrows, in the manner of a look-out on a hill or tower peering into the distance in various directions (Athenaeus 14.629f; Pollux 4.103). The speaker may be the satyrs' new patron, disparaging their old way of life.

ΘΡΗΙΣΣΑΙ

83

καὶ τὸ ξίφος ἐκάμπτετο οὐδαμῇ ἐνδιδόντος τοῦ χρωτὸς
τῇ σφαγῇ, τόξον ὥς τις ἐντείνων, πρὶν δή τις ... παρ-
οῦσα δαίμων ἔδειξεν αὐτῷ κατὰ ποῖον μέρος δεῖ χρή-
σασθαι τῇ σφαγῇ.

Scholia to Sophocles, *Ajax* 833

There have been many attempts to restore the poet's words;
combining what seem to me the best proposals, one may suggest:

> καὶ χρωτὸς ἐνδιδόντος οὐδαμοῦ σφαγῇ
> ἔκαμπτε, τόξον ὥς τις ἐντείνων, ξίφος,
> πρὶν δὴ παροῦσα δαιμόνων ἔδειξέ τις.

1 so Hartung   2 so Bothe (placing it before 1); first
placed here (but with ἔκαμψε) by Hartung   3 so Sidgwick

100

THRACIAN WOMEN

We learn from scholia on Sophocles' Ajax (on lines 134, 815 and 833) that this play included the suicide of Ajax, which was narrated by a messenger; that Ajax was invulnerable except in one spot (because, when he was a baby, Heracles had covered him with his lion-skin), and as a result was unable to strike himself the fatal blow until "a goddess" (Athena?) showed him the right place to do so (the armpit); and that the "Thracian women" of the chorus were war captives. The play almost certainly followed The Award of the Arms *(q.v.), and the third play of the trilogy is likely to have been* Women of Salamis *(q.v.)*

83

And, since his skin would not yield anywhere to the fatal blow, he kept bending his sword, like a man drawing a bow, until some goddess appeared and showed him the place.

From the messenger's report of Ajax's suicide.

84a

τρόποι δ' ἀμεμφεῖς, φιλόμουσοι, φιλοσυμπόται

Herodian, *General Prosody* fr. 11 Hunger

ΙΕΡΕΙΑΙ

86

στέλλειν ὅπως τάχιστα· ταῦτα γὰρ πατὴρ
Ζεὺς ἐγκαθίει Λοξίᾳ θεσπίσματα

Scholia to Sophocles, *Oedipus at Colonus* 893; Macrobius, *Saturnalia* 5.22.13

87

εὐφαμεῖτε· μελισσονόμοι δόμον Ἀρτέμιδος πέλας
οἴγειν

Aristophanes, *Frogs* 1273–4 with scholia

---

[1] Since the chorus presumably consisted of priestesses, and the opening and closing of temples was an important priestly duty (indeed κληδοῦχος "keyholder" can be a virtual synonym of ἱερεύς or ἱέρεια: cf. *Supp.* 291), it is likely that they are here referring to themselves. The bee was an emblem of Artemis, especially

84a

And his habits were blameless, fond of music, fond of the symposium

From a choral song, possibly praising Ajax after his death.

PRIESTESSES

All we can say for sure about this play is that its setting was a temple of Artemis. It has more than once been suggested that the play was about Iphigeneia, but the mention (fr. 88) of Casolaba, a town in Caria, points to a setting in Asia Minor, and possibly to a connection with Carians *(q.v.)*

86

Send ⟨him/her/it/them⟩ as quickly as may be; for such is the oracle that Father Zeus has passed down to Loxias.

87

Keep silence: the Bee-wards[1] are at hand to open Artemis' temple.

From a choral song.

at Ephesus but also elsewhere (see A. B. Cook, *JHS* 15 [1895] 12–13; L. Bodson, *Hiera Zoia* [Brussels, 1978] 38–43; Euripides, *Hippolytus* 76 doubtless plays on this association), and her cult-personnel may have been called μελισσονόμοι (i) as servants of the bee-goddess, or (ii) as keepers of hives of bees sacred to her, or (iii) as supervisors of girl acolytes who were called Artemis' "bees" as those who served her at Brauron in Attica were called "bears" (see R. C. T. Parker, *Polytheism and Society at Athens* [Oxford, 2005] 228–249).

ΙΞΙΩΝ

Of the two well-known stories about Ixion, that of his treacherous murder of his father-in-law (D)eïoneus appears to have been dramatized by Aeschylus in Perrhaebian Women *(q.v.). This leaves for* Ixion *the other tale, which follows on from it, of how gods and men alike were so horrified at this murder (the first ever committed in which the victim was a kinsman) that none of them was willing to purify Ixion; of how Zeus at length took pity on him, and not only purified him but took him up to heaven; of how Ixion, despite having received this great boon from Zeus, committed the ultimate* hybris *of attempting to seduce Hera (Zeus deceived him into lying instead with a cloud in her shape); and of how in punishment he was bound to a wheel "on which he rolls around everywhere,*

90

βίου πονηροῦ θάνατος εὐκλεέστερος

Stobaeus 4.53.15

IXION

proclaiming to mortals that they must repay their benefactors with kind deeds in return" (Pindar, Pythian 2.21–24). Aeschylus refers twice in Eumenides (439–441, 717–8) to Ixion's successful supplication to Zeus (though not to its consequences). It is not clear, however, how the tale can have been adapted for dramatic treatment, nor even whether it was a tragedy or a satyr-drama (fr. 90 suggests the former, fr. 91 the latter). The setting, at any rate, was evidently on earth, not in heaven, so probably Ixion was depicted in his period of isolation as an abhorred, polluted murderer with whom no one would associate—except, maybe, the satyrs? The play need not have been produced together with Perrhaebian Women; no plausible suggestion has ever been made as to how they could have formed part of a connected trilogy or tetralogy.

90

Death is less disgraceful than a wretched[1] life.

[1] Or "wicked"; without context we cannot determine for sure the meaning of πονηρός here (the one other occurrence of the word in Aeschylus, at *Cho.* 1045, is of no assistance).

91

τὸν δ' ἡμίοπον
ταχέως ὁ μέγας καταπίνει

Athenaeus 4.182c

ΙΦΙΓΕΝΕΙΑ

94

οὔτοι γυναιξὶ <χρὴ> κυδάζεσθαι· τί γαρ;

Scholia to Sophocles, *Ajax* 722; *Suda* κ2603

<χρὴ> add. Blomfield: om. schol., *Suda*

91

The half-size[1] pipe is easily trounced by the big one.

[1] lit. "half-holed", i.e. with three finger-holes instead of six. Since the verb καταπίνω "swallow whole, gulp down"—here apparently used metaphorically to mean "vanquish easily"—is not found in tragedy proper, this fragment should probably be assigned to a satyr chorus and indicates the genre of the play. It has sometimes been found tempting to interpret the fragment as applying figuratively to the transgressions of Ixion, but it is more likely to relate to something of more interest to satyrs.

IPHIGENEIA

We cannot tell whether this play was parallel in subject to Euripides' Iphigeneia at Aulis *(and to Sophocles'* Iphigeneia) *or to his* Iphigeneia in Tauris; *we only know that in it a woman, whether Iphigeneia or another, was involved in a quarrel in which high words were spoken (fr. 94); one possibility is that this woman was Clytaemestra, who appeared both in Sophocles' and in Euripides' plays about the Aulis sacrifice.*

94

It is not right to revile women.[1] How could it be?

[1] In itself the phrase could also mean "to be reviled by women" (for the two senses compare, respectively, Epicharmus fr. 32.6 K-A and Sophocles, *Ajax* 722); but χρὴ (the only other possible supplement, δεῖ, means in Aeschylus "it is needed", "it is necessary", or "it is destined", none of which fits the context here) asserts an ethical or social *duty*, and it makes no sense to speak of an ethical or social duty not to be reviled by women. The speaker is thus probably a woman, and quite possibly Clytaemestra, who in *Agamemnon* is very sensitive to male disparagement or condescension.

ΚΑΒΕΙΡΟΙ

The Cabeiri were minor gods, with varying attributes and functions, worshipped at various locations in Boeotia and the northern Aegean, especially Thebes and Lemnos. From Athenaeus (10.428f) we learn that Jason and his companions appeared in this play, and that in one scene they were drunk; since the passage blames Aeschylus for being "the first to introduce the sight of drunken men into tragedy", it is clear that this play was a tragedy, not a satyrdrama, in which drunkenness would have been nothing unusual. The play included a catalogue of the Argonauts (so the scholia to Pindar, Pythian 4.[171] 303). It has usually been associated with the Argonauts' stay in Lemnos, as a sequel to Hypsipyle *(q.v.). Deforge (see below) has suggested that the play may rather have dealt with a subse-*

95

ὄρνιθα δ' οὐ ποιῶ σε τῆς ἐμῆς ὁδοῦ

Athenaeus 9.373d

96

μήποτε κρωσσοὺς
μήτ' οἰνηροὺς μήθ' ὑδατηροὺς
λείπειν ἀφνεοῖσι δόμοισι

Pollux 6.23 (not naming the play), cf. Antiatticist in *Anecdota Bekkeri* 1.115.3 ὑδρηροὺς πίθους καὶ οἰνηρούς· Αἰσχύλος Καβείροις (Blomfield: καιείροις cod.)

1 μήποτε Pollux^{FS}: μήτε Pollux^{AB}: μήτ' αὖ or μηδ' αὖ Blomfield   3 λείπειν Heath: λιπεῖν codd.

CABEIRI

*quent visit they made to Samothrace, where according to
Apollonius Rhodius (1.915–921) they were initiated into
the local mysteries of the Great Gods—who in the fifth century and later were widely identified, rightly or wrongly,
with the Cabeiri (Herodotus 2.51.2; Stesimbrotus, FGrH
107 F 20; Plutarch, Marcellus 30.6); but the wine/drunken-
ness theme (evident also in frr. 96 and 97) points strongly to
Lemnos, where wine vessels were the most characteristic
dedication at the Cabeiri's sanctuary.[1] If the play followed
Hypsipyle within a tetralogy, the other companion plays
were probably Lemnian Women and The Argo (qq.v.)*

Recent studies: B. Deforge, "Eschyle et la légende des Argonautes", REG 100 (1987) 30–44, esp. 39–41; Podlecki 12–13.

95

But I do not treat you as an omen of my journey.

96

That there shall never be a dearth
of jars, either of wine or of water,
in ⟨this/your⟩ wealthy home.

A blessing chanted by the Cabeiri.[1]

[1] According to Plutarch (*Moralia* 632f–633a), the Cabeiri in
this play also "playfully threatened" to make the house "run short
of vinegar" (ὄξους σπανίζειν δῶμα); the three Greek words cited
are clearly a direct quotation from the play (fr. 97), but they cannot come from the same context as fr. 96, since their rhythm is
iambic and fr. 96 is in anapaests.

ΚΑΛΛΙΣΤΩ

The maiden Callisto was a hunting companion of Artemis in Arcadia; she was made pregnant by Zeus, and before giving birth was transformed into a bear (by Zeus or Hera or Artemis); her child, however (who in some accounts had to be taken from her womb after Artemis had shot her), was a human one, Arcas, the eponymous ancestor of the Arcadians. Callisto's ultimate destiny, by order of Zeus, was to be placed in the heavens as the constellation of the Great Bear. There are very many variant forms of this story (see for example Hesiod fr. 163; Pausanias 8.3.6–

ΚΑΡΕΣ Η ΕΥΡΩΠΗ

Europa, who in most accounts is a Phoenician by birth and a sister of Cadmus, was abducted by Zeus in the form of a bull (or, in this play, by a bull sent by Zeus [fr. 99.1–2]) and taken to Crete, where she gave birth to Minos and Rhadamanthys; in some accounts, including the one followed in this play, she also has a third son, Sarpedon, destined to be killed at Troy (so Hesiod frr. 140, 141). In this play Europa, who must now be elderly, is evidently living in Caria—which, as Strabo (14.3.3) complains, the dramatist seems to have identified or confused with Sarpedon's homeland of Lycia; Minos is dead (implied by fr. 99.12), Rhadamanthys though immortal has departed from earth, and she is anxious about the welfare of Sarpedon. There can be little doubt that the play culminated in the arrival of news of Sarpedon's death, followed probably by the return

CALLISTO

8.4.1; [Apollodorus], Library 3.8.1–2; Ovid, Metamorpho-
ses 1.211–240, 2.401–530; full particulars in Gantz 725–
9), some of which involve horrors or near-horrors of the
kind that tragedy loved to exploit (e.g. Arcas killed and cut
up by his grandfather Lycaon to make a cannibalistic meal
for Zeus, or unknowingly pursuing his bear-mother into an
inviolable sanctuary so that both of them are nearly sacri-
ficed). We do not know how Aeschylus treated the subject,
and only one two-word fragment of the play survives.

CARIANS *or* EUROPA

home of his body, conveyed from Troy by the divine powers
Sleep and Death (cf. Iliad 16.453–7, 666–683).

   West (see below) has put forward the attractive hypoth-
esis that Carians *was the first play of a trilogy which also*
included Memnon *and* The Weighing of Souls *(qq.v.), and*
the daring one that of these three plays only Memnon *was*
by Aeschylus, the others having been written (or com-
pleted, or revised) by his son Euphorion, whom West re-
gards (rightly, I believe) as the author of Prometheus
Bound *and* Unbound.

Recent studies: M. L. West, "*Iliad* and *Aethiopis* on stage: Aeschy-
lus and son", *CQ* 50 (2000) 338–352, esp. 347–350; A. G. Keen,
"Lycians in the *Kares* of Aeschylus", in F. McHardy et al. ed. *Lost
Dramas of Classical Athens* (Exeter, 2005) 63–82; W. S. Barrett,
"A detail of tragic usage: the application to persons of verbal
nouns in -μα", in *Greek Lyric, Tragedy, and Textual Criticism*
(Oxford, 2007) 351–367, at 355–57.

99

ΕΥΡΩΠΗ

ταύρῳ τε λειμῶ ξένια πάμβοτον †παραν†.
τοιόνδε μὲν Ζεὺς κλέμμα πρεσβύτου πατρὸς
αὐτοῦ μένων ἄμοχθος ἤνυσεν λαβεῖν.
τί οὖν; τὰ πολλὰ κεῖνα διὰ παύρων λέγω.
5 γυνὴ θεῷ μειχθεῖσα παρθένου σέβας
ἤμειψα, παίδων δ' ἐζύγην ξυνάονι.
καὶ †τριαγωνεις† τοὺς γυναικείους πόνους
ἐκαρτέρης‘, ἄρουρα δ' οὐκ ἐμέμψατο
τοῦ μὴ 'ξενεγκεῖν σπέρμα γενναῖον πατρός.
10 ἐκ τῶν μεγίστων δ' ἠρξάμην φυτευμάτων
Μίνων τεκοῦσα <

                                                    >

Ῥαδάμανθυν, ὅσπερ ἄφθιτος παίδων ἐμῶν.
ἀλλ' οὐκ ἐν αὐγαῖς ταῖς ἐμαῖς ζόην ἔχει,

1 λειμῶ West: λιμω Π   πάμβοτον West (-ος Weil): πανποδος
Π   πορῶν Platt   2 τοιοντε Π   προςβυτον Π
3 ἄμοχθος Wilamowitz: αμοχθον Π   ἤνυσεν (ἤνυσεν) Blass:
ηνοσον Π   4 τί οὖν Wecklein: τειουν Π   παυρω Π
5 θεου Π   6 εμιψε Π   εσυγη Π   ξυνάονι Blass: ξυν-
αγωνει Π   7 τριαγωνεις Π: τρίς γοναῖσι Wecklein: τρισὶν
ἀγῶσι Weil   8 ἄρουρα δ' οὐκ van Herwerden: αρουρας και
ουκ Π   9 του μεν ξεναικειν Π   γενναῖον Schenkl: γεναι
Π   10 ερξαμην ψυδευματων Π   11 Μίνων West:
μινω Π   lacuna (of at least 1½ lines) posited by Buecheler and
others   12 ραλαμανθον ωσπερ αφθιδος Π   13 αλλακ
Π   ἐν αὐγαῖς Wecklein, Gomperz, Kock: εμαγαις Π   ζόην
ἔχει Buecheler: ζοας εχειν Π

99

EUROPA

[My father unwittingly facilitated my abduction by welcoming Zeus's treacherous agent (?)] and <providing (?)>
for the bull a rich grazing meadow as a guest-gift. Such was
the theft that Zeus succeeded in committing at the ex-
pense of my aged father, without moving from his place
and without any toil. Well then, I shall tell the long tale of
the past in a few words. I, a mortal woman, united with a
god, gave up the honour of virginity, and was joined to a
partner in parenthood; three times I endured a woman's
pains in childbirth,[1] and my fertile field did not complain
nor refuse to bear to the end the noble seed of the Father. I
began with the greatest of my offspring, giving birth to
Minos . . .

*Here at least a line and a half, probably more, are lost: Europa may
well have said something about Minos' wealth and his rule over
Crete and beyond, and will certainly have mentioned that he is
now dead.*

[Secondly I bore] Rhadamanthys, who is the immortal one
among my children; but the life he has is not seen by my

---

[1] Adopting Wecklein's emendation rather than Weil's ("I endured a woman's pains in three struggles").

τὸ μὴ παρὸν δὲ τέρψιν οὐκ ἔχει φίλοις.
15 τρίτον δέ, τοῦ νῦν φροντίςιν χειμάζομαι,
Σαρπηδόν᾽, αἰχμὴ μὴ ᾿ξ Ἄρεως καθίκετο.
κ̣λέος γὰρ ἥκειν <
          > Ἑλλάδος λωτίϲματα
π̣άϲηϲ, ὑπερφέρονταϲ ἀλκίμῳ σθένει,
α̣ὐχεῖν δὲ Τρώων ἄϲτυ πορθήϲειν βίᾳ·
<
                              >
20 πρὸς οὓϲ δέδοικα μή τι μαργαίνων δορὶ
ἀνυπέρβατον δράϲῃ τε καὶ πάθῃ κακόν.
λεπτὴ γὰρ ἐλπίϲ, ἠδ᾽ ἐπὶ ξυροῦ μένει
μὴ πάντα παίϲαϲ᾽ ἐκχέω πρὸϲ ἕρματι

Didot papyrus ed. H. Weil, *Un papyrus inédit de la biblio-
thèque de M. Ambroise Firmin-Didot* (Paris, 1879), recto coll. IV
9–V 9

Corrections not otherwise attributed are Weil's.

14 παρων τε Π   φιλουϲ Π   15 δέ τοῦ νῦν Buecheler:
δετουνουν Π   φορντιζειν Π   χειμάζομαι Buecheler:
χειμάζεται Π   16 ϲαλφηδον Π   αἰχμὴ μὴ ᾿ξ Ἄρεωϲ
Francken: αιχμηϲ δ εξ αρεοϲ Π   17 κλεο Π   lacuna posited by Barrett, who suggests e.g. < Ἀϲιάδ᾽ εἰϲ πολύϲπορον /
ἄνδραϲ δορυϲϲούϲ,>   ἥκειν Bergk, Ἑλλάδοϲ Blass,
λωτίϲματα Weil: ηκειεν λοτιϲ λοτιϲματοϲ Π   18 ὑπερφέρονταϲ Wilamowitz (-τοϲ Weil): υπερπερωντεϲ Π   ἀλκίμῳ
ϲθένει Bergk, Gomperz: αλκιμουϲτενηϲ Π   19 αὐχεῖν van
Herwerden: αυχει Π   τρωαν Π   παρθηϲη βιον Π
19/20 lacuna posited by Barrett: perh. e.g. <ἔβη δ᾽ ἐκεῖϲε παῖϲ
ἐμὸϲ λαοὺϲ ἄγων, / Τροίαϲ ἀπείρξων ἐχθρὸν Ἀργείων

eyes,[2] and absence brings no joy to loved ones. The third
child I bore was the one over whom I am now storm-tossed
with anxiety, Sarpedon—anxiety lest an enemy spear-
point[3] may have pierced him. The story is that ‹spear-
wielding men (?),› the best in all Greece, have come ‹to
fertile Asia (?)›,[4] men outstanding in martial strength, and
boast that they will storm and sack the city of the Trojans.
‹My son has gone there at the head of his troops to keep
the hostile army of the Argives out of Troy;› I fear that
against them he may go berserk with his spear and both do
and suffer the greatest possible harm.[5] My hope is slender,
and it rests on the razor's edge whether I may strike a rock
and lose everything.

    [2] We are probably to assume that he is in the Isles of the
Blest, where he is already to be found in the *Odyssey* (4.564),
doubtless because of his great wisdom and justice (e.g. Hesiod fr.
141.13, Theognis 701).   [3] lit. "a spear-point from Ares".
[4] The lacuna posited here by Barrett is necessary because otherwise "have come" (ἥκειν) would have to mean, absurdly, "have
come to where I now am", i.e. Caria; the further lacuna which he
posits two lines later is required because if Europa feels her hear-
ers need to be told that a Greek army is attacking Troy, she cannot
possibly leave it to them to infer, as something too obvious to mention, that her son has gone to fight in this war on the other side of
Asia Minor. There need be no surprise that the careless schoolboy
who wrote this text has managed to omit (probably) three lines
from an eight-line passage.   [5] lit. "unsurpassable harm".

στρατόν›   20 πρὸς οὓς Bergk: προσου Π   δεδωκα
μητεῖ μαργαια (μαργανα Π^{pc}) δορει Π   21 αστυβερ-
βαρτον Π   22 ελπιςι Π   ἠδ᾽ ἐπὶ ξυροῦ Weil, μένει Blass:
ηδη επι ξυρημενηι Π   23 ἔρματι Blass: αρματει Π

100

ἀλλ' Ἄρης φιλεῖ
ἀεὶ τὰ λῷστα πάντ' ἀπανθίζειν στρατοῦ

Stobaeus 4.10.24

2 πάντ' ἀπανθίζειν Porson: πάντα τἀνθρώπων codd.

ΚΕΡΚΤΩΝ

*This play is stated to be a satyr-drama by Hesychius on two
(α6122, ε6960) of the four occasions when he quotes it.
Cercyon was a king of Eleusis (Aeschylus' home town)
who forced all passers-by to wrestle with him, and always killed them, until challenged by Theseus; one of the
metopes of the Athenian Hephaisteion confirms the fifth-
century currency of the account found in [Apollodorus],
Epitome 1.3, that Theseus defeated him by lifting him up
and dashing him against the ground, and there is vaguer
reference to Theseus "closing Cercyon's wrestling school"*

102

ἀμφωτίδες τοι τοῖς ἐνῳδίοις πέλας

Pollux 10.175

ἐνῳδίοις Radt, cf. Aesch. fr. 424b (Photius s.v. ἐνῳδία):
ἐνωτίοις codd.

100

But Ares is always in the habit of plucking off all that is best in an army.

CERCYON

in Bacchylides 18.26–27. The pattern of the play may have been similar to that of Euripides' Cyclops, with the satyrs (perhaps hitherto enslaved by Cercyon) losing no opportunity of displaying their selfishness and cowardice. The association—indeed partial identification—between the satyrs' true master Dionysus and Iacchus, the principal male divinity worshipped in the Eleusinian Mysteries, may well have featured in the play in one way or another.

Recent studies: A. Wessels and R. Krumeich in KPS 149–151; Podlecki 4–5.

102

Ear-guards[1] next to his earrings.

[1] Worn by wrestlers for protection. The person being described evidently has a luxurious lifestyle, but it is not clear whether he is Cercyon, or Theseus (thought of as an aristocratic youth of the kind who frequented the wrestling-schools of classical Athens), or even Dionysus.

ATTRIBUTED FRAGMENTS

ΚΗΡΥΚΕΣ

References in Pollux (10.68, 10.186) and Photius (s.v. πυρσοκόρσου λέοντος) establish that this was a satyr-play, and fr. 109 shows that it was concerned with one or another of the exploits of Heracles. B. A. van Groningen (Mnemosyne 58 [1930] 134) made the very attractive conjecture that it referred to one of the first of them, narrated by [Apollodorus], Library 2.4.9–11. At the age of eighteen, Heracles, then living in Thebes, slew a lion on Mount Cithaeron and dressed himself in its skin (cf. frr. 109, 110). On his way back, he happened to meet the heralds who had been sent to Thebes by Erginus, king of the Minyans of Orchomenus, to demand Thebes' annual tribute of a hundred cattle; he cut off the heralds' ears, noses and hands, tied them round their necks, and sent them back to Erginus

109

καὶ τῆς σισύρνης τῆς λεοντείου δορᾶς

Pollux 10.186

καὶ F S B A: κατὰ C L   σισύρνης C F S: τε σύρνης B A: κύρνης L   λεοντείου δορᾶς Mette (<δορᾶς> already Toup), cf. Hesychius λ646: λεοντέας B A: λεοντίας C L F S

HERALDS

with the message that that was his tribute. Erginus then attacked Thebes; his army was routed, and he was killed by Heracles.

This story in this form cannot, of course, have been converted directly into a satyr-play with the satyrs as the heralds, since the dramatist could not allow the satyrs to be mutilated. However, the satyrs might have usurped *the role of the heralds (as they seem to have usurped the role of Theban councillors in* The Sphinx, q.v.*), changed sides out of fear of Heracles and/or because of a promise of reward, and encouraged him in his confrontation with the real heralds when they arrived.*

Recent studies: A. Wessels and R. Krumeich in KPS 152–6; Podlecki 5.

109

And his leather jerkin made of the lion's skin

KIPKH

113a

μανόϲποροϲ ὤφθη
ὠχρόν, ὃ ἔϲχατόν ἐϲτιν .. ε πλάνηϲ[

Herodian, *General Prosody* fr. 12 Hunger: the first three words are certainly quoted from *Circe*, but it is not clear whether the rest is a continuation of the quotation or whether it is Herodian's comment

1–2 μανόϲπορος . . . ὠχρός or μανόσπορον . . . ὠχρόν Radt
2 ὅ τ' Radt (if these words are part of the Aeschylean quotation)
ὀψὲ Radt

CIRCE

Once again, the evidence of quoting authors (here He-rodian, General Prosody *fr. 12 Hunger and Hesychius ζ200) shows this to have been a satyr-play, and it has usually been associated with the "Odyssean trilogy" of* Ghost-Raisers, Penelope *and* Bone-Gatherers *(qq.v.) It presumably dealt with Odysseus' first visit to Circe after his companions had been transformed into pigs: were the satyrs Circe's swineherds (cf. Seaford on Euripides,* Cyclops *41–81), as in Euripides'* Cyclops *they were Polyphemus' shepherds? The fragments shed no light on the plot.*

Recent studies: A. Wessels and R. Krumeich in KPS 157–160; Podlecki 5.

113a

He was seen thinly sown in yellow, which is the ultimate . . . of wandering [. . .]

Scarcely intelligible, and surely corrupt.

ΚΡΗΣΣΑΙ

Our only clue to the subject of this play is fr. 116, a description of the varying colours of the blackberry as it ripens; this almost certainly links it to the story of Polyidus, which was the subject of Sophocles' Seers *and Euripides'* Polyidus. *The story is told by [Apollodorus],* Library *3.3.1– 2 and Hyginus,* Fabulae *136. Glaucus, son of Minos, went missing when a child, and Minos was told that he would be found by the person who could suggest the best analogy to describe a marvellous cow in Minos' herd which continually changed colour—now black, now white, now red. The seer Polyidus compared it to a blackberry, and was duly asked to find the boy; but he found him dead, drowned in a vat of honey. Minos demanded that he restore the boy to life; Polyidus did not know how to achieve this, but*

116

λευκοῖς τε γὰρ μόροισι καὶ μελαγχίμοις
καὶ μιλτοπρέπτοις βρίθεται ταὐτοῦ χρόνου

Athenaeus 2.51d; Eustathius on *Iliad* 22.13

CRETAN WOMEN

*while shut up with the corpse, he saw a snake bring an-
other snake back from the dead by the application of a
certain herb, and Polyidus then used the same herb to re-
vive Glaucus. Minos then demanded that Polyidus teach
Glaucus the art of divination as the price of being allowed
to leave Crete, and Polyidus did so, but when his ship was
getting under way for home he told Glaucus to spit into his
mouth, and Glaucus instantly forgot all that Polyidus had
taught him. That this story, in something very like this
form, was already current in the fifth century we know
from a white-ground cup of about 440 BC (London D5)
which shows a man and boy in a tomb and also two snakes.
Aeschylus' play clearly covered at least the first part of this
story; how far it continued we do not know.*

*See further on fr. 451h, which I have suggested may
come from this play.*

116

For it[1] is weighed down by white berries and black ones
and bright red ones, all at the same time.

*Presumably Polyidus, putting forward the blackberry bush as the
object most fit to be compared with Minos' wonderful cow.*

[1] The blackberry bush. Athenaeus states specifically that Aes-
chylus was referring to this plant ($\beta \acute{a} \tau o \varsigma$) and not to the mulberry
bush ($\sigma \upsilon \kappa \acute{a} \mu \iota \nu o \varsigma$) whose berries were also called $\mu \acute{o} \rho a$: doubtless
there had been a mention of $\beta \acute{a} \tau o \varsigma$ in the preceding line or two of
Aeschylus' text.

ΛΑΙΟΣ

This was the first play of the Theban tetralogy of 467 BC; its possible content is discussed in the Introduction to Seven against Thebes. *There was reference to the practice of exposing new-born infants in pots (χυτρίζειν, fr. 122; this is one of only two words that survive from the actual text of the play) and to a murderer who tasted and spat out his*

ΛΕΩΝ

123

ὁδοιπόρων δήλημα, χωρίτης δράκων

Stephanus of Byzantium, *Ethnics* p.699.13–14 Meineke

124

LAIUS

*victim's blood (fr. 122a). A fragment of a messenger-speech
that refers to a junction of three roads at Potniae near
Thebes (fr. 387a) may well be part of a narrative of the
murder of Laius, but we do not know enough either about
Laius or about Oedipus (q.v.) to be able to say with confidence which of these two plays it comes from.*

THE LION

*Stephanus of Byzantium, who quotes the only line that sur-
vives from this play (fr. 123), refers to it as a satyr-drama.
The mythical lion par excellence is surely the Nemean Lion
which Heracles killed as the first of his Labours, and this
will have been another instance of the familiar "hero vs.
monster" scenario in a satyr-play.*

Recent discussions: S. Scheurer and R. Krumeich in KPS 161–3;
Podlecki 6.

123

The bane of travellers, the serpent of the place[1]

[1] This *may* be a metaphorical description of the Nemean Lion;
but it might also refer to the Lernaean hydra, which was to be
Heracles' second Labour—in which case Heracles will presumably here be giving a catalogue of all the tasks that Eurystheus has
set him.

ΛΗΜΝΙΑΙ

"The Lemnian crime", the murder by the women of Lemnos of their husbands, was proverbially the acme and paradigm of human wickedness (Libation-Bearers 631–7; Herodotus 6.138.4). Since Aeschylus' Hypsipyle (q.v.) presented the aftermath of this crime, with the Argonauts arriving at an island with no surviving male inhabitants, it is reasonable to suppose that Lemnian Women *preceded it in a trilogy and dramatized the crime itself. The other plays in the same production were probably* Cabeiri *and* The Argo *(qq.v.)*

The play is named only three times in our sources, and while Herodian (General Prosody *frr. 13, 14 Hunger) twice names it as* Λήμνιαι (Lemnian Women), *the medieval*

ΛΥΚΟΥΡΓΟΣ

The scholia to Aristophanes, Thesmophoriazusae *135, name this as the satyr-play of the Lycurgus tetralogy, following* Edonians, Bassarids *and* Youths *(qq.v.) [Apollodorus],* Library *3.5.1, mentions that Lycurgus, in his persecution of Dionysus and his followers, took captive not only the female bacchants (whose miraculous release was one of the high points of* Edonians*) but also the satyrs; this detail can hardly be derived from any other source than a satyr-drama about Lycurgus. Since the dramatic time of* Lycurgus *must logically have been the same as that of* Edonians *(which began with the first news of the arrival of Dionysiac worshippers in Lycurgus' kingdom, and*

LEMNIAN WOMEN

catalogue of Aeschylus' plays calls it Λήμνιοι *(Lemnians).*
As in the cases of Women of Argos *and* Women of Salamis,
it is probably the catalogue that is in error; but Deforge
(see below) accepts Λήμνιοι *as the title and suggests, with-*
out any positive evidence, that the play was a satyr-
drama—a speculation which the contributors to KPS do
not even deem worthy of being recorded.

The two single-word fragments cited by Herodian, and
published from a Vienna palimpsest in 1967, are the only
ones known from this play.

Recent studies: B. Deforge, "Eschyle et la légende des Argonautes", REG 100 (1987) 30–44, esp. 42–43.

LYCURGUS

ended with the disgrace and downfall of the king) it must
have presented an alternative scenario for the story; this
would be the only case we know of in which, within a con-
nected tetralogy, the plot of the satyr-drama was blatantly
inconsistent with that of the tragic part of the produc-
tion. If Hermann's interpretation of fr. 124 (q.v.) is correct,
Lycurgus was presented as an inhuman tyrant; it has also
been suggested, on the basis of Nonnus, Dionysiaca
20.226–7 and 248–250, that he tried to "domesticate" the
satyrs, intending to cut off their equine tails and make
them sing at his feasts (in honour not of Dionysus, but of
himself and Ares).

124

κἀκ τῶνδ᾽ ἔπινε βρῦτον ἰσχναίνων χρόνῳ
κἀσεμνοκόμπει τοῦτ᾽ ἐν ἀνδρείᾳ στέγῃ

Athenaeus 10.447c

2 κἀσεμνοκόμπει Dindorf: καὶ σεμνοκοπτει cod.

MEMNΩN

Memnon the Ethiopian, son of the goddess Eos and her mortal husband Tithonus, came to aid his uncle Priam and the Trojans not long after the death of Hector; he killed Nestor's son, Antilochus, but was then himself killed by Achilles. The cyclic epic, the Aethiopis, *was named after him. Our sources make no acknowledged quotations from* Memnon, *but three quotations ascribed to* Agamemnon *do not occur in that play, and it is generally and reasonably supposed that copyists have each time substituted the more familiar play-title for the less familiar. In addition, another fragment (fr. 126a [300]), speaking of a person of Ethio-*

Recent studies: West, *Studies* 26, 47–48; F. Jouan, "Dionysos chez Eschyle", *Kernos* 5 (1992) 71–86, esp. 76; R. Germar and R. Krumeich in KPS 164–8; Podlecki 6.

124

And he would allow time for these[1] to dry, and then drink beer out of them, and make a proud boast of this in his banqueting room.[2]

[1] Probably the skulls of men he had killed, as Hermann brilliantly conjectured on the basis of Nonnus, *Dionysiaca* 20.149–153, 166–181. Thirteen centuries after Aeschylus, in AD 811, another ruler in Thrace—Krum, khan of the Bulgars—allegedly made a drinking cup of the skull of the Byzantine emperor Nikephoros I (Theophanes Confessor, *Chronographia* p.491.17–22 de Boor).　　[2] lit. "men's room", a poetic equivalent of the more common ἀνδρών. Part of the sting of the remark is that Greeks considered beer-drinking unmanly; cf. *Suppliants* 952–3, and see my article in *Museum Criticum* 25–28 (1990–3) 59–64.

MEMNON

pian origin and his native land, can also be plausibly ascribed to this play; if that is so, since the speaker has apparently not yet met Memnon, the play must have included his arrival at Troy, and may have been climaxed by his killing of Antilochus; the continuation of the story, and Memnon's own death, will have been presented in The Weighing of Souls *(q.v.) For a possible third (or rather first) play to complete a trilogy, see note on* The Carians.

In addition to what can be gleaned from the textual fragments, our sources offer three other significant details about the play: (1) Aristophanes, Frogs *963, makes*

Euripides speak of Aeschylus as creating characters like Memnon "with bells on the cheek-plates of their horses" (κωδωνοφαλαροπώλους), which suggests that the play probably included a detailed description of Memnon's armour, equipage and retinue (cf. [Euripides], Rhesus 300–313). (2) Pausanias (10.31.7) says that Memnon arrived at Troy not from Ethiopia but "from Susa in Persia and the river Choaspes" (no source given); Strabo (15.3.2) says that Susa was founded by Memnon's father Tithonus, and that Aeschylus called Memnon's mother (Eos) a Cissian,

126a (300)

γένος μὲν αἰνεῖν ἐκμαθὼν ἐπίσταμαι
Αἰθιοπίδος γῆς, Νεῖλος ἔνθ' ἑπτάρροος
γάνος κυλίνδει ῥευμάτων ἐπομβρίᾳ·
ἐν ᾗ πυρωπὸν †ἥλιος† ἐκλάμψαν φλόγα
5 τήκει πετραίαν χιόνα· πᾶσα δ' εὐθαλὴς
Αἴγυπτος ἁγνοῦ νάματος πληρουμένη
φερέσβιον Δήμητρος ἀντέλλει στάχυν

Anonymous, *On the Overflowing of the Nile* (= FGrH 647 F 1); Tzetzes on *Iliad* 1.427 (not identifying the play); attributed to *Memnon* by Butler and Hermann

1 ἐκμαθὼν Schweighaeuser: ἐκλαθὼν Anon.C: καὶ μαθὼν Anon.F: καὶ μαθεῖν Tzetzes   2 Νεῖλος ἔνθ' ἑπτάρροος Dindorf: ἔνθα (ἐντάδε Anon.C) Νεῖλος ἑπτάρρους codd. 3 γάνος Hermann: γαῖαν codd.   ῥευμάτων I. Voss: πνευμάτων codd.   4 πυρωπὸν Tzetzes: πυρωπὸς Anon.C: πυρωτὸν Anon.F   ἥλιος Anon.C: μηνὸς Anon.F Tzetzes: γλῆνος Burges: ἄστρον Zakas   ἐκλάμψαν Anon.F: ἐκλάμψας Anon.C Tzetzes

i.e. an inhabitant of the region around Susa. It thus appears that Aeschylus represented Memnon as a Persian by residence and partly by birth—which would obviously give the play powerful contemporary resonances. (3) Pollux (4.110) says that "they say" a fourth actor was used briefly in Memnon; *whether or not this is correct, it strongly suggests that the play did have three (main) actors, and thus was fairly late.*

Recent studies: M. L. West, "*Iliad* and *Aethiopis* on the stage: Aeschylus and son", *CQ* 50 (2000) 338–352, esp. 343–7.

126a (300)

I have learned definitely, and know, that I can speak of his origin[1] as being from the land of Ethiopia, from which the seven-mouthed Nile rolls down its fertilizing stream in overflowing abundance: the land where the fiery sun shines out in flame and melts the snows on the mountains, so that all of fruitful Egypt is covered by the flow of the sacred river and sprouts with the ears of Demeter's life-giving grain.[2]

Priam (?) speaking about Memnon, before they have met.

[1] The presence of the particle μέν indicates that the speaker probably went on to distinguish between Memnon's country of origin and some other country with which he was associated, doubtless Persia (Cissia); see introductory note to this play.

[2] Cf. *Supp.* 559; Euripides, *Helen* 2–3; Anaxagoras 59 A 91 Diels-Kranz; Herodotus 2.22.1.

127

καὶ μὴν πελάζει καὶ καταψύχει πνοὴ
ἄρκειος ὡς ναύταισιν ἀσκεύοις μολών

Aelius Dionysius α173; Eustathius on *Iliad* 18.487; *Anecdota Bekkeri* 1.445.18–19; Photius, *Lexicon* α2826 (none identifying author or play); cf. Hesychius α7698 ἀσκεύοις· ψιλοῖς, ἀπαρα-σκεύοις. Αἰσχύλος { Ἀγα}μέμνονι

2 ἄρκειος Lobeck: ἄρκιος codd.

128

χαλκὸν †ἀθέριτον† ἀσπίδος θ᾽ ὑπερτενῆ

Anecdota Bekkeri 1.353.10; Photius, *Lexicon* α474 (both Αἰσχύλος { Ἀγα}μέμνονι)

ἀθέριτον *Anecd.*: ἀνθερητὸν Photius: ἀθέρητον Reitzenstein: τὸν ἀθερῆ M. Schmidt[1]   θ᾽ add. Boissonade   the next line may have begun e.g. <δοράν>, cf. Aristotle fr. 498 Rose, Aelian *On the Nature of Animals* 2.16

[1] The lemma in the two lexicon entries is ἀθερής (ἀθηρής codd., corr. Wagner on the basis of similar entries in Hesychius [α1562] and the *Etymologicum Magnum*).

127

And now his (?) approach is chilling us, like a north wind
coming upon sailors unprepared for it.[1]

[1] If the "chilling approach" is indeed that of a person, then,
given that the action of the play is apparently set among the Trojans and their allies, the person in question is most likely Achilles.

128

The cold (?)[1] bronze and the ⟨leather (?)⟩ stretched over
the shield.

[1] It is clear from the lexica that ancient grammarians found
an adjective ἀθερής in Aeschylus' text but had no idea what it
meant. Their etymological explanations are all implausible; I
would derive the adjective from θέρειν "to heat", cf. εἰληθερής,
ἠλιοθερής, and *Iliad* 5.75 ψυχρὸν δ᾽ ἕλε χαλκὸν ὀδοῦσιν.

ΜΥΡΜΙΔΟΝΕΣ

This was the first play of a trilogy based on the Iliad, *being followed by* Nereids *and* Phrygians *(qq.v.) and perhaps by the satyr-drama* Chamber-Makers *(q.v.) It corresponded approximately to books 9–18 of the epic, and its setting appears to have been within the hut of Achilles (fr. 131.3–4; for imaginary interior settings in the pre-*skene *theatre, cf.* Persians *140–1). Achilles sat silent and veiled for a long time (cf. Aristophanes,* Frogs *911–5), ignoring the pleas of his followers the Myrmidons (frr. 131, 132). Eventually his old tutor Phoenix persuaded him to break his silence (fr. 132b), but only to emphasize, and explain, his determination not to go to the aid of the Achaean army (fr. 132c). Eventually, when word came that the ships were being set on fire (fr. 134), Patroclus, we may presume, as in the* Iliad, *persuaded Achilles—in Aeschylus' treatment the two were lovers (Plato,* Symposium *180a; cf. frr. 135–7)— to let him go into battle in Achilles' armour; and presently Antilochus (fr. 138) brought Achilles the shattering news of Patroclus' death after splendid heroic exploits (cf. Aristophanes,* Frogs *1041), which was soon followed by the arrival of Patroclus' corpse (cf. frr. 135–7). Achilles, as in*

MYRMIDONS

*Homer, blamed himself for sending Patroclus to his doom
(fr. 139) and was desperate to go into battle and avenge him
(fr. 140), but could not, because he now had no armour.*

*A series of vase paintings, showing Odysseus address-
ing an Achilles who is muffled up in his cloak, is probably to be associated with our play, particularly since there
is a parallel series linkable to* Nereids. *By the generally
accepted dating, the earliest of these vases belongs to the
490s, but vase dating is not an exact science, and it is unlikely that this tetralogy, which was one of Aeschylus' most
famous productions, predates his first victory in 484. It
may very well, indeed, have been the production with
which he won that victory and made his name for life.*

Recent studies: A. Garzya, "Sui frammenti dei Mirmidoni di
Eschilo", in J. A. López Férez ed. *De Homero a Libanio* (Madrid,
1995) 41–56; A. Moreau, "Eschyle et les tranches des repas
d'Homère: la trilogie d'Achille", *CGITA* 9 (1996) 3–29; Sommerstein *AT* 338–343; M. L. West, "*Iliad* and *Aethiopis* on the
stage: Aeschylus and son", *CQ* 50 (2000) 338–352, esp. 340–1; P.
Michelakis, *Achilles in Greek Tragedy* (Cambridge, 2002) 22–57.

131

τάδε μὲν λεύσσεις, φαίδιμ' Ἀχιλλεῦ,
δορικλυμάντους Δαναῶν μόχθους,
οὓς σὺ προπίνεις <θάσσων> εἴσω
κλισίας

Oxyrhynchus Papyrus 2163 fr. 1 (5–6 letters at the start of
lines 2–4, and remains of four further lines); Harpocration π100;
Aristophanes, *Frogs* 992 (line 1), with scholia; Eustathius on
Odyssey 23.124 (line 1)

3 προπίνεις Blomfield, θάσσων Taplin: π[Π: om. Harpocration (whose lemma is προπεπωκότες): προπίνων θάσσεις (or
μίμνεις) Hermann

132

Φθιῶτ' Ἀχιλλεῦ, τί ποτ' ἀνδροδάικτον ἀκούων
ἰὴ κόπον οὐ πελάθεις ἐπ' ἀρωγάν;

Aristophanes, *Frogs* 1264–5 with scholia (line 2 repeated at
1267, 1271, 1275, 1277)

1 Ἀχιλεῦ several mss.   2 ἰὴ κόπον Heath, cf. schol.
Frogs 1275: ἰήκοπον codd.

131

Do you see this, glorious Achilles—
the toils of the spear-ravaged Danaans,
whom you are betraying by sitting idle within
your hut . . . ?

*The opening lines of the play: chanted anapaests, almost certainly
the chorus addressing the seated, silent Achilles.*

132

Phthian Achilles, why, when you hear of the suffering
            and slaughter of men—
iehhh!—do you not advance to their succour?

*Probably the beginning of a sung choral ode that followed the
anapaestic prelude.*

*What is called fr. 132a actually consists of eight fragments
(Oxyrhynchus Papyrus 2163, frr. 2–9), in only two of which can
complete or nearly complete words be read; their relative placing,
and even (in all cases but one) their attribution to Myrmidons, are
quite uncertain. The fragment which can be attributed with some
confidence (8) is lyric, at least in its first five lines, and may well
come from the same choral song as fr. 132; we can read ἀνόνητον
profitless (line 1), διαφθοράς destruction (line 2), θάςςεις you
sit (line 3), ἄναξ Ἀχιλλεῦ lord Achilles (line 4), ['E]λλανα μὴ
προδῶς ς[τρατόν] (suppl. Lobel) don't betray the [G]reek a[rmy]
(line 5), [ἀμ]φιστόνως with much groaning (line 6), [ζε]ύγνυται is
joined (line 7), φράςαι to tell (line 9). In column I of fragment 4,
which appears to contain spoken iambics, the intelligible words
are κακανδρίᾳ by cowardice (line 2) and ἄτερ δίκης without
justice (line 3).*

132b

ΦΟΙΝΙΞ

[*remains of two lines*]

    ]. ἐπῳδὴν οὐκ ἔχω co[φωτέραν

    ]πεcειcαπαcαν ἡνίαν [

5   ].. δ᾽, Ἀχιλλεῦ, πρᾶcc᾽ ὅπῃ [

ΑΧΙΛΛΕΥΣ

Φοῖ]νιξ γεραιέ, τῶν ἐμῶν φρε[νῶν

πολ]λῶν ἀκούων δυ̣c̣τόμων λ[

πάλ]αι cιωπῶ κο̣ὐδὲν̣ [.]c̣τ̣. μ[

    ] ἀντέλεξα. c̣ὲ δὲ̣. [..]αξιωτ[

PSI 1472[1] + *Oxyrhynchus Papyrus* 2163 fr. 11 (parts of the same copy)

3 (beginning) [ἄλλη]ν̣ or [ταύτη]ς̣ Bartoletti   co[φω-
τέραν] Bartoletti   4 ἔσεισα πᾶσαν Radt   5 [κλυ]ὼ̣ν̣
δ᾽ Snell, [ἐκ τ]ῶ̣ν̣δ᾽ Radt   ὅπῃ [γέ σοι δοκῇ] Mette
6 suppl. Bartoletti   at end [τριβή] Bartoletti, [σέβας] Radt
7 [πολ]λῶν Bartoletti   λ[αλημάτων] Bartoletti, λ[όγων
ῥόθον] Snell: perh. λ[όγων ἐγώ]   8 [πάλ]αι Bartoletti
8–9 κοὐδὲν [ἀ]ν̣τ̣αμ[είβομαι | οὐδ᾽] Mette   9 τ̣[ὸν]
ἀξιώτ[ατον] Bartoletti

[1] This fragment, which gives us the left-hand side of the column, was destroyed in an air raid in 1944, and its text is now known only from G. Vitelli's transcript.

132b

PHOENIX

[. . .] I have no cl[everer] healing charm [. . .] I have shaken out every rein[1] (?) [. . . After hearing this (?),] Achilles, act in whatever way [you think right (?)].

ACHILLES

Aged [Phoe]nix, whom my sou[l reveres (?)], while hearing [ma]ny slanderous w[ords] I have [lo]ng been silent and [made] no [reply nor (?)] spoken in opposition. But you, [the] worthi[est of men, I will answer (?) . . .]

Probably the moment at which Achilles finally breaks his famous silence.

[1] i.e. "I have made every possible effort"; both this and the preceding expression indicate that we have here the end of a long speech in which Phoenix has desperately striven to persuade Achilles to modify his intransigence.

132c

ΑΧΙΛΛΕΥΣ

λεύcουcι τοὐμὸν cῶμα; μὴ δόκει ποτὲ
πέτρ[ο]ιc καταξανθέντα Πηλέωc γόνον
...]. . [.]. (.)ήcειν Τρωϊκὴν ἀνὰ χθόνα
..]ημένοιcι Τρωcὶ τὴν ἄ[ν]ευ δορόc.

5   ...]η γένοιτ᾽ ἂν εὐπετεστερ .. λεχουc
   ...]τουτο δὴ βροτοῖcιν ἰατρὸν πόνων.
   ....]ι δ᾽ Ἀχαιῶν χεῖρ᾽ ἐφορμήcω δορὶ
   ...]ῶcαν ὀργῇ ποιμένοc κακοῦ διαί
   ....]περ εἷc ὤν, ὡc λέγουcι cύμμαχοι,

10   ....]ν τοcαύτην ἔκτιc᾽ οὐ παρὼν μάχη
   ....]μ᾽ ἐγὼ τὰ πάντ᾽ Ἀχαϊκῷ cτρατῷ
   τοιόν]δ᾽ ἀφεῖναι τοὔποc οὐκ αἰδώc μ᾽ ἔχει.
   ......] τοιούτ[ο]υc εὐγενεcτέρουc ἐμοῦ

PSI 1211

1 λεύccουcι Π^{ac}   3 [ἀλκ]ὴν Diggle, then [π]αρησειν Fritsch
4 [ὀν]ημένοιcι Fritsch   5–6 assigned to a different speaker
(Phoenix? Odysseus? Patroclus?) by Norsa & Vitelli
5 [οὖτο]ι Körte: perh. [τί δ]ὴ   6 [τού]του, τὸ δὴ Körte: [. . .]
τοῦθ᾽, ὃ δὴ Diggle   ἰατρον Π: ἰατρὸς Diggle   7 [φόβω]ι
Schadewaldt   8 [χαλ]ῶσαν Fritsch   9 (διαί;) [ἀλλ᾽
εἴ]περ (. . . μάχῃ,) Norsa & Vitelli: (διαί,) [ὃς καί]περ (. . . μάχῃ;)
Steffen   10 [βλάβη]ν Pfeiffer, Eitrem: [λύμη]ν Diggle
11 [εἷς εἰ]μ᾽ Norsa & Vitelli: [οὐκ εἴ]μ᾽ (. . . στρατῷ;) Schadewaldt
εγω Π^{pc}: ετωι Π^{ac}   12 suppl. Körte   μ᾽ Π^{pc}: om. Π^{ac}
ἔχει Norsa & Vitelli: εκει Π   13 [τίς γὰρ] Fritsch

132c

ACHILLES

They'll stone me, will they? Never imagine that the son of
Peleus, if his body is shredded by stones, will [slacken in
giving aid to (?)] the [. . .] Trojans, in the land of Troy,
without weapons.[1] [What (?)] could be easier [than to accept death (?),] which men call the healer of their troubles?[2] Shall I, for [fear (?)] of the Achaeans, set myself in
motion, with a spear in the hand which is now [idle (?)]
through anger because of bad leadership?[3] [If] all on my
own, as our allies claim, I caused so much [harm] by my absence from battle, then I [alone] am everything to the
Achaean army:[4] I have no compunction about uttering
words like that. [For who (?)] would [say (?)] that [leaders

---

[1] Achilles' point is that by stoning him the Achaean army would be
doing themselves no good: he would still, even in death, be bene-
fiting the Trojans by depriving their enemies of his fighting
strength.   [2] This rendering does not claim to do more than
give the apparent general sense of the sentence. For death as the
"healer of troubles" cf. frr. 255, 353.   [3] lit. "because of a bad
shepherd" (i.e. Agamemnon, "shepherd of the people" in Homeric phrase).   [4] I have followed Norsa & Vitelli's restorations and sentence-divisions in lines 9 and 11. The main alternative, represented by Steffen's restoration in line 9 (see apparatus),
would make the sense run approximately: "Shall I, for fear of the
Achaeans, set myself in motion . . . , I who all on my own . . . caused
so much harm by my absence from battle? I alone am everything to the Achaean army."

......]ν ... οι καὶ ϲτρατοῦ τὰ βέλτατα;

15 ......].. [..].. ὑμᾶϲ εἰϲ ἀνὴρ ἠκίζετο

......] . ἀράϲϲων καὶ πολυϲκεδεὶϲ ϲυθείϲ,

......]α τεύχ[η π]ερὶ νέοιϲ βραχ[ίο]ϲιν

......]. ϲυ. [..] .. δὲ †πανθιμων† ϲτρατὸν

] ... [..]ων εὐμαρῶϲ ἐτρ[έ]ψατο;

20] .. [.] . δ .. ϲ προδοϲίαν ... [.]μεμοι,

] . [. ἄ]νδρα τόνδ' α ... [...]θανεῖν.

[*Remains of fifteen more lines, in which the intelligible expressions
are* εἶπον οὐ ψευδῆ λέγων (26), τόνδ' ἀποφθερεῖ ϲτρατόν (27),
ὁρᾶν πάρα (28), κατήγοροϲ (30), ἐλε[ύ]θερον λέγειϲ (31), εὐτυ-
χέϲτερα (32), οὐδεὶϲ φρονεῖ (33), [ο]ὐδαμῶϲ πρέπει τόδε (34),
διαλ[λα]γαί (35), μειλί[γ]ματι (36)]

14 [ταγοὺϲ ἂ]ν εἴποι Norsa & Vitelli   16 [πάντας]
(perh. rather [Κύκνοϲ], which Schadewaldt proposed in 15)
ταράϲϲων Norsa & Vitelli   ϲυθειϲ Πᵖᶜ: the second letter is
corrected from ι or χ   17 [τίϲ θεὶϲ τ]ὰ Snell
18 [ἔϲωϲε]ν ϲυ εὖ π[ωϲ τ]όνδε Snell   πάνθιμων Πᵖᶜ, πάνθιμον
Πᵃᶜ: πάνθ' ὑμῶν Schadewaldt   19 [πλῆθος] Schadewaldt,
then δὲ Τ[ρώ]ων Snell   20 [νῦν δ' ὢν] ἄν[α]νδρος Snell
ἔνε[ι]μ' ἐμοί Snell   21 (beginning) [κεῖνοϲ, θέλει γ]ὰ[ρ]
Snell   αἰϲχ[ρῶϲ] θανεῖν Norsa & Vitelli

⁵ The demonstrative adjective implies a gesture, possibly towards Odysseus if he is present (but even if there was an "em-
bassy" scene in the play—for which we have only the uncertain
evidence of the vase-paintings—Achilles could not have made this
speech before Phoenix had succeeded in breaking his silence, and
to have Odysseus present at that stage would require three actors,

(?)] like these[5] are nobler men than I am, and the best in the army? [When Cycnus (?)] on his own was mauling you [all (?)], throwing you into confusion (?), rushing upon you and scattering you on all sides,[6] [who was it who put (?) hi]s armou[r o]n his young ar[m]s [and somehow (?)] bravely [saved (?) t]his whole army of yours, easily putting [the masses (?)] of [the Trojans (?)] to flight? [And yet now that (?)] unmanly (?) person[7] [has labelled (?)] me a traitor, [because he wants (?)] this [m]an here[8] to die [a disgraceful death (?)]

In the fifteen remaining lines, the intelligible expressions are I have said, and I have not spoken falsely *(26),* he[9] will destroy this army *(27),* one can see *(28),* accuser *(30),* you speak freely (?) *(31),* more fortunate *(32),* no one has thoughts *(33),* this is in no way appropriate *(34),* recon[ci]liation *(35),* propi[ti]ation *(36). It is likely that from line 28 a different character is speaking, arguing with some bluntness that Achilles is in the wrong and should try to compose his quarrel with Agamemnon; this may still be Phoenix, but Phoenix's earlier speech seems to have been rather diffident (cf. fr. 132b.5), and it is at least as likely that the speaker now is Patroclus, whose intimacy with Achilles would enable him to speak more boldly (cf.* Iliad *16.29–35).*

impossible in an earlyish play), more likely an angry wave in the direction in which the rest of the Achaean camp is supposed to lie. (Achilles and his men were right at one end of the encampment: *Iliad* 8.225–6, 11.8–9.)   [6] Cycnus was killed by Achilles at the very beginning of the Trojan War (*Cypria* Arg. §10 West); that Achilles is speaking of an event early in the war is clear from his reference to his "young arms".   [7] If this reading, or something like it, is correct, the person meant is evidently Agamemnon. [8] Achilles is referring to himself.   [9] Hector?

143

134

†ἀπὸ δ᾽ αὖτε† ξουθὸς ἱππαλεκτρυὼν
στάζει †κηρόθεν τῶν† φαρμάκων πολὺς πόνος

Scholia to Aristophanes, *Peace* 1177 and *Frogs* 932

1 ἀπὸ δ᾽ αὖτε schol. *Peace*: ἐπὶ δ᾽ αἰετὸς schol. *Frogs*:
<δεινῶς> δ᾽ ἀπ᾽ αὐτῆς Bothe: perh. στάζει δ᾽ ἀπ᾽ αὐτῆς
2 στάζει κηρόθεν τῶν codd.: perh. κηρός, χυθέντων (κηρός
λυθέντων Dindorf, positing a lost line before 2 beginning with
στάζει: κράζει [sic], χυθέντων Blaydes)

135

σέβας δὲ μηρῶν ἁγνὸν οὐ κατηδέσω,
ὦ δυσχάριστε τῶν πυκνῶν φιλημάτων

Plutarch, *Moralia* 61a (line 2 only) and 751c; Athenaeus
13.602e

1 ἁγνὸν Th. Canter: ἅγιον Athenaeus: om. Plutarch (751c)
οὐ κατηδέσω Plutarch (751c): οὐκ ἐπηδέσω Athenaeus

134

And the tawny horsecock,[1] the product of much labour with liquefied (?) dyes, was dripping off the ship (?) like wax (?)

A messenger (?) describing the critical moment of the firing of the ships.

[1] A fabulous creature, with the front end of a horse, the rear end of a cock, and wings, which appears frequently in Athenian art of the sixth and early fifth centuries; here it is imagined as being painted as an emblem on a ship. The paint melts with the heat and drips away when the ship (or perhaps an adjacent one) is set on fire.

135

And you did not respect the sacred honour of the thigh-bond,[1] ungrateful that you were for those countless kisses!

Probably Achilles reproaching the dead Patroclus for having disobeyed his instructions not to advance too far towards Troy.

[1] i.e. the bond created by intercrural sex; see K. J. Dover, *Greek Homosexuality* (London, 1978) 96–99, 197.

ATTRIBUTED FRAGMENTS

136

ΑΧΙΛΛΕΥΣ

μηρῶν τε τῶν σῶν ηὐσέβησ' ὁμιλίαν
κλαίων

[Lucian], *Erotes* 54 (στένων . . . Ἀχιλλεὺς τὸν Πατρόκλου
θάνατον: author and play not specified)

1 ηὐσέβησ' (εὐσέβησ') ὁμιλίαν Hermann: εὐσεβὴς (om. L)
ὁμιλία codd.   2 κλαίων Dobree: καλλίω codd.

The letters]ησομιλ[*in line 3 of a five-line scrap of papyrus
(Oxyrhynchus Papyrus 2256 [= Aesch. fr. dub. 451s], frag. 55)
have been identified by Snell and others as coming from line 1 of
the above fragment. The scanty remains of the surrounding lines
are not incompatible with this identification; if it is correct, line 2
of this fragment of* Myrmidons *may have ended* [κατ]ᾳ σκότο[ν]
"down in(to) the darkness".

137

ΑΧΙΛΛΕΥΣ

καὶ μὴν, φιλῶ γάρ, ἀβδέλυκτ' ἐμοὶ τάδε

Photius, *Lexicon* α33; *Suda* α25 (identifying author and play);
Anecdota Bekkeri i 321.22 (identifying only the author); Zonaras,
Lexicon 9 Tittmann; Cramer, *Anecdota Parisina* iv 85.23 (identi-
fying neither)

136

ACHILLES

And I honoured the intimacy of your thighs by bewailing
you.

Again addressing the dead Patroclus.

137

ACHILLES

And yet to me, because I love him, this[1] is not loathsome.

[1] Referring either to the sight of Patroclus' bloody corpse (if,
for example, Achilles is asking for it to be uncovered) or, as has
also been suggested, to the act of affectionately touching or even
kissing it.

138

ΑΧΙΛΛΕΥΣ

Ἀντίλοχ’, ἀποίμωξόν με τοῦ τεθνηκότος
τὸν ζῶντα μᾶλλον· τἀμὰ γὰρ διοίχεται

Aristophanes, *Assemblywomen* 392–3 (where τεθνηκότος is comically replaced by τριωβόλου) with scholia (whence *Suda* α3715)

139

ΑΧΙΛΛΕΥΣ

ὧδ’ ἐστὶ μύθων τῶν Λιβυστικῶν κλέος,
πληγέντ’ ἀτρακτῷ τοξικῷ τὸν αἰετὸν
εἰπεῖν ἰδόντα μηχανὴν πτερώματος·
"τάδ’ οὐχ ὑπ’ ἄλλων, ἀλλὰ τοῖς αὑτῶν πτεροῖς
5 ἁλισκόμεσθα"

Aristophanes, *Birds* 807 (line 4 only); the whole passage is quoted in the scholia and *Suda* ο992 (line 1 omitted) and τ183; Diogenianus, *Proverbs* Preface *ad fin.* (line 1 only); Philo, *On the Indestructibility of the Universe* 49; Galen, *On the Doctrines of Hippocrates and Plato* 4.5.17; Arsenius, *Sayings* 15.88a (these three quote lines 4–5 only); many other writers allude to the passage

1 ὧδ’ Diogenianus: ὁ δέ *Suda* τ183: ὡς δέ vel sim. cett. κλέος Schneidewin: τὸ κλέος Diogenianus: λόγος cett.

138

ACHILLES

Cry for me the living, Antilochus,[1] more than for the dead: all I had is gone!

[1] In the *Iliad* too (17.651–701, 18.1–34) it had been Antilochus, son of Nestor, who brought Achilles the news of Patroclus' death.

139

ACHILLES

This is what is said about a fable they tell in Africa: an eagle was hit with an arrow from the bow, saw the way it was flighted,[1] and said, "In this way we are vanquished, not by others, but with our own feathers!"

Achilles' reflection on the fact that by sending Patroclus into battle he has been the cause of the anguish he is now suffering.

[1] viz. with eagle feathers.

ΜΥΣΟΙ

The central character of Mysians *was Telephus. This can be inferred from the mention in the play (fr. 145) of Oeum, a village near Telephus' birthplace Tegea in Arcadia, and also from Aristotle's criticism (Poetics 1460a30–32) of "the man in* Mysians *who came from Tegea to Mysia without ever speaking"—for though Sophocles also wrote a play called* Mysians *in which a man, almost certainly Telephus, arrives in Mysia from abroad, we know that in Sophocles' play this man immediately asks a native what country he is in (Sophocles fr. 411). The Aeschylean Telephus had been silent because he was under blood-pollution (cf. Eumenides 448–450), having killed his maternal uncles, the sons*

143

ἰὼ Κάικε Μύσιαί τ᾽ ἐπιρροαί

Strabo 13.1.70 (εἰπεῖν Αἰσχύλον κατὰ τὴν εἰσβολὴν τοῦ ἐν Μυρμιδόσι [so codd.: Μυσοῖς Pauw] προλόγου); Macrobius, *Saturnalia* 5.20.16 (play not named); Sacerdos, *Ars Grammatica* 3.4 (play not named); *Zenon Papyrus* 59651 (author and play not named)

144

ποταμοῦ Καΐκου χαῖρε πρῶτος ὀργεών,
εὐχαῖς δὲ σῴζοις δεσπότας παιωνίοις

Photius, *Lexicon* s.v. ὀργεῶνες; Suda ο511

MYSIANS

*of Aleos; the play may well have included his purification
(cf. fr. 144, which is addressed to a priest). In several accounts Telephus either arrives in Mysia together with his
mother Auge, or is reunited with her there; if Aeschylus
used such a version, Auge may have acted as Telephus'
spokesperson.*

*Telephus (q.v.) is widely thought to have been a sequel
to Mysians.*

Recent studies: C. Preiser, *Euripides: Telephos* (Hildesheim,
2000) 51–52.

143

Hail, Caïcus,[1] and you tributary streams of Mysia!

The opening words of the play.[2]

[1] The chief river of Mysia.   [2] Taplin, *Stagecraft* 424,
shrewdly notes that we need not rule out Telephus as the speaker
of these words, if he was at this point alone on stage.

144

Greeting, chief priest of the river Caïcus, and may you
bring safety to your masters[1] by your prayers for their
health!

[1] i.e., presumably, the Mysian royal house; several versions of
the Telephus story mention a king Teuthras, who usually marries
Auge and eventually bequeaths his kingdom to Telephus.

144a

εὗδον
καλπάζοντας ἐν αἰχμαῖς

Photius, *Lexicon* α1514

ΝΕΑΝΙΣΚΟΙ

146

αὔρας ὑποσκίοισιν ἐν ψυκτηρίοις

Athenaeus 11.503c

αὔρας Valckenaer: σαύρας codd.   ὑποσκίοισιν C E: ὑπη-
κόοισιν A

YOUTHS

144a

I saw them
trotting among the spears

Lyric; probably from a choral song.

YOUTHS

*This was the third play of the Lycurgus tetralogy, follow-
ing* Edonians *and* Bassarids *and preceding the satyr-play*
Lycurgus *(qq.v.) The fragments give us little clue to its content; but it has been attractively suggested by West and by
Seaford (see below) that, after the violent overthrow by Dionysus and his devotees, first of Lycurgus who had rejected
him, and then of Orpheus who had exalted Apollo/Helios
above him,* Youths *presented a reconciliation in which
cults of Dionysus and of Apollo/Helios were both firmly established in Thrace.*

Recent studies: West, *Studies* 46–47; F. Jouan, "Dionysos chez
Eschyle", *Kernos* 5 (1992) 71–86, esp. 75–76; M. Di Marco, "Dioniso ed Orfeo nelle *Bassaridi* di Eschilo", in A. Masaracchia ed.
Orfeo e l'orfismo (Rome, 1993) 101–153; R. A. S. Seaford, "Mystic
light in Aeschylus' *Bassarai*", *CQ* 55 (2005) 602–6, esp. 605–6.

146

Breezes in cool shaded spots.

146a

πρὸς δ' ἐπὶ τοῖς ἀμφιλαφῆ πήματ' ἔχων ἀθανάτων

Photius, *Lexicon* α1346

146b

καὶ καρτερὸς γὰρ †καὶ πολεμικὸς† ἀρείφατος

Etymologicum Genuinum s.v. ἀρειμάνιος

καὶ πολεμικὸς ἀρείφατος codd.: ἐν μάχῃ κἀρείφατος Theo-
doridis: καὶ τὸ λῆμ' ἀρείφατος Kassel, comparing Hesychius
α7117 (= Aesch. fr. 147) ἀρείφατον λῆμα· ἰσχυρόν . . .· Αἰσχύλος Νεανίσκοις

NEMEA

Unless this play took its title from the town of Nemea
or from the Nemean Games (which would be very abnor-
mal, either for a tragedy or for a satyr-drama), the title
must refer to the only known mythical character of that
name, and probably to the only story about her that is at-
tested (by an introductory scholium to Pindar's Nemeans),
namely that she was the mother of the child Archemorus
who was killed by a snake at Phlius while the expedition of
the Seven against Thebes was passing through the town,
and in whose memory their leader, Adrastus, founded the
Nemean Games. If so, the play will have corresponded

146a

And having, in addition to that, abundant suffering from
the immortals.

*Lyric (choriambs), so probably from a choral ode; we cannot tell
who is referred to (it may well be a character in an entirely different myth, mentioned by way of example).*

146b

For he was both strong and warlike <of spirit (?)>.

*This, on the other hand, is apparently an iambic trimeter, and
more likely to refer to someone who had featured in the trilogy
(Lycurgus?).*

NEMEA

in subject to Euripides' late play Hypsipyle, *where, how-
ever, the boy's original name is Opheltes (he is renamed
Archemorus after his death) and his mother's Eurydice
(Hypsipyle, in exile from Lemnos, being his nurse). There
is, however, no reason to believe that Hypsipyle figured in
Aeschylus' play. No quotations survive.*

It is very tempting to associate this play with Eleusinians, Women of Argos, *and* Epigoni *(qq.v.), in all of
which Adrastus was probably a character; if so, it must
have been a satyr-drama—with an athletic connection, as
in* The Sacred Delegation.

ΝΗΡΕΙΔΕΣ

This play has nearly always been regarded as the second play of the Achilles trilogy, following Myrmidons *and preceding* Phrygians *(qq.v.) In the* Iliad *(18.35–147), Thetis is accompanied by her sisters the Nereids when she comes to comfort Achilles after the death of Patroclus, and later (19.1–39) she returns alone bringing him the new armour which Hephaestus has made. Aeschylus merged these two visits into one, making Thetis and the Nereids together bring Achilles his armour; the play then probably continued with Achilles' preparations for battle, a report of his exploits including the killing of Hector, the funeral of Patroclus (cf. fr. 153) and perhaps Achilles' abusive treatment of Hector's body—roughly the material contained in books 19–23 of the* Iliad.

However, the few surviving fragments explicitly attributed to the play contain nothing that obviously refers to Hector, Patroclus, or Achilles' new armour, and it has been possible for West (see below) to argue that Nereids *was the third, not the second, play of the trilogy, and that its subject was the death of Achilles. West's arguments are not*

150

δελφινηρὸν πεδίον πόντου
διαμειψάμεναι

Scholia to Euripides, *Phoenician Maidens* 209

1 δελφινηρὸν Vr: δελφίνορον cett.

NEREIDS

strong (the main one being that he cannot imagine what a chorus of Nereids would do in the presence of Hector's body), and are all but conclusively refuted by the artistic evidence: simultaneously with the well-known series of vase paintings apparently inspired by Myrmidons, *there begins another series (LIMC Achilles nos. 510–525), showing Thetis bringing Achilles his new armour, in which, contrary to earlier literary and artistic evidence, Thetis is accompanied by Nereids (often riding on dolphins or other sea-creatures) and Achilles is seated and often muffled just as on the* Myrmidons *vases. See A. Kossatz-Deissmann,* LIMC *i.1 (1981) 127. See also below on frr. 150a and 151.*

Recent studies: A. Moreau, "Eschyle et les tranches des repas d'Homère: la trilogie d'Achille", *CGITA* 9 (1996) 3–29; Sommerstein *AT* 343–4; W. Luppe, "Das Aischyleische Nereiden-Fragment 151 Radt: Überlegungen zu einer übergangenen Konjektur", *RhM* 141 (1998) 407–9; M. L. West, "*Iliad* and *Aethiopis* on the stage: Aeschylus and son", *CQ* 50 (2000) 338–352, esp. 341–3; P. Michelakis, *Achilles in Greek Tragedy* (Cambridge, 2002) 53–56.

150

Crossing the expanse of the sea
where dolphins play

Anapaests, doubtless at the entry of the chorus.[1]

[1] In view of the evidence of vase-paintings, it has been suggested that the chorus actually entered riding on dolphins; this may well, however, be artistic imagination based on the words of the text.

150a (296)

πᾶσα γὰρ Τροία δέδορκεν Ἕκτορος τύχης διαί

Epimerismi Homerici δ68 Dyck (author not specified, but immediately followed by *Ag.* 448 cited as καὶ ἐν Ἀγαμέμνονι, implying that this too is Aeschylean;[1] ascribed to this play by Haupt).

[1] Furthermore, διαί occurs 10 or 11 times in Aeschylus, never in Sophocles or Euripides.

151

ἐναροκτάντας δὲ †φθογγ[...]κότος† ὑψοῦ
τέλος ἀθανάτων ἀπολείψει

Hesychius ε2679; he says that "the commentators" offer the paraphrase ὁ δὲ ἐναροκτάντας θάνατος (Heinsius: -ον cod.) μοι ἐπικαυχώμενος τὸ ἐκ τῶν θεῶν τέλος ὑψοῦ ἀπολείψει... καὶ ἐπὶ τοὺς ἐχθροὺς ἥξει

1 φθογγ[...]κότος cod. (Musurus wrote ος over the erasure): perh. φθόγγος < > ἔγκοτον (so Latte, proposing <ἐμοὶ>, but the lacuna may be longer)   2 ἀπολείψει Musurus in cod.: ἀπολέψει cod.

152

κάμακος δ' ἱεὶς γλώσσημα διπλοῦν

Scholia to Pindar, *Nemean* 6.50[85]

δ' ἱεὶς Heimsoeth: εἶσι κάμακος codd.   διπλοῦν Hermann, Dindorf: διπλάσιον codd.

150a (296)

For all Troy sees light[1] because of Hector's good fortune.

[1] i.e. has new hope; lit. "has sight". The reference is doubtless to the death of Patroclus. E. A. J. Ahrens and Hermann ascribed this fragment to *Phrygians* (but the statement would not be true after Hector's death), Schadewaldt to *Myrmidons* (but the reference to the feelings of "all Troy" would be more appropriate when the Trojans had had a little time to receive and digest the news of Hector's success). The line is a trochaic tetrameter.

151

Words ⟨of boasting (?)⟩ over a killing in battle
will make the power of the immortals on high
angry ⟨with me (?)⟩[1]

Anapaests again, but apparently "lyric" rather than "marching"; the μοι of the commentators whom Hesychius cites suggests that Achilles was the speaker, presumably after the death of Hector.

[1] The text was probably already corrupt in the time of the (Hellenistic?) commentators cited by Hesychius, whose paraphrase is hardly intelligible and ignores κότος (cod.) entirely.

152

And, throwing his spear with its double point[1] . . .

Anapaests again, describing or imagining Achilles in battle.

[1] For Achilles' double-pointed spear (which Homer either does not know of, or deliberately ignores) cf. *Little Iliad* fr. 5 West, Sophocles fr. 152. The spear was the only piece of Achilles' equipment which Patroclus did not take into battle, because only Achilles could wield it (*Iliad* 16.140–4).

153

λεπτὸς δὲ σινδὼν ἀμφιβαλλέσθω χροΐ

Herodian, *On the Declension of Nouns* ed. A. Hilgard, *Excerpta ex libris Herodiani technici* (Leipzig, 1887) p. 22.31.

NIOBH

Niobe, daughter of Tantalus and wife of Amphion of Thebes, offended Apollo and Artemis (and/or their mother Leto) by boasting that she had had many fine children (in Aeschylus the number was fourteen) while Leto had had only two; Apollo and Artemis punished her by destroying all her children, and she wept inconsolably until the gods transformed her into a rock at Mount Sipylus in Lydia which continued to shed tears (Iliad 24.602–617). Aeschylus' play began after the catastrophe, with Niobe sitting veiled and wordless at her children's tomb (fr. 154a.6–7; Aristophanes, Frogs 911–920; Life of Aeschylus 5); later her father came to Thebes (frr. 154a.10, 158, 159), presumably to comfort her so far as he could and to take her home to Lydia, her husband Amphion being probably also dead (cf. Ovid, Metamorphoses 6.271). It is hard to see how there can have been much plot development, and the play is likely to have concerned itself mainly with Tantalus' efforts to understand, and to come to terms with, so appalling a disaster, and to persuade his daughter to do likewise.

Two lines from the play (now fr. 154a.15–16) attained notoriety through being quoted and criticized by Plato

153

Let fine linen be cast over his body.

Achilles giving instructions for the laying-out of Patroclus (cf. Iliad *18.352–3).*

NIOBE

(Republic *380a) as propagating an unacceptable belief in divine malevolence; however, now that a papyrus has given us an idea of their context, we can see that Plato was making tendentious use of the lines, and that they were designed, not primarily to blame the gods, but to introduce a criticism of Niobe.*

Two fragments of a line or more ascribed by Radt to this play, 157a and 164, have here been omitted. There is no adequate reason to suppose that fr. 157a (= Aristophanes, Thesmophoriazusae *889–890, from a scene parodying Euripides'* Helen) *is quoted or adapted from Aeschylus; on fr. 164, see de Lucia (below).*

Recent studies: A. Garzya, "Sur la Niobé d'Eschyle", *REG* 100 (1987) 185–202; R. de Lucia, "Eschilo, fr. 164 Radt (Niobe): una fonte sconosciuta e alcune osservazione", *Atti dell'Accademia Pontaniana* 38 (1989) 113–120; A. Moreau, "La Niobé d'Eschyle: quelques jalons", *REG* 108 (1995) 288–307; M. Alfani, "Note sulla Niobe di Eschilo", *Rivista di Cultura Classica e Medioevale* 39 (1997) 261–9, and "La 'Niobe' di Eschilo: una storia degli studi", *Appunti Romani di Filologia* 1 (1999) 1–26; R. A. S. Seaford, "Death and wedding in Aeschylus' *Niobe*", in F. McHardy et al. ed. *Lost Dramas of Classical Athens* (Exeter, 2005) 113–127.

154a

ο]ὐδὲν εἰ μὴ πατέρ' ἀναστενάζε[ται
τὸν] δόντα καὶ φύϲαντα, Ταντάλου β[ίαν,
εἰϲ οἷ]ον ἐξώκειλεν ἀλίμενον γάμον·
]ϲ κακοῦ γὰρ πνεῦμα προϲβ[άλλε]ι̣ δο[
]δ' ὁρᾶτε τοὐπι[τ]έρμιον γάμου·
τριταῖ]ον ἦμαρ τόνδ' ἐφημένη τάφον
τέκνοιϲ ἐπῴζει ζῶϲα τοῖϲ τεθνηκόϲιν,
]υϲα τὴν τάλαιναν εὔμορφον φυήν·
]ϲ κακωθεὶϲ δ' οὐδὲν ἄλλ' ε[ἰ] μὴ ϲκιά̣.

PSI 1208; Hesychius ε5579 (lines 6–7 Αἰϲχύλος Νιόβη· ἐφιμένη [sic] . . . τεθνηκόϲιν); lines 15–16 are quoted by Plato, *Republic* 380a (as by Aeschylus, and as referring to τὰ τῆς Νιόβης πάθη), by Menander, *Aspis* 412–3 (as by Aeschylus), and, without naming the author, by Plutarch, *Moralia* 17b and 1065e, and Stobaeus 3.3.37

1 [ἀλλ'] or [ἢ δ'] Maas   [ο]ὐδέν Norsa & Vitelli: οὐδέν' Schadewaldt   ἀναϲτενάζε[ται] Schadewaldt   2 suppl. Norsa & Vitelli   3 suppl. Schadewaldt   γαμ(ον) Π^pc: βιον Π^ac   4 [παντὸ]ς Pfeiffer   προϲβ[αλλε]ι Norsa & Vitelli   δό[μοις] Latte, δό[ρει] Pfeiffer   5 [ὑμεῖϲ] Norsa & Vitelli, [αὐταί] Schadewaldt, [αὐτοί] Reinhardt   6 suppl. Wolff   7 ἐπῴζει ζῶϲα Latte: ἔπωζε Hesychius: εποιμω-ζουϲα Π   8 [τήκ]ουϲα Camerer   9 βροτὸ]ς Körte, Maas, Fraenkel

---

1 Cf. Sophocles, *Oedipus the King* 422–3 (Teiresias to Oedipus) "the marriage into which you sailed on a fair wind, but which offered your house no good anchorage".

NIOBE

154a

[She is] groaning loudly over nothing so much as that her father [who] begot her and gave her in marriage, the m[ighty] Tantalus, ran her aground [on suc]h a harbourless shore of a union;[1] for a storm of [every kind of (?)] evil has as[saile]d [this] h[ouse (?)]. And you [yourselves] can see the final outcome of this marriage: this is the [third (?)] day that she has been sitting at this tomb, a living mother brooding[2] over her dead children, with the unhappy beauty of her form [melt]ing away. A [mortal] afflicted is noth-

This speech is delivered to the chorus (cf. line 14), in the presence of the silent Niobe, by a character who cannot be identified with certainty but must be a person close to Niobe and well informed about recent events in the family. It cannot be Tantalus or Amphion, both of whom are referred to in the third person. Niobe's mother, a surprisingly popular candidate among recent scholars (Garzya, Moreau), can also be excluded: even if we were to suppose that she had somehow arrived in Thebes before her husband, she could not be in a position to inform the chorus about events there. The only remaining possibilities deserving serious consideration are Antiope, the mother of Amphion, and Niobe's nurse; the speech's focus on Niobe, and especially line 14 with its anxiety lest frank speech cause harm to her, points strongly to the nurse, since Amphion's mother might be expected to be more concerned with her son, and indeed to be hostile to the woman whose folly had destroyed his family. The chorus must be residents of Thebes (since Tantalus, and any retinue he may have, have not yet arrived) but not members of Amphion's household; we cannot tell, either from this fragment or in any other way, whether they were men or women, unless fr. 155 refers to them.

[2] lit. "sitting ‹like a mother-bird› over her eggs".

10   ] μὲν ἥξει δεῦρο Ταντάλου βία
      ]κόμιστρα τῆϲδε καὶ πεφα[.....]ν.
      ]δε μῆνιν τίνα φέρων Ἀμφίονι
      ]. ον ἀικῶϲ ἐξεφύλλαϲεν γένοϲ;
      πρ]ὸϲ ὑμᾶϲ, οὐ γάρ ἐϲτε δύϲφρονε[ϲ,
15   ] θεὸϲ μὲν αἰτίαν φύει βροτοῖϲ,
      ὅταν κακῶϲαι δῶμα παμπήδην θέλῃ·
      ]ε θνητὸν ὄντα χρὴ τὸν . [
      π]εριϲτέλλοντα μὴ θραϲυϲτομ[εῖν.
      ] εὖ πράϲϲοντεϲ οὔποτ' ἤλπιϲα[ν
20   ]ντεϲ ἐκχεῖν ἣν ἔχωϲ[
      γ]ὰρ ἐξαρθεῖϲα [κ]αλλιϲ[τ
      [Remains of one further line]

10 [καὶ νῦν] Latte   11 (beginning) [οὔϲων] Schadewaldt,
[ἔχων] Muscolino   12 [Φοῖβοϲ] δὲ Maas; [πατὴρ] δὲ Lesky
13 [ἀκμά]ζον Lobel   αικωϲ Πᵃᶜ; αινωϲ Πᵖᶜ   14 [ἐγὼ
πρ]ὸϲ Norsa & Vitelli   15 [φράϲω·] Maas   17 [ὅμωϲ
δ]ὲ Norsa & Vitelli   τὸν ἐ[κ θεῶν] Norsa & Vitelli
18 [ὄλβον π]εριϲτέλλοντα Körte, Latte, Cazzaniga
19 [ἀλλ' οἱ μὲν] Norsa & Vitelli, [ἀλλ' οἱ γὰρ] Maas, [οἱ δ' αἰὲν]
Lesky   20 [ϲφαλέ]ντεϲ Fraenkel   ἔχωϲ' [εὐπραξίαν]
Norsa & Vitelli   21 [αὕτη γ]ὰρ Lloyd-Jones   [κ]αλ-
λιϲ[τεύματι] Norsa & Vitelli, then [πλήθει τε παίδων] Körte, cf.
schol. *Iliad* 24.602

ing but a shadow. [And now (?)] mighty Tantalus will be coming here [to apply (?)] means to bring her home and [. . .]. And what anger did [Phoebus (?)[3]] bear towards Amphion, that he so humbled this [flourish]ing family and stripped it bare? [I will tell] you, for you are not unfriendly.[4] When god wishes to ruin a family completely, he plants a cause[5] among its members; [but all the same], seeing that one is mortal, one should cherish the [prosperity that comes from the gods (?)] and not be rash in speech. [But those who] enjoy [continuing (?)] success never expect to [slip up (?)] and lose the [prosperity (?)] they have. For [this woman], elated by [her (?)] surpassing beauty [and the number of her children (?) . . .]

---

3 Or "the Father" (i.e. Zeus).

4 Implying "I can speak to you frankly without fearing you may use the knowledge to Niobe's detriment".

5 The context suggests that this refers to a cause *of temptation* (such as great prosperity, which encourages arrogant behaviour) rather than a character flaw.

155

Ἴστρος τοιαύτας παρθένους ἐξεύχεται
τρέφειν ὅ θ᾽ ἁγνὸς Φᾶσις

Choeroboscus (i), *On Hephaestion's Enchiridion* p.190.13–14
Consbruch; line 1 only (or part of it) is cited by Hephaestion himself (*Enchiridion* p.3.15 Consbruch); Choeroboscus (ii) *op.cit.*
p.190.9; Eustathius on *Odyssey* 10.492–5; Priscian, *Institutiones
Grammaticae* 1.52, and an anonymous commentator on him (i
192 Hertz); scholia to Sophocles, *Oedipus the King* 1264; and
Tzetzes on *Iliad* 1.342 and Aristophanes, *Wealth* 14, 44, 116, 943
and 946.

1 ἐξεύχεται Choeroboscus (i): μνηστεύεται Eustathius: λο-
χεύεται cett.

158

ΤΑΝΤΑΛΟΣ

σπείρω δ᾽ ἄρουραν δώδεχ᾽ ἡμερῶν ὁδόν,
Βερέκυντα χώραν, ἔνθ᾽ Ἀδραστείας ἕδος
Ἴδη τε μυκηθμοῖσι καὶ βληχήμασιν
βρέμουσι μήλων, πᾶν τ᾽ Ἐρέχθειον πέδον

Strabo 12.8.21; also (first eight words only) Plutarch, *Moralia*
603a and 778b.

2 χώραν Blaydes: χῶρον codd.
3 Ἴδη Casaubon: Ἴδης codd.   βληχήμασιν West: βρυ-
χήμασιν codd.
4 τ᾽ Ἐρέχθειον Meineke: δ᾽ ἐρέχθεον D h i: δ᾽ ἐρέχθει C g l r
v w: ὀρεχθεῖ u x

155

Ister[1] and holy Phasis[2] boast that they rear such maidens as
these.[3]

[1] The Danube, which separated Thrace from Scythia.   [2] The
principal river of Colchis, now the Rioni in Georgia.   [3] Or "as
this". It is not clear what maiden or maidens are being described
(the chorus? the daughters of Niobe?) or what is being asserted
about them. It may or may not be relevant that in *Prometheus
Bound* (415–6) the Amazon warrior-maidens live in Colchis, and
in Herodotus (4.110–117) their descendants live in Scythia.

158

TANTALUS

The land I sow extends for twelve days' journey: the country of the Berecyntians,[1] where the territory of Adrasteia[2]
and Mount Ida resound with the lowing and bleating of
livestock, and all of the Erechthean plain.[3]

[1] A Phrygian tribe.   [2] The land on the Asian shore of the
Propontis (Sea of Marmara) at its western end, between Parium
and Cyzicus.   [3] Meaning here, apparently, the Troad, after Erichthonius son of Dardanus (*Iliad* 20.219–230), owner of
three thousand horses and great-great-grandfather of Priam.
Thus Tantalus is describing himself as ruler of the whole region
known to fifth-century Greeks as Phrygia.

159

ΤΑΝΤΑΛΟΣ

θυμός ποθ᾽ ἁμὸς οὐρανῷ κυρῶν ἄνω
ἔραζε πίπτει καί με προσφωνεῖ τάδε·
"γίγνωσκε τἀνθρώπεια μὴ σέβειν ἄγαν"

Plutarch, *Moralia* 603a

1 ποθ᾽ Fritzsche: δέ ποθ᾽ codd.

160

<× – (∪)> μέλαθρα καὶ δόμους Ἀμφίονος

Aristophanes, *Birds* 1247 (μέλαθρα μὲν αὐτοῦ καὶ . . .) with
scholia; many scholars have held that the scholiast's note ἔστι δὲ
ἐκ Νιόβης Αἰσχύλου applies not only to this line but to other
paratragic material in its vicinity, especially 1248 (καταιθαλώσω
πυρφόροισιν αἰετοῖς: claimed for Aeschylus by Stanley)

161

μόνος θεῶν γὰρ Θάνατος οὐ δώρων ἐρᾷ,
οὐδ᾽ ἄν τι θύων οὐδ᾽ ἐπισπένδων ἄνοις,
οὐδ᾽ ἔστι βωμὸς οὐδὲ παιωνίζεται·
μόνου δὲ Πειθὼ δαιμόνων ἀποστατεῖ

Stobaeus 4.51.1; scholia to *Iliad* 9.158 (lines 1–3); Eustathius
on same passage (lines 1–3); line 1 is quoted by Aristophanes,
Frogs 1392 with scholia; scholia to Euripides, *Alcestis* 55 and
Sophocles, *Electra* 39; and *Suda* θ45 and μ1235.

2 οὐδ᾽ . . . οὐδ᾽ schol. *Iliad* 9.158, Eustathius: οὔτ᾽ . . . οὔτ᾽
Stobaeus   ἄνοις Dobree: ναοῖς Stobaeus: λάβοις schol.,
Eustathius

159

TANTALUS

My spirit, which once reached up to the high heavens, has fallen to earth[1] and says this to me: "Learn not to give too much honour to anything that is human".

Probably part of the same speech as fr. 158.[2]

[1] Probably as a result of his notorious sins and their punishment, which he may have narrated earlier in the same speech.
[2] According to Plutarch, Tantalus says fr. 158, εἶτα μετ᾽ ὀλίγον fr. 159.

160

. . . the halls and home of Amphion.[1]

[1] In Aristophanes' play this is part of a response by the hero, Peisetaerus, to a threatening tirade by the goddess Iris. She had said: "Fool, fool, do not provoke the formidable souls of the gods, lest all your race be utterly overthrown by Justice with the mattock of Zeus, and smoky flame reduce to ashes your person and the enclosure of your house with Licymnian bolts!" (*Birds* 1238–42), to which Peisetaerus replies *inter alia*: "Do you know that if Zeus annoys me any further, I will reduce his halls and the home of Amphion [sic] to ashes with incendiary eagles . . . ?" (1246–8), after which his menaces become more bird-centred, more comic, and finally obscene.

161

Alone of the gods, Death desires no gifts; one can gain nothing by making sacrifice or pouring libation to him, nor has he any altar, nor is he addressed in songs of praise; from him, alone among divinities, Persuasion stands aloof.[1]

[1] i.e. Death is immune to all persuasion.

169

162

NIOBH

οἱ θεῶν ἀγχίσποροι,
οἱ Ζηνὸς ἐγγύς, ὧν κατ᾽ Ἰδαῖον πάγον
Διὸς πατρῴου βωμός ἐστ᾽ ἐν αἰθέρι,
κοὔ πώ σφιν ἐξίτηλον αἷμα δαιμόνων

Plato, *Republic* 391e (author and play not specified); Strabo
12.8.21 (lines 2b-3a, cited from Αἰσχύλος . . . ἐν τῇ Νιόβῃ: οἷς ἐν
Ἰδαίῳ πάγῳ Διὸς πατρῴου βωμός ἐστι); lines 1–2a are mis-
quoted (Ζηνὸς ἐγγὺς καὶ θεῶν ἀγχίσποροι) by [Lucian], *Enco-
mium of Demosthenes* 13

2 οἱ Bekker: om. Codd.   ὧν Plato: οἷς Strabo   κατ᾽
Ἰδαῖον πάγον Plato: ἐν Ἰδαίῳ πάγῳ Strabo

ΞΑΝΤΡΙΑΙ

*This play is known to have dealt with the fate of an enemy
of Dionysus at the hands of female bacchants: in fr. 169
Lyssa, the goddess of madness, urges them on to tear
their victim in pieces. The death of Pentheus was certainly
mentioned in the play (fr. 172b), and its location was
Mount Cithaeron, as in Euripides'* Bacchae. *Since an ancient headnote (Hypothesis) to* Bacchae *names* Pentheus
(q.v.) *as the Aeschylean play running parallel to it, it has
often been suspected that Pentheus' death was not part of
the action of* Wool-Carders *but was only predicted in it. In
view of fr. 169, however, we would then have to suppose
that in the play named after him Pentheus only appeared
as a corpse, if at all—for which there would be no parallel*

162

NIOBE[1]

Those who are near of kin to the gods and close to Zeus,[2] whose altar of Ancestral Zeus is high in the upper air on the crags of Ida, and in whom the divine blood has not yet lost its potency.

[1] Strabo states that Niobe is the speaker, and that she is referring to the family of Tantalus. [2] No text earlier than or contemporary with Aeschylus specifies Tantalus' parentage, but in all later sources bar one (starting with Euripides, *Orestes* 5) he is a son of Zeus (the exception is a scholium to the same Euripidean passage, which names the mountain-god Tmolus as his father).

see 220a

WOOL-CARDERS

in what we know of Greek tragedy. This is probably, all the same, the least bad of the available hypotheses. Alternative possibilities are (i) that Wool-Carders *and* Pentheus *are two names for the same play (but Galen quotes lines from both plays [frr. 170, 183], each under its own title, in the same passage) and (ii) that the plot of* Wool-Carders *had nothing to do with Pentheus at all but dealt with another Dionysiac story, such as that of the daughters of Minyas who resisted Dionysus, were driven mad, and tore the son of one of themselves in pieces (but the late Hellenistic scholar Asclepiades—see on fr. 220a—clearly associated* Wool-Carders *with the Cadmus-Semele-Pentheus story). A further complication is the existence of a set of papyrus*

171

fragments (168, 168a, 168b Radt = 220a, b, c in this edition) which contain two lines that are quoted elsewhere as from Wool-Carders; *the content of the fragments, however, strongly suggests that they actually come from* Semele *(q.v.) Many scholars have grouped* Wool-Carders *with* Semele *and* Pentheus *in a trilogy, often with* The Nurses of Dionysus *(q.v.) as the satyr-drama; but* Archeresses *(q.v.) is another candidate for a place in such a grouping.*

169

ΛΥΣΣΑ

ἐκ ποδῶν δ' ἄνω

ὑπέρχεται σπαραγμὸς εἰς ἄκρον κάρα·
κέντημα λύσσης, σκορπίου βέλος λέγω

Pausanias the Atticist o15 Erbse (= Photius s.v. ὀκτώπουν); Suda o130

2 ὑπέρχεται codd.: perh. ὑπελθέτω? 3 λύσσης Lobeck: γλώσσης codd.

170

ἃς οὔτε πέμφιξ ἡλίου προσδέρκεται
οὔτ' ἀστερωπὸν ὄμμα Λητῴας κόρης

Galen, *Commentary on Hippocrates' Epidemiae Book VI* (xvii a 880.8–9 Kühn); πέμφιξ is also cited from this play by Photius s.v.

1 (ἐν Ξαντρίαις)· ἃς Bentley, Koraes (the Arabic version of Galen reads *ksntria*): ἐξαντοιαίας cod. 2 ἀστερωπὸν ὄμμα Bentley, Koraes (and the Arabic version appears to render this): ἀστέρων πῶμα cod.

The "wool-carders" of the title will have been the cho-rus, shown at first as engaged in ordinary womanly activi-ties, but later "driven in madness by Dionysus from their looms and shuttles" (Euripides, Bacchae 118–9).

Recent studies: F. Jouan, "Dionysos chez Eschyle", *Kernos* 5 (1992) 71–86, esp. 77–78.

169
LYSSA[1]

And the rending goes up[2] from the feet to the top of the head: I speak of the prick of madness, the sting of the scor-pion.

[1] The quoting sources say that she is "inspiring the bac-chants". In Euripides, *Bacchae* 977 the bacchants who will shortly be tearing Pentheus apart are called "swift hounds of Lyssa".
[2] One would have expected Lyssa to say "And let the rending go up . . ."

170

Which[1] neither the flaming orb[2] of the sun looks upon, nor the starlike eye of Leto's daughter.[3]

[1] Or "whom"; the Greek relative pronoun is feminine and plu-ral, but it is not clear to whom or what it refers.   [2] lit. "pus-tule".   3 This is the earliest known text in which the moon is identified with Artemis (cf. on *Bassarids*, in which Orpheus ap-parently identified the sun with Apollo).

171

κάμακες πεύκης οἱ πυρίφλεκτοι

Pollux 10.117

ΟΙΔΙΠΟΥΣ

ΟΠΛΩΝ ΚΡΙΣΙΣ

171

Spears of pine blazing with fire.[1]

[1] i.e. torches; cf. Euripides, *Bacchae* 144–7.

OEDIPUS

This was the second play of the Theban tetralogy, following Laius *and preceding* Seven against Thebes *and* The Sphinx; *its possible content is discussed in the introduction to* Seven against Thebes. *No fragments survive, unless fr. 387a, part of a narrative about the murder of Laius, comes from this play.*

THE AWARD OF THE ARMS

The subject of this play was the contest for the armour of Achilles, in which Ajax was defeated by Odysseus; the play probably formed a trilogy with Thracian Women *and* Women of Salamis *(qq.v.). It is likely, in view of fr. 174, that Thetis, who offered the armour as a prize for the best man in the Achaean army, was a character in the play. The play was apparently imitated by the Roman dramatists Pacuvius and Accius in tragedies entitled* Armorum Iudicium, *and was probably a major source for the accounts of the episode by Ovid (*Metamorphoses *12.620– 13.381) and Quintus of Smyrna (*Posthomerica *5.1–332).*

Recent studies: M. Librán Moreno, "Philostr. *Her.* 20.2: una posible alusión a *El juicio de las armas* de Ésquilo", *Cuadernos de Filología Clásica: estudios griegos y indoeuropeos* 16 (2006) 195–209.

174

δέσποινα πεντήκοντα Νηρῄδων κορῶν

Scholia to Aristophanes, *Acharnians* 883

κορῶν L (i.e. Triclinius): χορόν ΕΓ: κορᾶν R (as in Aristophanes' text, where the speaker is a Boeotian)

175

ἀλλ' Ἀντικλείας ἆσσον ἦλθε Σίσυφος,
τῆς σῆς λέγω τοι μητρός, ἥ σ' ἐγείνατο

Scholia to Sophocles, *Ajax* 190

176

ἁπλᾶ γάρ ἐστι τῆς ἀληθείας ἔπη

Stobaeus 3.11.14; Anon. in *The Theosophy of the Sibyls* 3.30 Erbse; Arsenius, *Apophthegmata* 3.60k

174

Mistress of fifty Nereid maidens.

Addressed to Thetis.[1]

[1] The scholiast says that the speaker was "inviting the Nereids to come out ‹of the sea› and judge ‹the contest›", but this may be an error: one would not expect goddesses to give an unjust verdict unless (like Athena, cf. *Little Iliad* fr. 2 West) they were prejudiced, and there would be no reason for the Nereids to be prejudiced in favour of Odysseus or against Ajax. The established account in the first half of the fifth century was that the contest was decided by a vote of the army (Pindar, *Nemean* 8.27; two paintings by the Brygos Painter, *LIMC* Aias I 83 and 84), and Sophocles (*Ajax* 449, 1135–7) assumes that his audience know this.

175

AJAX

But Sisyphus came close to Anticleia[1]—to your mother, I tell you, to her who gave birth to you!

[1] The allegation that Odysseus was really the son of Sisyphus, not of Laertes, is repeatedly made in tragedy by his enemies (Sophocles, *Ajax* 189; *Philoctetes* 417, 625; fr. 567). The story was that he had slept with Anticleia when visiting her father Autolycus to reclaim his stolen cattle, or had raped her when she was on her way to Ithaca, so that she was already pregnant with Odysseus when Laertes married her (scholia to Sophocles, *Ajax* 190).

176

The words of truth are simple.

Doubtless Ajax, contrasting his plain honesty with the tricky oratory of Odysseus.

177

177

τί γὰρ καλὸν ζῆν †βίον ὃς† λύπας φέρει;

Stobaeus 4.53.24

βίον ὃς codd.: βίοτον ὃς Stanley: ᾧ βίος Nauck

177a

καὶ διὰ πλευμόνων
θερμῶν ἄησιν ὕπνον

Photius α447

1 πλευμόνων Radt: πνευμόνων cod.　　2 θερμῶν cod.ᵖᶜ:
θερμὸν cod.ᵃᶜ

ΟΣΤΟΛΟΓΟΙ

The two surviving fragments of this play both come from a speech or speeches by Odysseus, describing the indignities inflicted upon him, while he was in disguise as a beggar in his own palace, by Penelope's suitors, whose bodies, or perhaps rather their ash-urns, are visible on stage (cf. fr. 180.1 ὅδ'). Since ὀστολογία is the collection of ashes for burial after a body has been cremated (see e.g. Menander, The Shield 77), it is generally accepted that the play was based on the episode in the Odyssey *(24.413ff) where the families of the suitors collect and bury their bodies (or ship them home) and then meet to plot revenge on Odysseus. In the epic, however, Odysseus has left the palace for his father's*

177

For what honour is there in living a life that brings[1] only
pain?

Ajax's reaction to defeat in the contest?

[1] Or, with Nauck, "... in living for one to whom life brings ..."

177a

And through his fevered lungs
he[1] breathes sleep.

From a choral song.

[1] Or "she" or "it". We do not know what the subject of the sentence was—it need not necessarily have been the owner of the
lungs; compare e.g. Pindar, *Pythian* 1.1–9, on the effect of music
in quenching the fire of Zeus's thunderbolt and lulling his eagle to
sleep.

BONE-GATHERERS

*country estate; in the play he stands his ground and
justifies his actions. The play was probably the third in an
Odyssean trilogy, following* Ghost-Raisers *and* Penelope
(qq.v.); the accompanying satyr-play was no doubt Circe
(q.v.)

*The references to symposiac games in fr. 179, and to a
chamber-pot being thrown at Odysseus in fr. 180, have led
many scholars to believe that* Bone-Gatherers *was a satyr-
play. To accept this, however, would force us to abandon
the notion of an Odyssean tetralogy; moreover, Athenaeus
(1.17c) criticizes Aeschylus (and Sophocles [fr. 565], who
closely imitates fr. 180 of this play) for presenting drunken*

ATTRIBUTED FRAGMENTS

179

ΟΔΥΣΣΕΥΣ

Εὐρύμαχος οὗτος ἄλλος οὐδὲν ἥσσονας
ὕβριζ᾽ ὑβρισμοὺς οὐκ ἐναισίους ἐμοί·
ἦν μὲν γὰρ αὐτῷ σκοπὸς ἀεὶ τοὐμὸν κάρα,
τοῦ δ᾽ ἀγκυλητοῖς κοσσάβοις ἐπίσκοπος
5 †ἐκτεμὼν† ἡβῶσα χεὶρ ἐφίετο

Athenaeus 15.667c; the phrase ἀγκυλητοὺς κοσσάβους is
also ascribed to Aeschylus (play not specified) by Athenaeus 11
(epitome) 782e and Eustathius on *Iliad* 2.774

1 οὗτος Hermann: οὐ cod.   ἥσσονας Musurus: ἥσσον
cod.   2 ἐναισίους Valckenaer, Porson, Koraes: αινεσιους
cod.   3 σκοπὸς Dobree: κότταβος cod.   τοὐμὸν Petit:
τοῦ μὲν cod.   4 ἀγκυλητοῖς κοσσάβοις Schweighaeuser
(all our sources say that Aeschylus spoke of ἀγκυλητοὺς κοσσάβους): ἀγκυλητοῦ κοσσάβιός cod.   ἐπίσκοπος Bothe
(ἐπίσκοπα Dobree): εστιν σκοπὸς cod.   5 ἐκτεμὼν cod.:
perh. e.g. ὀσ<σων> τ᾽ ἐμῶν (ὅσσων ἐμῶν Dobree, σκ<ύτων>
τ᾽ ἐμῶν Holwerda)

180

heroes throwing chamber-pots at each other—which in a satyr-drama could hardly have been regarded as objectionable—and Pollux (2.224) says that οὐράνη "chamber-pot", used here, is the tragic equivalent of the comic term ἀμίς. Compare also (to take only one example) Libation-Bearers 755–760, on babies' nappies and their contents.

Recent discussions: D. Holwerda, "Zur Interpretation und Emendation zweier Aischylos-Fragmente", in H. Hofmann and A. M. Harder ed. *Fragmenta Dramatica* (Göttingen, 1991) 3–7; M. G. Palutan, "La parodia del cottabo nei Syndeipnoi di Sofocle e negli Ostologoi di Eschilo", *SIFC* 14 (1996) 10–27; A. Wessels and R. Krumeich in KPS 205–7; P. Grossardt, "The title of Aeschylus' *Ostologoi*", *HSCP* 101 (2003) 155–8; A. H. Sommerstein, "The anger of Achilles, Mark One: Sophocles' *Syndeipnoi*", in Sommerstein ed. *Shards from Kolonos: Studies in Sophoclean Fragments* (Bari, 2003) 355–371, at 363–4, 368–370; id., "*Syndeipnoi*", in Sommerstein et al. *Sophocles: Selected Fragmentary Plays* (Oxford, 2006) 84–140, at 124–7; Podlecki 16.

179

ODYSSEUS

This other one, Eurymachus,[1] used to commit against me unseemly outrages no less grave. He was always using my head as a target,[2] and his vigorous arm took accurate aim at it, and at my eyes (?), with bent-armed wine-flicks.

[1] Odysseus has evidently just been speaking of the behaviour of the most prominent and most wicked of the suitors, Antinous, and now passes to Eurymachus as the second-ranking in both respects. In the *Odyssey* (18.394–8) Eurymachus throws a footstool at the disguised Odysseus; it misses and knocks down a servant.

[2] In the game of *kottabos*, which consisted of throwing the dregs of one's wine-cup at a (normally inanimate) target.

180

ΟΔΥΣΣΕΥΣ

ὅδ᾽ ἐστίν, ὅς ποτ᾽ ἀμφ᾽ ἐμοὶ βέλος
γελωτοποιόν, τὴν κάκοσμον οὐράνην,
ἔρριψεν οὐδ᾽ ἥμαρτε· περὶ δ᾽ ἐμῷ κάρᾳ
πληγεῖσ᾽ ἐναυάγησεν ὀστρακουμένη,
5   χωρὶς μυρηρῶν τευχέων πνέουσ᾽ ἐμοί

Athenaeus 1.17c; Eustathius on *Odyssey* 17.462; Philodemus, *On Poems* 213 Janko (τὴν κά[κ]οσμον αὐράνην [sic] ἔρρι[ψ]εν);[1]
several grammarians mention that Aeschylus used the word
οὐράνη

[1] None of these authors names the play, but both Athenaeus
and Philodemus make it clear that the victim of the assault was
Odysseus.

ΠΑΛΑΜΗΔΗΣ

*Palamedes is a figure unknown to, or ignored by, the
poet(s) of the* Iliad *and* Odyssey, *but the tale of how he was
treacherously murdered during the Trojan War, by Odysseus—in some versions alone, in others with Diomedes
and sometimes Agamemnon as accomplices—was a popular one from the cyclic epics onwards, and was dramatized
by all three of the great tragedians. Odysseus' motive
is sometimes revenge, Palamedes having unmasked him
when he tried to avoid serving in the war by pretending to
be mad (Cypria Arg. §5 West), sometimes jealousy of his
cleverness. The later accounts, doubtless deriving from one
or more of the tragic treatments, regularly have Palamedes*

PALAMEDES

180

ODYSSEUS

This[1] is the man who once threw in my direction an object designed to make me a laughing-stock, the evil-smelling chamber-pot, and he did not miss his aim; it struck me on the head and smashed into fragments, wafting over me an odour very unlike that of perfume-jars.

[1] Not certainly identifiable, but most likely Ctesippus, in the *Odyssey* (20.287–302) the only suitor other than Antinous and Eurymachus who throws an object (a cow's hoof) at the disguised Odysseus; later he is appropriately killed by the oxherd Philoetius.

PALAMEDES

being condemned by the army on a trumped-up charge of treason and put to death by stoning; frr. 181a and 182 would fit well into such a scenario as part of a defence speech. Aeschylus' play, however, went on beyond Palamedes' condemnation and execution, since fr. 181 shows that Palamedes' father, Nauplius, came to Troy (as Sophocles later made him do in The Arrival of Nauplius) *and protested, doubtless to little effect, about what had been done to his son; the story was that he took revenge later by causing the Greek fleet to be wrecked on its way home and/or by encouraging the leaders' wives to have adulterous affairs.*

    I have tried to establish, in the article cited below, what can be inferred with greater or lesser confidence about the structure of this play; I also argue there that fr. 451k Radt (here fr. 180a) gives us the opening lines of its prologue, on the grounds that none of the ten other known Trojan War plays of Aeschylus (except Myrmidons *[q.v.], which we*

183

180a (451k)

μ]ὲν εὐχαῖc πρῶτα πρεcβεύων cέβ[αc
ἱ]κνοῦμαι φέγγ[οc] ἡλίου τὸ νῦν
αμ]εῖψαι ξὺ[ν] τύχαιc εὐημέρ[οιc
](.).. [.] Ἑλλάδοc λοχαγέταιc
5   Με]νέλεῳ τὴν βίαιον ἁρπαγὴν
]πράccουcι Πρ[ι]αμ[ί]δην Πάριν
]c εὐμενῆ cυνα[λ]λ[α]γήν·

[Remains of three more lines; then a gap of uncertain length;
then remains of another three lines ending] . ονοc,] . . . Τρωϊκόν,]
. τοῦ θεοῦ]

Oxyrhynchus Papyrus 2253

1 [Διὸς μ]ὲν Vaio ([μ]ὲν Lobel)   σέβ[αs] Snell
2 (beginning) [αἰτῶν θ'] Snell: [ἔπειθ'] Mette   3 [πόνους
ἀμ]εῖψαι Snell ([ἀμ]εῖψαι Lobel)   5 (beginning) οἵπερ
Snell: οἳ ξὺν Stark   6 [γυναικὸς ἐκ]πράσσουσι Snell
7 [νείκης βαρεία]s Lloyd-Jones   ευμενηι Π

*know began differently) could have opened, as this one
did, with a character hoping for a "friendly reconciliation"
among the "captains of Greece" (lines 5–6, which speak of
these leaders as "seeking revenge" for the "violent seizure"
of Helen, rule out the possibility that the reconciliation envisaged was one with the Trojans).*

Recent studies: C. W. Müller, "Der Palamedesmythos im Philoktet
des Euripides", *RhM* 133 (1990) 193–209 (esp. 204–8); A. H.
Sommerstein, "The prologue of Aeschylus' *Palamedes*", *RhM* 143
(2000) 118–127; F. Jouan and H. van Looy, *Euripide* viii.2 (Paris,
2000) 487–507, esp. 490–4.

180a (451k)

Giving pride of place in my prayers to the maj[esty of Zeus,
I beg and (?) b]eseech him that this present lig[ht of the
sun may [exc]hange [our sufferings (?)] for a good day's
fortune, [and to grant to (??)] the captains of Greece, [who
together with (?) Me]nelaus are seeking revenge from
Paris, son of Pr[i]am, for the violent seizure [of his wife],
a friendly reco[n]c[i]liation [of their grievous quarrel (?).
. . .]

[. . .] Trojan [. . .] of the god [. . .]

*The beginning of the play: apparently the accusation of treason
against Palamedes has already been made, and a Greek not himself involved in the quarrel (Calchas? Nestor?) prays that it may
be resolved peacefully.*

ATTRIBUTED FRAGMENTS

181

τίνος κατέκας ἕνεκα παῖδ᾽ ἐμὸν βλάβης;

Scholia (A) to *Iliad* 4.319 = Herodian, *On Iliadic Prosody* p. 46.13 Lentz

181a

ΠΑΛΑΜΗΔΗΣ

ἔπειτα πάσης Ἑλλάδος καὶ ξυμμάχων
βίον διῴκησ᾽ ὄντα πρὶν πεφυρμένον
θηρσίν θ᾽ ὅμοιον· πρῶτα μὲν τὸν πάνσοφον
ἀριθμὸν ηὕρηκ᾽, ἔξοχον σοφισμάτων

Stobaeus 1, Prologue, extract 1a (tacked on to *Prometheus Bound* 454–9, as if it were a continuation of that passage; ascribed to *Palamedes* by Blomfield tentatively, by Wachsmuth firmly; cf. Plato, *Republic* 522d ἐν ταῖς τραγῳδίαις Παλαμήδης . . . φησὶν ἀριθμὸν εὑρὼν τάς . . . τάξεις τῷ στρατοπέδῳ καταστῆσαι [~ fr. 182])

3 θηρσίν Hermann (θηρσί anon. [Amsterdam, 1736]): θερσί cod.

181

On account of what injury did you kill my son?

Nauplius protesting to Odysseus (or perhaps to Agamemnon).

181a

PALAMEDES

Then I organized the life of all the Greeks and their allies, which previously had been as chaotic as that of beasts. To begin with, I invented the ingenious art of number, supreme among all techniques.[1]

---

[1] *Prometheus Bound* 447–450, 459–460 are either a close parallel to this passage or, if not by Aeschylus, an imitation of it. A scholium on *Prometheus* 457–9 states that Aeschylus "also ascribed this invention to Palamedes", but the scholium is differently placed in different manuscripts, and it is not clear whether it is referring to arithmetic (as in our fragment) or astronomy.

182

ΠΑΛΑΜΗΔΗΣ

καὶ ταξιάρχας χἀκατοντάρχας στρατῷ
ἔταξα, σῖτον δ᾽ εἰδέναι διώρισα,
ἄριστα, δεῖπνα δόρπα θ᾽ αἱρεῖσθαι τρίτα

Athenaeus 1.11d; scholia to *Iliad* 2.381 and *Odyssey* 2.20 (line
3 only); Eustathius on *Odyssey* 16.2 (lines 2–3, from σῖτον) and
on *Iliad* 2.381, 24.444 and *Odyssey* 2.20, 17.599 (each time citing
all or part of line 3); all sources cite Aeschylus as author, none
names the play, but Athenaeus, and Eustathius on *Odyssey* 16.2,
name Palamedes as the speaker

1 χἀκατοντάρχας Heath (after Pauw), στρατῷ Schweighaeuser: καὶ στρατάρχας καὶ ἑκατοντάρχας codd.   3 τρίτα
Athenaeus, schol. *Od.*: τρία Eustathius on *Il.* 24.444, *Od.* 2.20,
16.2 (on *Il.* 2.381 he records both readings); in schol. *Il.* the mss.
are divided; Eustathius on *Od.* 17.599 omits the word.

ΠΕΝΘΕΥΣ

*One of the Hypotheses to Euripides' Bacchae says that
the same story (sc. in essentials) was told by Aeschylus
in* Pentheus. *This raises problems, which are briefly discussed above in the introductory note to* Wool-Carders,
*where it is also considered what other plays may have been
produced with these two. If we accept what was there
described as "the least bad of the available hypotheses",*

182

PALAMEDES

And I appointed brigade and company commanders[1] for
the army, and I taught them to distinguish their meals, to
take breakfast, dinner and thirdly supper.

[1] lit. "taxiarchs and commanders of hundreds". In classical
Athens a taxiarch was the commander of the hoplite troops of one
of the ten tribes into which the citizen body was divided.

PENTHEUS

Pentheus *will have dealt only with the arrival at Thebes of
the news of Pentheus' death on Mount Cithaeron at the
hands of the bacchants, and the reactions of his family, the
Theban community and perhaps Dionysus himself. Only
one fragment of the text survives.*

Recent discussions: F. Jouan, "Dionysos chez Eschyle", *Kernos* 5
(1992) 71–86, esp. 78; V. Di Benedetto, "Eschilo e Dioniso: pos-
tille", *Lexis* 22 (2004) 37–42.

ATTRIBUTED FRAGMENTS

183

μηδ᾽ αἵματος πέμφιγα πρὸς πέδῳ βάλῃς

Galen, *Commentary on Hippocrates' Epidemiae Book VI* (xvii a 880.14 Kühn)

πέμφιγα Gemusaeus: πέμφιγγα cod.

ΠΕΡΡΑΙΒΙΔΕΣ

184

ποῦ μοι τὰ πολλὰ δῶρα κἀκροθίνια;
ποῦ χρυσότευκτα κἀργυρᾶ σκυφώματα;

Athenaeus 11.499a; Eustathius on *Odyssey* 15.85 (line 2 only).

183

And do not spill a gout[1] of blood on the ground.

[1] lit. "a pustule", i.e. a round, bright drop.

PERRHAEBIAN WOMEN

This play is generally considered to have dealt with the story of Ixion's treacherous murder of his father-in-law, Eioneus or Deioneus. Ixion was king of Gyrton, a city in Perrhaebia (northern Thessaly) (Strabo 9.5.19), and the three surviving quotations fit very well the story of how Ixion, in order to avoid paying (D)eioneus the gifts due by custom in exchange for his daughter, invited his father-in-law as if to a feast and enticed him into entering a room which he had booby-trapped; (D)eioneus fell into a fiery pit and perished in the flames (Pindar, Pythian *2.21–48 with scholia; Diodorus Siculus 4.69.3–5). The sequel to this murder was presented in* Ixion *(q.v.), which may or may not have been part of the same production.*

184

Where are my many choice gifts? Where are the cups wrought in gold and silver?

Presumably Ixion's father-in-law demanding his bride-gifts.

185

ἀργυρηλάτοις
κέρασι χρυσᾶ στόμια προσβεβλημένοις

Athenaeus 11.476c; Eustathius on *Iliad* 13.21.

186

τέθνηκεν αἰσχρῶς χρημάτων ἀπαιόλῃ

Eustathius on *Iliad* 2.816; ἀπαιόλη is cited from this play by Hesychius α5725.

ΠΗΝΕΛΟΠΗ

185

With silver drinking-horns that had golden mouthpieces
attached to them.

*Perhaps referring to the gifts, perhaps to the luxurious appurte-
nances of Ixion's treacherous feast.*

186

He has died a disgraceful death by a scheme to defraud
him of what was his.

PENELOPE

*From the title and the only surviving fragment (187) we
can see that this play dramatized the section of the* Odyssey
*during which Odysseus returned to his own house in the
guise of a beggar, and that it included a version of the interview between him and Penelope which fills most of book 19
of the epic. We cannot tell what other episodes were included, or how closely Aeschylus followed the Homeric
story, though it is tempting to imagine that the play culminated in the (offstage) slaying of Penelope's suitors and the
reunion of husband and wife.*

*Penelope was probably the second play of an Odyssean
tetralogy, preceded by* Ghost-Raisers *(q.v.) and followed
by* Bone-Gatherers *and the satyr-drama* Circe *(qq.v.)*

187

ΟΔΥΣΣΕΥΣ

ἐγὼ γένος μέν εἰμι Κρὴς ἀρχέστατον

Etymologicum Genuinum s.v. αἰδοιέστατον and ἀφθονέστατον; *Etymologicum Symeonis* and *Etymologicum Magnum* s.v.
αἰδοιέστατον (or -ος)

ΠΟΛΥΔΕΚΤΗΣ

*Polydectes was the king of Seriphos who, wishing to marry
Perseus' mother Danaë, sent Perseus in quest of the head of
the Gorgon Medusa in the expectation that he would not
return; Perseus did return, with the head, and used it to
turn Polydectes to stone. We know of this play only from its
inclusion in the medieval catalogue of Aeschylus' plays;
no quotations or other references to its content survive,
and we cannot tell whether it dealt with the events lead-*

ΠΡΟΜΗΘΕΥΣ

In addition to the fragments cited from Prometheus Unbound *and* Prometheus the Fire-Bearer *or* Fire-Kindler
*(qq.v.), there are a number of surviving quotations which
are ascribed by the source authors either simply to* Prometheus, *or incorrectly to* Prometheus Bound. *In some cases*

187

ODYSSEUS

I am a Cretan of most kingly lineage.[1]

[1] "In his made-up tales [in the *Odyssey*] Odysseus always pretends to be a Cretan" (Hoekstra on *Odyssey* 13.256–286); but only in one of them does he claim to be a member of the Cretan royal house—the tale he tells Penelope during their interview (*Odyssey* 19.165–307), where he presents himself as a grandson of Minos and brother of Idomeneus, the leader of the Cretans at Troy (19.178–184).

POLYDECTES

ing to Perseus' departure from Seriphos, or with those surrounding his return. If the play formed part of a Perseus tetralogy, it may either have preceded or followed Phorcides *(q.v.), and the accompanying satyr-drama will certainly have been* Net-Haulers *(q.v.), which featured Danaë, the infant Perseus, and Polydectes' brother Dictys; however, no third serious play can be identified that would make such a tetralogy complete.*

PROMETHEUS

it is possible to identify the play with fair confidence, but of others, including the two printed below, we can say no more than that they come from one of the lost Prometheus-plays in the Aeschylean corpus.

188

πολλοῖς γάρ ἐστι κέρδος ἡ σιγὴ βροτῶν

Scholia (M B D) to Aelius Aristeides, *Oration* 3.97 (p.190 Frommel; p.501.17–18 Dindorf) (Αἰσχύλος . . . ἐν Προμηθεῖ δεσμώτῃ)

189a

ΠΡΟΜΗΘΕΤΣ

ἵππων ὄνων τ᾽ ὀχεῖα καὶ ταύρων γονὰς
δοὺς ἀντίδουλα καὶ πόνων ἐκδέκτορα

Plutarch, *Moralia* 98c (ὁ Προμηθεὺς . . . κατ᾽ Αἰσχύλον), 965a (ὁ Αἰσχύλου Προμηθεὺς δοῦναί φησιν ἡμῖν . . .); Porphyry, *On Abstinence* 3.18 (Αἰσχύλος)

ΠΡΟΜΗΘΕΤΣ ΛΤΟΜΕΝΟΣ

Prometheus Unbound *was the sequel to* Prometheus Bound, *and matches it so well in content, theme and technique as to make it safe to say that "if ever two plays were composed together, these two were" (M. L. West, JHS 99 [1979] 130). On their authorship and date, see introduction to* Prometheus Bound.

*Prometheus had been told by Hermes (*Prometheus Bound *1020–5) that after a long period beneath the earth he would be brought back to its surface, but would then be persistently tormented by the eagle of Zeus eating at his liver. At the beginning of* Prometheus Unbound *this prediction has been fulfilled (fr. 193). Prometheus is visited by the chorus of his brother-Titans (frr. 190–3), who have ap-*

188

For to many mortals silence is advantageous.

189a

PROMETHEUS

Giving to them[1] the offspring of horses and asses, and the children of bulls,[2] to take over their labours and be the equivalent of slaves.

[1] sc. to humans.   [2] i.e. mules and (castrated) oxen, for transport and field-work respectively; cf. *Prometheus Bound* 462–5. For this interpretation of the fragment, see F. E. Romer, "'Οχεῖα, mules, and animal husbandry in a *Prometheus* play: amending *LSJ* and unemending Aeschylus fr. 189a R", *TAPA* 130 (2000) 67–87.

PROMETHEUS UNBOUND

parently been released by Zeus from their underground imprisonment, and tells them of his sufferings. Then— again as predicted in the previous play—Heracles arrives, having got lost on his way to attempt the most distant of his Labours, the taking of the apples of the Hesperides (cf. Strabo 4.1.7); he shoots the eagle (fr. 200) and is given directions for his journey (frr. 195–9). Prometheus and Zeus are still at enmity (fr. 201), but there was subsequently a reconciliation between them, with Prometheus revealing the secret with which he might otherwise have caused the overthrow of Zeus—that Thetis, for whom Zeus has conceived a passion, is destined to bear a son mightier than his father (cf. Philodemus, On Piety p.41.4–16 Gomperz): we learn of honours given to Prometheus in memory of his bondage (fr. 202), and it has often been suggested that there may have been mention of the establishment of his Athenian cult. The reconciliation may have been effected through Prometheus' mother, Ge-Themis, whose name is wrongly included, together with that of Heracles, in the list of dramatis personae *appended to the Hypothesis to* Prometheus Bound; *she had once before been responsible for effecting an alliance between Prometheus and Zeus (Prometheus Bound 209–218), and it would be appropriate if she were to do so again.*

Prometheus Unbound *appears to have been imitated or parodied by the comic dramatist Cratinus in his play* The Wealth-Gods (Πλοῦτοι), *probably produced in 429 BC. The "Wealth-Gods" of the chorus identify themselves as Titans (fr. 171.11): they had at one time been imprisoned (ib. 20, 21), but "now that the rule of tyranny [has been dis-*

190

ΧΟΡΟΣ

ἥκομεν <   >
τοὺς σοὺς ἄθλους τούσδε, Προμηθεῦ,
δεσμοῦ τε πάθος τόδ᾽ ἐποψόμενοι

Arrian, *Periplous of the Euxine Sea* 19.2; Anon., *Periplous of the Euxine Sea* p.131 Diller

1 lacuna posited by Jacobs: <ἡμεῖς> Walker: perh. <ἡμεῖς οἱ Τιτᾶνες>.

*solved] and the demos is in power" they have come in
search of their "old brother . . . even if he is now rotting
away" (ib. 22–26). We do not know whether Prometheus
himself appeared on stage in Cratinus' play.*

Recent discussions: K. DeVries, "The *Prometheis* in vase painting
and on the stage", in R. M. Rosen and J. J. Farrell ed. *Nomo-
deiktes: Studies in Honor of Martin Ostwald* (Ann Arbor, 1993)
517–523; G. Liberman, "Le *Prométhée délivré* attribué à Eschyle,
un passage de Valérius Flaccus et un vase d'Apulie", *Revue des
Études Anciennes* 98 (1996) 273–280; Sommerstein *AT* 315–9;
M. L. West, "A fragment of *Prometheus Lyomenos?*", *ZPE* 113
(1996) 21; E. Lefèvre, *Studien zu den Quellen und zum Ver-
ständnis des Prometheus Desmotes* (Göttingen, 2003); A. J. Podlecki, *Aeschylus: Prometheus Bound* (Oxford, 2005) 27–34.

190

CHORUS

We ⟨Titans (?)⟩ have come,
Prometheus, to behold these trials you undergo
and this bondage that you suffer.

*These chanted anapaests were probably the opening words of the
play (cf. Procopius, cited on fr. 191).*

ATTRIBUTED FRAGMENTS

191

ΧΟΡΟΣ

†πῇ μὲν† δίδυμον χθονὸς Εὐρώπης
μέγαν ἠδ' Ἀσίας τέρμονα Φᾶσιν

Arrian and Anon. as for fr. 190; cf. Procopius, *The Wars of Justinian* 8.6.15 ὁ τραγῳδοποιὸς Αἰσχύλος ἐν Προμηθεῖ τῷ λυομένῳ εὐθὺς ἀρχόμενος τῆς τραγῳδίας τὸν ποταμὸν Φᾶσιν τέρμονα καλεῖ γῆς τε τῆς Ἀσίας καὶ τῆς Εὐρώπης

1 πῇ μὲν Arrian, Anon. codd. A^pc B: τῇ μὲν Anon. cod. A^ac: ἐπὶ μὲν Bergk   2 μέγαν ἠδ' Anon. codd. A^pc(?) B: μέγαν ἢ δ' Arrian: μέγα πῇ δ' Anon. cod. A^ac

192

ΧΟΡΟΣ

φοινικόπεδον τ' ἐρυθρᾶς ἱερὸν
χεῦμα θαλάσσης
†χαλκοκέραυνόν† τε παρ' Ὠκεανῷ
λίμνην †παντότροφον† Αἰθιόπων,
ἵν' ὁ παντόπτης Ἥλιος αἰεὶ
χρῶτ' ἀθάνατον κάματόν θ' ἵππων
θερμαῖς ὕδατος
μαλακοῦ προχοαῖς ἀναπαύει.

Strabo 1.2.27

3 χαλκοκέραυνόν codd.: χαλκοστερόπον Weil, cf. *Iliad* 11.83: χαλκαμάρυγόν van Herwerden   4 παντότροφον codd. (παντο- from 5): <μελάνων> τροφὸν Diggle 5 παντόπτης Grotius: παντεπόπτας codd.   8 προχοαῖς ed. pr.: προχοαῖς τ' codd.

200

191

CHORUS

To (?) the Phasis,[1] the great twin boundary
of the lands of Europe and Asia.

Again from the chorus's anapaestic entrance-chant, following fr.
190 at a short interval (fr. 192 may have come between them).

[1] See on fr. 155. In *Prometheus Bound* (729–735) the boundary of Europe and Asia is a watercourse called the Bosporus; one
would have expected this to mean the Cimmerian Bosporus (the
Strait of Kerch, connecting the Black Sea with the Sea of Azov),
but I have argued *ad loc.* that the author, either inadvertently or
intentionally, has there confused the Cimmerian Bosporus with
the Phasis.

192

CHORUS

And the mighty, crimson-bottomed waters
of the Red Sea,[1]
and the bay beside the Ocean, flashing like bronze (?),
that gives sustenance to the black (?) Ethiopians,[2]
where the all-seeing Sun always
refreshes his immortal flesh and his fatigued horses
in its warm flow
of gentle water.

Another extract from the chorus's anapaestic entrance-chant; logi-
cally it should come between frr. 190 and 191 in a description of a
journey from the eastern ends of the earth to Prometheus' rock in
furthest Scythia.

[1] For classical Greeks this name denoted the whole Indian
Ocean with its gulfs.   [2] The close connection made between
the Ethiopian bay and the "Red Sea" implies that we are to place it
in the distant East: cf. *Prometheus Bound* 807–9, Herodotus 7.70,

193

PROMETHEUS

Titanum suboles, socia nostri sanguinis,
generata Caelo, aspicite religatum asperis
vinctumque saxis, navem ut horrisono freto
noctem paventes timidi adnectunt navitae.
5 Saturnius me sic infixit Iuppiter,
Iovisque numen Mulciberi adscivit manus.
hos ille cuneos fabrica crudeli inserens
perrupit artus; qua miser sollertia
transverberatus castrum hoc Furiarum incolo.
10 iam tertio me quoque funesto die
tristi advolatu aduncis lacerans unguibus
Iovis satelles pastu dilaniat fero;
tum iecure opimo farta et satiata adfatim

Cicero, *Tusculan Disputations* 2.23–25 (*apud eum [sc. Aeschy-
lum] Prometheus . . . poenas pendens adfixus ad Caucasum dicit
haec*), himself translating the Aeschylean text (cf. *ibid*. 2.26);
Priscian, *Institutiones Grammaticae* 10.53 (line 13 [*tum . . . satiata*]); Nonius Marcellus, *De Compendiosa Doctrina* 17.8 (lines
14–15 [*sublime . . . sanguinem*], ascribed to Accius' *Prometheus*);
Arusianus, *Exempla Elocutionum* (vii 457.7 Keil) (line 15 [*nostrum adulat sanguinem*])

and Euripides fr. 771 (from *Phaethon*) who speaks of "the first land on which the rising Sun casts his golden flame, [which] the neighbouring black men call the shining stables of Dawn and the Sun".

193

PROMETHEUS

Seed of the Titans, kin of my own blood, offspring of Uranus,[1] behold me bound and chained to these rugged rocks, as fearful sailors, terrified of the night, tie up their ship in a roaring strait. It was Zeus, son of Cronus, who thus fixed me here, and the hand of Hephaestus assented to Zeus's decree.[2] He, with cruel skill, thrust in these wedges,[3] breaking through my body; and, pierced through by his craftsmanship, I dwell in misery in this fortress of the Furies. Now, every other deadly day, the agent of Zeus wings its sinister way here, savages me with its curved talons and tears me apart to make its barbarous meal; then, amply stuffed and gorged with the fatness of my liver, it

---

[1] Cicero, like all Roman writers, latinizes the names of Greek gods—Uranus, Cronus, Zeus and Hephaestus become Caelum, Saturn, Jupiter and Mulciber (i.e. Vulcan); I have restored the conventional English renderings of the Greek names.

[2] Cf. *Prometheus Bound* 619.

[3] Cf. *Prometheus Bound* 64–65.

clangorem fundit vastum et sublime avolans
15   pinnata cauda nostrum adulat sanguinem.
cum vero adesum inflatu renovatumst iecur,
tum rursum taetros avida se ad pastus refert.
sic hanc custodem maesti cruciatus alo,
quae me perenni vivum foedat miseria.
20   namque, ut videtis, vinclis constrictus Iovis
arcere nequeo diram volucrem a pectore.
sic me ipse viduus pestes excipio anxias,
amore mortis terminum anquirens mali.
sed longe a leto numine aspellor Iovis,
25   atque haec vetusta saeclis glomerata horridis
luctifica clades nostro infixa est corpori;
e quo liquatae solis ardore excidunt
guttae, quae saxa adsidue instillant Caucasi

14 sublime avolans *Turnebus*: sublime advolans *codd. of Cicero*: tui mei volans *Nonius*   18–19 hanc . . . quae *Bentley*: hunc . . . qui *codd.*

---

[4] Thirteen human generations have passed since Prometheus was first bound to the rock (*Prometheus Bound* 774), during a long but undefined portion of which he was beneath the earth (*ibid.* 1020–1).

makes a vast racket and, as it flies off into the sky, it licks my blood with its tail feathers. And when the liver on which it has fed has been renewed and reinflated, then it comes back and sets itself greedily again to its cruel feeding. Thus I provide nourishment to this warder of my wretched torture, who defiles my living body with endless misery; for held fast, as you see I am, in Zeus's chains, I am unable to keep this terrible bird away from my breast. And so, bereaved of my own self, I endure a succession of anguishing torments, ever seeking an end to my suffering, longing for death. But the power of Zeus keeps death far away from me, and this ancient, lamentable atrocity, accumulated through generations of horror,[4] is indelibly imprinted in my body—my body, from which fall drops[5] melted by the heat of the sun, which continually drip on to the rocks of the Caucasus.[6]

[5] Drops of blood, or rather ichor. According to Apollonius Rhodius, *Argonautica* 3.845–866, these drops caused a plant to spring up, an ointment extracted from which was later used by Medea to make Jason invulnerable for a day; this tale may go back to Sophocles' *Women of Colchis* (cf. the Hypothesis to *Prometheus Bound*, and Sophocles fr. 340).

[6] Cicero, like most who wrote about Prometheus in antiquity, thought that the Caucasus was the scene of his binding; it certainly was not so in *Prometheus Bound* (cf. lines 719–720 of that play; the Hypothesis nevertheless asserts that the scene is "in Scythia on the Caucasian mountains"), and there is no reason to believe that it was so in *Prometheus Unbound* either (see A. Bonnafé, *Journal des Savants* [1991] 153–6). Cicero has doubtless added the word for metrical and/or stylistic reasons, unaware that he was introducing a geographical error.

*

195

ΠΡΟΜΗΘΕΥΣ

εὐθεῖαν ἕρπε τήνδε· καὶ πρώτιστα μὲν
βορεάδας ἥξεις πρὸς πνοάς, ἵν᾽ εὐλαβοῦ
βρόμον καταιγίζοντα, μή σ᾽ ἀναρπάσῃ
δυσχειμέρῳ πέμφιγι συστρέψας ἄφνω

Galen, *Commentary on Hippocrates' Epidemiae Book VI* (xvii
a 879.13–880.2 Kühn) (ἐν Προμηθεῖ δεσμώτῃ)

2 πρὸς πνοάς, ἵν᾽ Sophianus: πρὸ πνόαισιν cod.
4 πέμφιγι Gemusaeus, συστρέψας Sophianus: πέμφιγγι στρέ-
ψας cod.

196

ΠΡΟΜΗΘΕΥΣ

ἔπειτα δ᾽ ἥξεις δῆμον ἐνδικώτατον
<×–> ἁπάντων καὶ φιλοξενώτατον,
Γαβίους, ἵν᾽ οὔτ᾽ ἄροτρον οὔτε γατόμος
τέμνει δίκελλ᾽ ἄρουραν, ἀλλ᾽ αὐτόσποροι
γύαι φέρουσι βίοτον ἄφθονον βροτοῖς

Stephanus of Byzantium, *Ethnica* p.7.5–9 Meineke; the
scholia, and Eustathius, on *Iliad* 13.6 also report that Aeschylus
used the form Γαβίους

1 ἥξεις Stanley: ἥξει codd.   2 <θνητῶν> Grotius,
<βροτῶν> Hermann   4 δίκελλ᾽ Th. Canter: δικέλλης
codd.

•

195

PROMETHEUS

Keep straight on this way, and first of all you will come to the blasts of the north wind; here beware of its noisy squalls, lest one suddenly snatch you up and whirl you aloft in its stormy vortex.

Giving directions to Heracles.[1]

[1] Galen ascribes these lines to *Prometheus Bound*, doubtless through a confusion (on his part or his source's) between Prometheus' instructions to Io in *Bound* and those to Heracles in *Unbound*.

196

PROMETHEUS

And then you will come to the most righteous and most hospitable people of all ‹mankind›, the Gabians,[1] among whom neither the plough nor the earth-cutting mattock cleaves the soil, but self-sown fields yield men an ample livelihood.

Further instructions to Heracles.

[1] Evidently the same as the Ἄβιοι of *Iliad* 13.6, who seem there to be envisaged as living in or beyond what was later called Scythia. The added initial consonant has never been satisfactorily explained; it may be the poet's own arbitrary invention, if he felt that it would be paradoxical for a people to be called Ἄβιοι (understood as "without livelihood"; in fact in the *Iliad* it probably meant "without violence") when they gained an "ample livelihood" without having to toil for it.

ATTRIBUTED FRAGMENTS

199

ΠΡΟΜΗΘΕΥΣ

ἥξεις δὲ Λιγύων εἰς ἀτάρβητον στρατόν·
ἔνθ᾽ οὐ μάχης, σάφ᾽ οἶδα, καὶ θοῦρός περ ὢν
λύψῃ· πέπρωται γάρ σε καὶ βέλη λιπεῖν
ἐνταῦθ᾽· ἑλέσθαι δ᾽ οὔτιν᾽ ἐκ γαίας λίθον
5 ἕξεις, ἐπεὶ πᾶς χῶρός ἐστι μαλθακός.
ἰδὼν δ᾽ ἀμηχανοῦντά σ᾽ οἰκτιρεῖ πατήρ,
νεφέλην δ᾽ ὑπερσχὼν νιφάδι γογγύλων πέτρων
ὑπόσκιον θήσει χθον᾽· οἷς ἔπειτα σὺ
βάλλων διώσῃ ῥᾳδίως Λίγυν στρατόν

Strabo 4.1.7; Dionysius of Halicarnassus, *Roman Antiquities*
1.41.3 (lines 1–3)

3 λύψῃ Diels: μέμψῃ (A C Bᵖᶜ) or πέμψῃ (cett.) Strabo:
μέμψει (cett.) or μέμψιν (B) Dionysius.   4 γαίας C: γέας
cett.   6 οἰκτιρεῖ Nauck, πατήρ Cobet: ὁ Ζεὺς οἰκτερεῖ
codd.   7 ὑπερσχὼν Casaubon: ὑποσχὼν codd.
8–9 σὺ βάλλων Heath, διώσῃ (-σει) Koraes: συμβαλὼν δηώσει
(δηώεις B) codd.

200

ΗΡΑΚΛΗΣ

ἀγρεὺς δ᾽ Ἀπόλλων ὀρθὸν ἰθύνοι βέλος

Plutarch, *Moralia* 757e (naming Heracles as the speaker, and
saying he is shooting at "the bird", but not naming the play)

208

199

PROMETHEUS

Then you will come to the dauntless host of the Ligurians, where, bold as you are, you will not, I know for sure, be eager for battle; for it is fated that there you will run out of arrows, and you will not be able to take any stones from the ground,[1] because the whole place is soft soil. But your Father will see your distress and take pity on you: he will bring a cloud over the land and cover it completely[2] with a hail of round stones.[3] With these you will then pelt the Ligurian army and easily put them to flight.

Further instructions to Heracles for his journey to the Hesperides.

[1] For use as emergency weapons.   [2] lit. "put it under shadow".   [3] This story provides an aetiology for the existence of the "Plain of Stones"—the stony and arid (now partly irrigated) Plaine de la Crau, stretching east of the Rhône between Arles and the sea and once covering some 40,000 hectares (150 square miles), which will have been well known to Greeks through its proximity to the Phocaean colony of Massalia (Marseille).

200

HERACLES

And may Apollo the Hunter direct my arrow straight!

Heracles' prayer as he draws his bow to shoot the eagle.

201

ΠΡΟΜΗΘΕΥΣ

ἐχθροῦ πατρός μοι τοῦτο φίλτατον τέκνον

Plutarch, *Pompey* 1.1 (ὁ Αἰσχύλου Προμηθεὺς πρὸς τὸν Ἡρακλέα σωθεὶς ὑπ' αὐτοῦ)

ΠΡΟΜΗΘΕΥΣ ΠΥΡΦΟΡΟΣ

Apart from the surviving Prometheus Bound, *the considerable information we possess about* Prometheus Unbound *(q.v.), and a scattering of quotations (including frr. 188 and 189a: see above) ascribed to an unspecified* Prometheus *play, we have four further packages of evidence about* Prometheus *plays attributed to Aeschylus. (1) The medieval catalogue of his plays lists a* Προμηθεὺς πυρφόρος *(Prometheus the Fire-Bearer), and we have one quotation attributed to it (fr. 208) and one statement reported from it (fr. 208a).[1] (2) Pollux (9.156) states that there was an Aeschylean play called* Προμηθεὺς πυρκαεύς *(Prometheus the Fire-Kindler), and elsewhere (10.64) he quotes a line from this play (fr. 205); a metrical licence in this line proves that the play must have been a satyr-drama, not a tragedy. (3) The Hypothesis to* Persians *states*

[1] Namely, that Prometheus was bound for thirty thousand years—far longer than the thirteen generations spoken of in *Prometheus Bound* (774). We cannot tell from our sources whether this was a statement about the past or a prediction about the future, nor whether it was accurate or (as it might well be in a satyr-play) grossly exaggerated.

201

PROMETHEUS

This son, my dearest friend, of a father who is my enemy.

Speaking of Heracles.[1]

[1] Plutarch's phrase πρὸς τὸν Ἡρακλέα could mean either "addressing Heracles" or "in reference to Heracles", but τοῦτο in the actual quotation shows that Heracles is not being addressed and is probably not even present (otherwise the poet would probably have written e.g. τόνδε φίλτατον τόκον). Prometheus has been "saved" by Heracles (presumably from the eagle), so Plutarch tells us, but has evidently not yet been reconciled with Zeus; perhaps he is telling his mother (cf. introductory note to this play) about recent events?

PROMETHEUS THE FIRE-BEARER

that in the production of which it formed part, in 472 BC, the fourth play (i.e. the satyr-drama) was Prometheus. *(4) There are several papyrus fragments (frr. 204a-d), two quotations (frr. 206 [187a], 207), one other reference (fr. 207a, from the scholia to Hesiod,* Works and Days 89), *and several vase-paintings, which connect satyrs with Prometheus and/or with fire.*

From this evidence it is clear that there was an Aeschylean satyr-play, presumably the one produced in 472, in which Prometheus brought fire to the satyrs, who had never seen it before, were greatly delighted by it (particularly because they hoped its possession would make them more attractive to nymphs: fr. 204b), but had no idea how to handle it safely (frr. 206, 207). According to the Hesiod scholiast, Prometheus "received from the satyrs [presumably in exchange for fire] the jar of evils, and deposited it with [his brother] Epimetheus, warning him never to accept anything from Zeus, but Epimetheus ignored the warning and accepted Pandora"—with consequences that are well known; fr. 207b (369) fits well with this.

It has usually been supposed, on the basis of (2), that Prometheus the Fire-Kindler *was the satyr-drama, while* Prometheus the Fire-Bearer *was a serious play forming a trilogy with* Prometheus Bound *and* Unbound. *There are, however, two serious objections to this view. On the one hand, there is no possible place for* Prometheus the Fire-Bearer *in a tragic Prometheus-trilogy. It cannot have come first, because the exposition of the initial situation in* Prometheus Bound *(especially in 199–241) is so full and detailed as to preclude the possibility that the audience are being told all this for the second time; it cannot have come second, because Hermes' prophecy in* Prometheus Bound *1014–29 allows for no other events to intervene between Prometheus' return to the daylight and the beginning of his torment by the eagle; and it cannot have come third, because* Prometheus Unbound *is known to have wound up the story of Prometheus so completely that there can have been no scope for a further play about him (see introductory note to* Prometheus Unbound*). On the other hand, since epithets were attached to play-titles precisely for the purpose of distinguishing between plays of the same name*

204a

Small remains of 20 lines including φέγγοϲ *(line 2),].φλεκτο[(line 10),* τόδε *(line 12), and* παντελε[*(line 13).*

Oxyrhynchus Papyrus 2245 fr. 1 col. I

212

by the same author, it is very unlikely that two different Prometheus *plays should be given epithets so similar as* πυρφόρος *and* πυρκαεύς. *More probably one of these epithets is a corruption of the other, and all the evidence summarized under (1–4) above relates to the same play, the satyr-play of 472. Brown (see below) has argued convincingly that the proper title of this play is* Προμηθεὺς πυρφόρος, *and (following Dindorf in the 1829 edition of the* Thesaurus Graecae Linguae, *s.v.* πυρκαεύς) *that the epithet* πυρκαεύς, *known only to Pollux, is an error caused by the existence of a Sophoclean play entitled* Ναύπλιος πυρκαεύς. Prometheus, *unlike Nauplius, does not* kindle fire, *in the satyr-drama or anywhere else; he* brings *it to men or satyrs as the case may be. I have accordingly presented all the fragments attributable to the satyr-drama under the title* Prometheus the Fire-Bearer, *in addition to the one actually ascribed to a play so named.*

Recent discussions: A. L. Brown, "Prometheus Pyrphoros", *BICS* 37 (1990) 50–56; C. Serrano Aybar, "Aristippos A. fr. 204d.12 Radt", in *Actas del VIII Congreso Español de Estudios Clásicos* i (Madrid, 1994) 291–7; Sommerstein, *Aeschylean Tragedy* 314–5, 319–321; R. Germar, N. Pechstein and R. Krumeich in KPS 169–178; P. Yziquel, "Le drame satyrique eschyléen", *CGITA* 14 (2001) 1–22, esp. 7–10; A. J. Podlecki, *Aeschylus: Prometheus Bound* (Oxford, 2005) 27–28, 30–32, 34; Podlecki 6–7.

204a

Small remains of 20 lines including light *(line 2),* burnt (?) *(line 10),* this *(line 12), and* complete *(line 13).*

204b

ΧΟΡΟΣ

στρ. ⟨*two dochmiac metra*⟩
    -cίᾳ δέ μ' εὐμενὴc χορεύει χάριc·
    φ[α]ε̣ν̣ν[ὸ]ν ⟨∪ – ⟩
    χιτῶνα πάρ πυρὸc ἀκάματον αὐγάν.
    κλυοῦc' ἐμοῦ δὲ Ναΐδων τιc παρ' ἑc-
5 τιοῦχον cέλαc πολλὰ διώξεται.
    Νύμφαc δέ τοι πέποιθ' ἐγὼ
    cτήcει[ν] χοροὺc
    Προμηθέωc δῶρον ὡc cεβούcαc.

ἀντ. κα̣λ̣[ὸ]ν δ' ὕμνον ἀμφὶ τὸν δόντα μολ-
10 πάcειν [.]ολ[...]ῳ λεγούcαc τόδ', ὡc
    Προμηθε[ὺc βρο]τοιc
    φερέcβιόc τε [...]. [(.)] cπευcίδωρ[οc.
    χορεύcειν . [......]νί̈ ἐλπὶc ὡ-
    ρ]ίου χε̣[ί]ματ[οc ...]ερ . ι̣χ[..]..

Oxyrhynchus Papyrus 2245 fr. 1 col. II

1 [Νυ-] | cία Fraenkel   2 φ[α]ε̣ν̣ν[ὸ]ν Lobel   there
is then a gap in the papyrus which might have accommodated 3
letters, but no convincing supplement is so short   ⟨βάλε⟩
Snell: ⟨δ' ἄγω⟩ Mette: perh. ⟨δ' ἔχω⟩   10 [ἔ]ολ[π' ἐγ]ὼ
Lobel   11 suppl. Lobel   12 τε [κ]α̣[ὶ] rejected by
Lobel (too short for the space—unless there was an erasure)

204b

CHORUS

[*first line of strophe lost*]
And friendly [Ny]sian (?) delight[1] will set me dancing:
‹I will wear (?)› a g[l]eami[n]g
tunic by the unwearing brilliance of the fire.
And one of the Naiads,[2] when she hears about it from
    me,
will chase me hard[3] by the light that shines at my hearth!
And I am confident, I tell you, that the nymphs
will join in choral dances
because they honour the gift of Prometheus.

And [I have good hope (?)] that they will chant
a fine song about its giver, saying this—
that Prometheus is to humans
a bringer of life [and] eager to provide gifts.
My hope is that they will dance [. . .
. . .] of winter chill [. . .]

---

[1] i.e. (if Fraenkel's conjecture is correct) euphoria induced by
wine (with reference to Mount Nysa, Dionysus' childhood home).

[2] Water-nymphs.

[3] Whereas ordinarily it is satyrs who chase nymphs—and to little avail.

15 Νύμφας δέ τοι πέποιθ᾽ ἐγὼ
στήσειν χοροὺς
Προμη[θ]έως δῶρον ὡς σεβούσας.

[*Remains of nine further lines including* ποιμέν[ ]ς πρέπειν
(18), νυκτιπλαγ[κτ *(19–20),* β[α]θυξυλο[*(24).*]

15–17 partly restored from 6–8: gaps and doubtful letters marked
only where there is also a gap or doubt in 6–8

204c

*Remains of 29 lines, of which the first 13 were lyric; intelli-
gible words are* θελουσα[*(1),* λειμών[*(2),* χορευμας[*(3),*
ἱερὰ δ᾽ ἀκτὶς σελ[*(4),* τ]ηλέγνωτον *(5),* ἀ[ν]τισέληνον *(6)*

Oxyrhynchus Papyrus 2245 fr. 1 col. III

204d

*Eleven short fragments, only one of which (no. 12) contains
enough to be worth presenting here:*

[*remains of one line*]
.]. [...] δέ τοι τρ[
πέλας πυρὸς
... ροις μεθυ . [
5 .. αν ζε[.]μεν[.]. [
χιὼν δ᾽ ἀριστιππο[ς
]. ὄμβρου κ[.]ρα· . [

*Lines 2–4 appear to be a refrain of the same metrical structure
as fr. 204b.6–8 and 15–17; they are followed by a horizontal line,
indicating the beginning of a new (anti)strophe.*

And I am confident, I tell you, that the nymphs
will join in choral dances
because they honour the gift of Prometheus.

[*Remains of nine further lines including* that it is proper for shepherds (?) *(18)*, wandering by night *(19–20)*, thickly wooded *(24)*.]

204c

Remains of 29 lines including wishing *(1; the subject was
feminine)*, meadow *(2)*, dances *(3)*, the sacred ray [of the]
mo[on (?)] *(4)*, known afar *(5)*, moonlike *(6)*.

204d

A lyric refrain (lines 2–4) containing and, I tell you *(2; cf. fr.
204b.6)*, near the fire *(3) and* drunk (?) *(4); then a new (anti)stro-
phe containing* snow like the best horses[1] *(6) and* my (?) head from
(*or* in?) a shower *(7). The satyrs are evidently continuing to exult
in the benefits of having a fire in their home in winter (cf. fr.
204c.13–14).*

---

[1] i.e. white; for the excellence of white horses cf. Pindar,
Pythian 9.83, [Euripides], *Rhesus* 616–621, and the epithet
λεύκιππος applied to many gods and heroes, especially the
Dioscori. See C. Serrano Aybar, *Actas del VIII Congreso Español
de Estudios Clásicos* (Madrid, 1994) 291–7.

Oxyrhynchus Papyrus 2245 frr. 2–12

6 suppl. Snell   7 [ἐκ] τ᾽ ὄμβρου Mette: [ὑ]π᾽ ὄμβρου
inter alia Radt   κ[ά]ρα Snell

205

λινᾶ δὲ πεσσὰ κὠμολίνου μακροὶ τόνοι

Pollux 10.64 (Αἰσχύλου ἐν Προμηθεῖ πυρκαεῖ)

λινᾶ δὲ Bentley: λίνα δὲ C² L: λιναδὲ C: λινάδες F S
πεσσὰ Wilamowitz: πίσσα codd.   μακροὶ τόνοι F S:
μακρότονοι C: μακρότεροι L: μακροὶ τόμοι perhaps implied by
Wilamowitz's translation (giving the same sense as that adopted
here)

206 (187a)

ἐξευλαβοῦ δὲ μή σε προσβάλῃ στόμα
πέμφιξ· πικρὰ γὰρ †καὶ οὐ διὰ ζωῆς ἀτμοί†

Galen, *Commentary on Hippocrates' Epidemiae Book VI* (xvii
a 880.11–12 Kühn) (Αἰσχύλος . . . ἐν Προμηθεῖ)

1 βάλῃ Hermann: βάλλῃ cod.   2 καὶ . . . ἀτμοί cod.:
"and injures the throat" Arabic translation: κοὐλία λαιμῷ
<λίαν> Wenkebach

207

ΠΡΟΜΗΘΕΥΣ

τράγος γένειον ἆρα πενθήσεις σύ γε

Plutarch, *Moralia* 86f (τοῦ . . . σατύρου τὸ πῦρ, ὡς πρῶτον
ὤφθη, βουλομένου φιλῆσαι καὶ περιβαλεῖν, ὁ Προμηθεὺς sc.
λέγει); Eustathius on *Iliad* 3.277 (without indication of author or
work)

205

Linen plugs and long strips of raw flax

Possibly a recommendation (by Prometheus?) for how to treat a burn.

206

Take care the round drop[1] doesn't touch your mouth; it's bitter and very dangerous to the throat (?)

Presumably Prometheus warning Silenus (?), who has never before seen a pot boiling over a fire.

[1] Of boiling water, no doubt. The word here translated "round drop" literally means "pustule"; cf. frr. 170, 183, 195.4.

207

PROMETHEUS

Then you'll be mourning for your beard, like a billygoat!

To a satyr (or Silenus?) who, on first seeing fire, is eager to kiss and embrace it.

207b (369)

ἐκ πηλοπλάστου σπέρματος θνητὴ γυνή

Scholia to Hesiod, *Works and Days* 157 (κατὰ τὸν Αἰσχύλον)

ἐκ R: τοῦ cett.

208

σιγῶν θ᾽ ὅπου δεῖ καὶ λέγων τὰ καίρια

Aulus Gellius, *Attic Nights* 13.19.4 (*aput Aeschylum* ἐν τῷ πυρφόρῳ Προμηθεῖ)

θ᾽ (τε) cett.: γε Z

ΠΡΟΠΟΜΠΟΙ

ΠΡΩΤΕΥΣ

This was the satyr-drama that concluded the Oresteia *tetralogy; it is generally agreed that it must have presented the adventures of Menelaus in Egypt, which he narrates in the fourth book of the* Odyssey *(351–580). Proteus in the* Odyssey *was the prophetic, shape-changing "Old Man of the Sea"; in Stesichorus (Chamaeleon fr. 29 Wehrli = PMG 193), in Herodotus (2.112–120), and in Euripides'* Helen, *he was simply a human king of Egypt. We do not know how he was presented in Aeschylus, though the evidence, such as it is, tends to favour the Homeric over the Stesichorean model (see below). The play's focus on Menelaus seems to be prepared for, earlier in the tetralogy, by references to his*

207b (369)

A mortal woman created by the fashioning of clay.[1]

Referring to Pandora (so the scholiast who cites the line).

[1] lit. "from clay-fashioned seed".

208

Staying silent when appropriate and saying what suits the occasion.[1]

[1] This line is almost identical with *Cho*. 582, and very similar to *Seven* 619.

THE ESCORT

Nothing whatever is known about this play except for its title and a one-word citation (fr. 209), neither of which gives any clue to its subject-matter.

PROTEUS

disappearance on the homeward voyage from Troy, and his possible eventual return, in Agamemnon *(617–633, 674–9) and* Libation-Bearers *(1041). Some of the descriptions of Helen in* Agamemnon, *in particular those at 404–426 and 737–743, have also led Cunningham and Griffith (see below) to suggest that Aeschylus, like Euripides after him, used Stesichorus' idea that the Trojan War was fought for a phantom divinely substituted for Helen while the real Helen, unknown to Menelaus or anyone else, was in Egypt; but fr. 211 suggests that, as in the* Odyssey, *Menelaus was not on the Egyptian mainland but on a small island off its coast, where he and his party were forced to subsist*

210

σιτουμένην δύστηνον ἀθλίαν φάβα
μέσακτα πλευρὰ πρὸς πτύοις πεπληγμένην

Athenaeus 9.394a

2 πεπληγμένην Schweighaeuser: πεπλεγμένην cod.

ΣΑΛΑΜΙΝΙΑΙ

The medieval catalogue calls this play Σαλαμίνιοι, *implying a chorus of male Salaminians, but this has no support among the authors who cite the fragments, and there are other errors of the same type in the catalogue (see on* Women of Argos *and* Lemnian Women*). The most famous mythical episode to take place on Salamis was the return from Troy of Teucer, the half-brother of Ajax, and his*

unheroically on fish (cf. Odyssey 4.354–369)—and nei-
ther a human king Proteus, nor Helen as a guest of his,
would have been living in such a place. The satyrs, who
may have found themselves on the island as a result of ship-
wreck (as in Euripides' Cyclops), perhaps gave assistance
to Menelaus and escaped with him, though he may well
have had difficulty in ensuring that they kept their hands
off Helen. Eido (in Homer, Eidothea), the daughter of Pro-
teus, may have been a character in the play (fr. 212).

Recent discussions: M. Cunningham, "Thoughts on Aeschylus:
the satyr play *Proteus*—the ending of the *Oresteia*", *Liverpool*
Classical Monthly 19 (1994) 67–68; Sommerstein *AT* 189–190; R.
Germar and R. Krumeich in KPS 179–181; P. Yziquel, "Le drame
satyrique eschyléen", *CGITA* 14 (2001) 1–22, esp. 10–13; M.
Griffith, "Slaves of Dionysos: satyrs, audience, and the ends of the
Oresteia", *CA* 21 (2002) 195–258, esp. 237–254; D. Del Corno,
"Odisseo fra i Satiri", in G. Zanetto et al. ed. *Momenti della*
ricezione omerica (Milan, 2004) 187–195; Podlecki 7.

210

A poor wretched pigeon trying to feed,[1] which has been
struck by winnowing-fans and had its ribs clean broken.

[1] sc. on the grain that is being winnowed.

WOMEN OF SALAMIS

banishment by his angry father Telamon for having failed
to protect Ajax's life; he afterwards founded the city of Sa-
lamis in Cyprus. It is generally accepted that this was the
subject of this play, and that it probably followed The
Award of the Arms *and* Thracian Women *(qq.v.) as the*
third play in an Ajax trilogy.

ATTRIBUTED FRAGMENTS

215a (404)

Αἴγινα δ' αὔτη πρὸς νότου κεῖται πνοάς

Strabo 9.1.9 (not naming the play; he is discussing Salamis city which "faces Aegina and the south"); assigned to this play by Wagner

216

εἴ μοι γένοιτο φᾶρος †ἶσον† οὐρανῷ

Herodian, (i) *General Prosody* i.392.30 Lentz; id., (ii) *On Vowels of Doubtful Length* ii.16.6 Lentz; id., (iii) *On Anomalous Words* ii.942.4 Lentz

εἴ μοι (i, iii): ἐμοὶ (ii)   ἶσον (ii): ἴσον ἐν (i, iii): perh. εἰκὸς?

ΣΕΜΕΛΗ Η ΥΔΡΟΦΟΡΟΙ

Until fairly recently our main information about this play came from a scholium on Apollonius Rhodius' Argonautica (1.636) which stated that Aeschylus "brought [Semele] on stage pregnant and divinely possessed, and the women who touched her belly also became possessed". These women must evidently have been the chorus of the play. They may have been laying hands on Semele's belly to ease her labour pains (cf. Soranus, Gynaecology 2.4.1), and perhaps had brought (hot) water to warm their hands for this purpose.

The story of Semele's death is told in many variants, but is almost always the same in essentials. Semele, daughter of Cadmus of Thebes, having been made pregnant by Zeus, was persuaded by the jealous Hera, who visited her in disguise, to ask Zeus to come to her in his full divine glory;

215a (404)

And there lies Aegina, in the direction from which the south wind blows.

Probably from the prologue.

216

If I had[1] a robe that looked like (?) the heavens[2] . . .

[1] Or "If only I could have . . . !"   [2] i.e., probably, one spangled with stars. Cf. Euripides, *Ion* 1143–58 (a tapestry forming the roof of a tent); Nonnus, *Dionysiaca* 40.577–9 (a garment given by Heracles to Dionysus).

SEMELE *or* WATER-CARRIERS

Zeus, who had previously given her the right to have any one request granted, duly came, and Semele was destroyed by his lightnings and thunderbolts; Zeus, however, snatched the unborn Dionysus from her body, sewed him up in his own thigh, and kept him there till he was ready to come into the world. The actual or prospective birth of Dionysus was certainly a concern of our play, since there was mention of the Amphidromia (fr. 222), a household ritual for a new-born child; but the few short book-fragments that survive told us little more than this.

However, a papyrus published in 1941 (frr. 220a-c [168, 168a-b]) contains fragments of a choral song which mentions Semele and Cadmus, followed by hexameter verses some of which are referred to by Plato (Republic 381d) as having been spoken by Hera in the disguise of a mendicant priestess. Hera is not spoken of as having adopted this particular disguise in other versions of the Semele story, but no one would have doubted that these papyrus fragments were indeed from Semele, were it not for one conflicting piece of evidence: the ancient scholar Asclepiades, cited in the scholia to Aristophanes, Frogs 1344, ascribes the first two of the hexameter lines (here fr. 220a.16–17) to Wool-Carders *(q.v.) and claims to have found them in a manuscript he consulted at Athens. This is itself a statement that arouses some suspicion, since it implies that the lines were* not *in the texts of* Wool-Carders *regularly used by the scholars of Alexandria, and in fact Asclepiades is a far from reliable witness on matters of this kind.*[1] *We should certainly not feel it our duty to believe him if it entails supposing that Aeschylus brought a disguised Hera into* Wool-Carders, *a play set at a time when Dionysus had grown to maturity and begun to act violently against enemies such as Pentheus, when every other mention of a disguised Hera in connection with Dionysus refers to a time before his birth. We can safely assign the papyrus*

[1] Of the four other statements by Asclepiades about tragedy that survive in the Aristophanic scholia, one is certainly and one almost certainly wrong. In *Birds* 348 he detects parody of Euripides' *Andromeda*, which was not produced until two years after *Birds*; and he ascribes *Frogs* 1270 (= Aesch. fr. 238) to Aeschylus' *Iphigeneia* when another scholar, Timachidas, said it was from *Telephus* (they were probably both guessing: see introductory note to *Telephus*). It should be added, too, that *Frogs* 1344 itself can hardly be derived from *Wool-Carders* (as Asclepiades claimed), or from any other Aeschylean play, when it forms part of a song which is presented by the character "Aeschylus" as typically Euripidean, and which elsewhere parodies only Euripides!

226

fragments to Semele. *Hera's words, with their praise of the modest (and of course chaste) bride and their hints (fr. 220a.24–28) that the nymphs may be "harsh and hateful" to one who does not meet these standards, seem well designed to make the chorus—and Semele herself, if present—even more apprehensive than they must already be about the risk to her reputation if she is thought to have lost her virginity to a mortal, and therefore to put them in a mood to listen receptively to a suggestion that she demand that Zeus make it manifest to all that* he *is the father of her unborn child.*

On the question of a trilogy/tetralogy of which Semele *may have formed part, see introductory note to* Wool-Carders.

Recent discussions: F. Jouan, "Dionysos chez Eschyle", *Kernos* 5 (1992) 71–86, esp. 77; J. Hadjicosti, "Hera transformed on stage: Aeschylus fr. 168", *Kernos* 19 (2006) 291–301.

220a (168)

ΧΟΡΟΣ

[Remains of six lines including ἀλοιφᾷ (2), οὐ πλέον Ἥρας (3), ὁπλότεροι (4)]

7 -μενοι θεῶν . [.....]όϲιμος βιοτά·
   φίλοιϲιν ἐν μάκεϲι πίϲτις φθονερ[ὰ
   δόξα τ᾽ ἀεικής. Σεμέλας δ᾽ ε[ὐ-
10 χόμεθ᾽ εἶναι διὰ πᾶν
   εὐθύπορον λά[χος

   τὰ γὰρ ἄλλα τάδ᾽ [
   Κάδμῳ Σεμέ[λα
   τῷ[ι] παντοκρα[τ
15 Ζηνί γάμων δ[

Oxyrhynchus Papyrus 2164 fr. 1; scholia to Aristophanes, *Frogs* 1344 (lines 16–17: ἐκ τῶν Ξαντριῶν [sic] Αἰσχύλου according to Asclepiades); Plato, *Republic* 381d (line 17: author not stated, Hera named as speaker); [Diogenes], *Letter* 34.1 (lines 16–17: author not stated, Hera named as speaker)

8 φίλοισιν (or φιλοῦσιν) Lobel   μάκεσι Cantarella
πίστις φθονερ[ὰ] Mette   9 suppl. Lobel   11 suppl.
Latte, Cantarella: then e.g. αἰοῦς (Latte), ὄλβου (Lloyd-Jones)
after 11 (as also after 6 and 15) the papyrus has a horizontal line,
marking a structural break of some kind in the song
14 παντοκρα[τεῖ] Lasserre, παντοκρα[τοῦντι] Radt

SEMELE *or* WATER-CARRIERS

220a (168)

CHORUS

[*Remains of six lines including* with ointment *(2)*, not more than Hera *(3)*, younger *(masculine plural) (4)*]

... of the gods [...] ... life:
with her (?) family, in the long run, trust is invidious,
and their opinions are harmful (?).[1] But we pray
that Semele may always have
a for[tune] that steers a straight path [...]

For these other things [...]
to Cadmus, Seme[le ...]
to all-powerful [...]
Zeus [...] mating [...]

[*Enter* HERA, *disguised as a begging priestess.*]

---

[1] If this passage is correctly read, the reference will probably be to Semele's sisters, who in many accounts refused to believe that Zeus was the father of her child, though this story is not (otherwise) attested before Euripides' *Bacchae* (26–31).

ATTRIBUTED FRAGMENTS

HPA

νύμφαι ναμερτεῖς, κυδραὶ θεαί, αἷϲιν ἀγείρω
Ἰνάχου Ἀργείου ποταμοῦ παιϲὶν βιοδώροιϲ,
αἵ τε παριϲτανται πᾶϲιν βροτέοιϲιν ἐπ' ἔργ[οιϲ
ε. [(ca. 14 letters)]τε καὶ εὐμόλποιϲ ὑμ[εναίοιϲ
20 καὶ τ[(ca. 13 letters) ν]εολέκτρουϲ ἀρτιγάμ[
λευκο. [(ca. 13 letters)]μμαϲιν ε[ὔ]φρονεϲ[
φῶϲ δεκ[(ca. 14 letters)]περ ὄμματοϲ εϲτ[
αἰδὼϲ γὰρ καθαρὰ καὶ ν[υ]μφοκόμοϲ μέ[γ]' ἀρί[ϲτα,
παίδων δ' εὔκαρπον τε[λ]έθει γένοϲ, οἷϲ[
25 ἵλαοι ἀντιάϲουϲι μελίφ[ρον]α θυμὸν ἔχ[ουϲαι,
ἀμφότερον ϲύμεναι μ[
τραχεῖαι ϲτυγεραί τε καὶ [
ἀ]γχίμολοι· πολλὰϲ μεν[
.... (.)]γον εὐναίου φωτὸ[ϲ
30 .....]ελαϲιν τε μίτραιϲ[

16 so Lobel, Latte: νυμφαιναμερτεῖϲκ[......(.)]ιαιϲινα-
γειρ[Π: νύμφαι ὀρεϲιγόνιοι (V: -ιαι cett.: ὀρεϲϲίγονοι Ar. in
text) θεαῖϲιν ἀγείρω schol. Ar.: [Diogenes] speaks of Hera νύμ-
φαιϲ κρήναιϲιν (κρηναίαιϲιν Latte: perh. κρηναίαιϲ), κυδραῖϲ
θεαῖϲ, ἀγειρουϲαν   19 suppl. Lobel   20 ἀρτιγά-
μ[ουϲ τε] Lobel   21 [ὄ]μμαϲιν Diggle, but cf. 22: perh.
[καλύ]μμαϲιν, cf. Ag. 1178   ε[ὔ]φρονεϲ Lobel
22 [ὑ]πὲρ Cantarella   23 suppl. Lobel   24 οἷϲ[ιν
ἐκεῖναι] Cantarella   25 μελίφ[ρον]α Lobel   ἔχ[ουϲαι]
Cantarella   26 ἀμφότερον considered by Lobel:
αμφοτεραι Π   29 [ϲύζυ]γον Cantarella

230

HERA

Infallible nymphs, glorious goddesses, for whom I
    collect alms,
life-giving daughters of the Argive river Inachus,
who attend upon all mortal act[ivities,]
[. . .] and we[ddings] with their happy music,
and [. . . maidens (?)] new to the bed of wed[lock],
white [. . . e]yes (?)[2] [they are (?)] kindly,
light . . . [. . .] . . . of the eye . . . [. . .]
For modesty is pure and is by f[ar] the be[st] adorner of
    a bride,
and a rich crop of children are born to those whom
    [they]
come to meet in propitious mood, w[ith] a plea[san]t
    spirit,
goddesses who come in two ways, . . . [. . . and also (?)]
harsh, hateful, and [. . .]
in their approach; many women . . . [. . .]
[. . .] . . . of a wedded husba[nd . . .]
[. . .] and with . . . headbands [. . .]

---

[2] Another possible restoration would give the meaning "veils".

220b (168a)

Remains of the beginnings of nine lines (dactylic; very possibly hexameters), including [μέ]μφομα[ι] *(2; suppl. Lobel),* [ἐμ] φρεςίν *(4; suppl. Radt),* [εὐ]δαίμων *(5; suppl. Mette),* [χα]ίρετε *(6; suppl. Lobel),* εὔκλει[ά]ν θ' *(8), and* Κάδμου τ' *(9).*

Oxyrhynchus Papyrus 2164 fr. 2

220c (168b)

Remains of the ends of seven lyric lines (which could all be hexameters), including λέλᾱκ[*(2),* νόςοιςιν *(3),* φράζω *(4), and*].. ἐχεςθε *(5;* δέχεςθε *Lobel). Mette suggested that these are the ends of the same lines whose beginnings are preserved as fr. 220b.2–8.*

Oxyrhynchus Papyrus 2164 fr. 3

ΣΙΣΥΦΟΣ ΔΡΑΠΕΤΗΣ καὶ ΣΙΣΥΦΟΣ ΠΕΤΡΟΚΥΛΙΣΤΗΣ

These two plays clearly dealt with two phases of a well-known story about Sisyphus, the renowned trickster and king of Corinth, told by a scholiast on Iliad *6.153 who cites Pherecydes (fr. 119 Fowler) as his authority. Sisyphus having incurred the wrath of Zeus, Zeus sent Death to take him away, but Sisyphus bound Death in chains so that no one died until Hades[1] released Death from his bonds. Sisyphus*

[1] Fowler prefers the reading "Ares" found in one ms. (which here depends on a different source from the rest) and in Eustathius.

220b (168a)

Remains of the beginnings of nine lines, including I
[b]lame *(2),* [in] the mind *(4),* [ha]ppy *(5),* [h]ail *(6), and*
good repute *(8), and* and of Cadmus *(9).*

220c (168b)

Remains of the ends of seven lines, including [I] proclaim
or [he] proclaim[s] *(2),* ailments *(3),* I speak *(4), and per-*
haps accept *(5).*[1]

---

[1] The verb (which may be indicative or imperative) is second
person plural; if this is indeed part of the hexameter speech of the
disguised Hera, the addressees will be either the chorus or the
nymphs whose priestess she is pretending to be.

SISYPHUS THE RUNAWAY *and*
SISYPHUS THE STONE-ROLLER

*had time before he died to instruct his wife, Merope, not to
make the customary offerings at his tomb, and eventually,
as he had planned, Hades sent him home to Corinth to re-
monstrate with her—and he stayed there. When, however,
he finally died of old age, he was punished in the underworld by being made to roll a great stone uphill, only for it
always to roll down again before he had reached the top
(cf. Odyssey 11.593–600).*

It is plausible to suppose that Sisyphus the Runaway
was set in Corinth and presented Sisyphus' return from the

underworld (perhaps with Merope as a character), while
Sisyphus the Stone-Roller *was set in Hades. The latter was*
certainly a satyr-play, as fr. 233 shows, and it is highly
probable that Sisyphus the Runaway *was one too, though*
we have no clue to how the satyrs were worked into their
plots.

There are only two fragments (fr. 233 and the one-word
fr. 234) for which we have an ancient ascription to one of
the two plays (in each case the Stone-Roller*); but most of*
the longer ones can be assigned with fair confidence to one

225

καὶ *νίπτρα* δὴ χρὴ θεοφόρων ποδῶν φέρειν.
λεοντοβάμων ποῦ σκάφη χαλκήλατος;

Pollux 10.77 (Αἰσχύλον . . . ἐν Σισύφῳ); cf. Horace, *Satires*
2.3.20–21 *olim nam quaerere amabam | quo vafer ille pedes*
lavisset Sisyphus aere

226

σὺ δ᾽ ὁ σταθμοῦχος εὖ κατιλλώψας ἄθρει

Pollux 10.20 (ἐν Αἰσχύλου Σισύφῳ)

play or the other (frr. 225, 226, 228 to the Runaway; *229
and 230 to the* Stone-Roller; *227 uncertain). It has sometimes been suggested (most recently by Gantz 174) that the
two plays were actually one and the same; but as Germar et
al. (below) 182 n.1 point out, the existence of two clearly
distinct epithets shows that ancient scholars knew of two
plays and needed to distinguish them.*

Recent discussions: R. Germar, N. Pechstein and R. Krumeich in
KPS 182–8; Podlecki 13.

225

And we must certainly provide a wash for these feet that
carry a god. Where is the bronze basin with feet like lion's
paws?

Presumably from Runaway, *in view of the household setting.*[1]

[1] The Horace passage (cf. opposite) suggests that this foot-
washing was performed by Sisyphus (rather than, say, Merope)
and that there was something cunning (*vafer*) about it; Germar et
al. attractively suggest as a possibility that the feet are those of
Death, and that the invitation to have them washed is a ruse to fa-
cilitate his being seized and bound. Alternatively this may be
Merope welcoming Sisyphus back from the dead and treating him
(wrongly) as one who is now immortal.

226

And you, the head of the household, should take a close,
squinting look at this.

Probably also from Runaway: *Silenus to Sisyphus?*

227

ἀλλ' ἀρουραῖός τίς ἐστι σμίνθος ὧδ' ὑπερφυής;

Aelian, *On the Nature of Animals* 12.5 (Αἰσχύλος ἐν τῷ Σισύφῳ)

228

ΣΙΣΤΦΟΣ

Ζαγρεῖ τε νῦν μοι καὶ πολυξένῳ <πατρὶ>
χαίρειν

Etymologicum Gudianum s.v. Ζαγρεύς (578.9–10 de Stefani) (Αἰσχύλος ἐν Σισύφῳ [Fiorillo: σκύφῳ codd.]); *Anecdota Oxoniensia* 2.443.11 (Αἰσχύλος)

1 <πατρί> add. Hermann, cf. context in *Et. Gud.* and *An. Ox.* (τινές δὲ τὸν Ζαγρέα υἱὸν Ἅιδου φασίν)

229

†καὶ θανόντων† οἷσιν οὐκ ἔνεστ' ἰκμάς

Etymologicum Gudianum s.v. κῖκυς (Αἰσχύλος ἐν Σισύφῳ)

καὶ θανόντων codd.: καὶ τῶν θανόντων Dindorf: τῶν κατθανόντων Bergk   οἷσιν J. G. Schneider: εἰσὶν codd.   οὐκ ἔνεστ' ἰκμάς Seebode: οὐκ ἐνεστιγμάσει w: οὐκέτι ἰμάσι b (both blending the quoted words with the beginning of the lexicographer's next following word, εἶτα)

227

Then is it some kind of field-mouse that is so enormous?

Most likely the satyrs, or Silenus, trying to identify an object from clues provided by another character (cf. Sophocles, Trackers 298–324).[1]

[1] What is the object? Perhaps Sisyphus' stone, in the *Stone-Roller*; the *Trackers* parallel shows that there is no need to assume the object is present on stage.

228

SISYPHUS

I now bid farewell to Zagreus and his ever-hospitable father.[1]

Evidently from Runaway, *after his return to earth.*

[1] Hades-Pluto. Zagreus was a chthonic god, whom in *Egyptians* Aeschylus actually identified with Hades; starting with Euripides (fr. 472) he tends to become partly syncretized with Dionysus.

229

(And) of the dead, in whom there is no moisture.

Cited together with fr. 230 (below) and, we may safely presume, from the same play.

230

σοὶ δ' οὐκ ἔνεστι κῖκυς οὐδ' αἱμόρρυτοι
φλέβες

Etymologicum Gudianum s.v. κῖκυς (immediately following
fr. 229, linked by εἶτα)

233

Αἰτναῖός ἐστι κάνθαρος βίᾳ πονῶν

Scholia to Aristophanes, *Peace* 73 (Αἰσχύλος . . . ἐν Σισύφῳ
πετροκυλιστῇ)

ΣΦΙΓΞ

*This was the satyr-drama that concluded the Theban te-
tralogy of 467 BC, following* Laius, Oedipus *(qq.v.) and*
Seven against Thebes. *Its subject will have been the defeat of the Sphinx by Oedipus, who must surely be the
"stranger" of fr. 235. A contemporary vase-painting
(LIMC Oidipous 72; often called "the Fujita hydria")
probably throws light on the role of the satyrs in the play:
it shows five of them, white-bearded, richly robed and car-
rying long sceptres, sitting on high-backed, cloth-draped
chairs looking at, and apparently listening to, the Sphinx*

230

But in you there is no strength, nor do your veins have blood flowing in them.[1]

The addressee (Sisyphus?) is evidently a dead person in the underworld (i.e. this fragment is from the Stone-Roller); the speaker will be either one of the underworld gods, or a visitor (Silenus?) who has descended alive to Hades.

[1] Cf. *Odyssey* 11.141–9, 393.

233

He is like a beetle from Mount Etna,[1] toiling powerfully.

A description of Sisyphus rolling his stone.

[1] The comparison is with a dung-beetle rolling a large ball of dung. Mount Etna was widely believed to be the home of a race of giant beetles; cf. Epicharmus fr. 65 K-A; Sophocles, *Trackers* 307; Sophocles fr. 162; Aristophanes, *Peace* 73; Plato comicus fr. 36 K-A.

THE SPHINX

seated on a rock.[1] They seem to have usurped the role of Theban councillors, perhaps in the hope of securing the reward offered by Creon to whoever should solve the Sphinx's riddle and so save the Thebans from destruction; they will have failed to do so, and perhaps found them-

[1] For what seems to be another version of the same scene see Tiverios (above). These images suggest that the Sphinx herself was a speaking character in the play; on the Fujita hydria her trunk and legs suggest, not a lion, but an actor wearing a lion costume.

235

τῷ δὲ ξένῳ γε στέφανος, ἀρχαῖον †στέφος†,
δεσμῶν ἄριστος ἐκ Προμηθέως λόγου

Athenaeus 674d

1 στέφανος Grotius: στέφανον cod.　στέφος cod.: γέρας
or γάνος Blaydes

selves in danger of making a meal for the Sphinx, until res-
cued by Oedipus. A few other, later vase-paintings also
bring satyrs and the Sphinx together, but there is no partic-
ular reason to associate them specifically with Aeschylus'
play (the overcoming of a monster was a common theme of
satyr-drama).

Recent discussions: Sommerstein *AT* 129–130; R. Germar and R.
Krumeich in KPS 189–196; M. A. Tiverios, "The satyr-play *Sphinx*
of Aeschylus again", in P. Linant de Bellefonds ed. *Agathos
Daimon: mythes et cultes: études d'iconographie en l'honneur de
Lilly Kahil* (Athens, 2000) 477–487; P. Yziquel, "Le drame
satyrique eschyléen", *CGITA* 14 (2001) 1–22, esp. 19–22;
Podlecki 7–8.

235

And for the stranger a garland,[1] the ancient ‹mark of honour (?)›, the best of bonds according to the tale of Prometheus.[2]

[1] The particles δέ . . . γε contrast this reward rather strongly to
one which has apparently just been proposed for someone else. Is
this Silenus, suggesting to Creon that Oedipus should be given a
token reward while he himself should get the substantive one
(presumably the kingship of Thebes and the hand of Iocaste)?
[2] Athenaeus, just before quoting these lines, has stated that "Aeschylus in *Prometheus Unbound* says clearly that we put garlands
on our heads in honour of Prometheus, in recompense for his
binding"; since the Prometheus plays, whether by Aeschylus or
not, are almost certainly later than *The Sphinx*, our fragment
shows that this aetiology is of pre-Aeschylean origin.

236

Σφίγγα, δυσαμεριᾶν πρύτανιν κύνα

Aristophanes, *Frogs* 1287 with scholia

ΤΗΛΕΦΟΣ

After becoming king of Mysia (see on Mysians*), Telephus was wounded by Achilles when Agamemnon's army landed in his country in the belief that they had arrived near Troy. Being told by an oracle that his wounder would also be his healer, he went to Argos (or Mycenae), where the army was assembled, pleaded for assistance, and was eventually healed by the verdigris from Achilles' spear-point; in return he agreed to guide the fleet on its voyage to Troy. This story was as old as the cyclic epic, the* Cypria *(Arg. §7 West), and was famously dramatized by Euripides in 438* BC. *The most sensational episode in Euripides' play, Telephus' seizure of the infant Orestes as a hostage, may have featured already, in a somewhat different (and less violent) form, in Aeschylus' play; this is stated by a scholiast on Aristophanes,* Acharnians 332, *and Csapo and Preiser*

236[1]

The Sphinx, the bitch[2] that presided over days of ill-fortune

[1] The verse is lyric (dactylic). The Aristophanic scholia explicitly ascribe it to *The Sphinx*, in which the most plausible place for it would be in a retrospective song after the monster's destruction; but Naeke may have been right to suggest that the ascription is erroneous and that the line actually came from *Oedipus*.

[2] The Sphinx is called a dog because she snatched up her prey; in *Seven against Thebes* (776–7) she is τὰν ἁρπαξάνδραν κῆρα, in Sophocles (*Oedipus the King* 391) ἡ ῥαψῳδὸς . . . κύων.

TELEPHUS

(see below) have argued that iconographic evidence supports the view that Orestes was first brought into the Telephus story not in 438 but in or around the 460s.

This play seems to have been lost, or at least to have become a bibliographic rarity, at an unusually early date. There is only one unequivocal citation of it by any author later than the mid fourth century; and fr. 238, which is ascribed by one Hellenistic scholar (Timachidas) to Telephus *and by another (Asclepiades) to* Iphigeneia, *was not to be found in any Aeschylean text in the Alexandrian Library in the time of the great Aristarchus (mid second century BC).*

Recent discussions: E. G. Csapo, "Hikesia in the *Telephus* of Aeschylus", *QUCC* 63 (1990) 41–52; C. Preiser, *Euripides: Telephos* (Hildesheim, 2000) 51–59.

238

κύδιστ' Ἀχαιῶν Ἀτρέως πολυκοίρανε μάνθανέ μου
παῖ

Aristophanes, *Frogs* 1270 with scholia (Ἀρίσταρχος καὶ
Ἀπολλώνιος ἐπισκέψασθαι πόθεν εἰσιν· Τιμαχίδας δὲ ἐκ
Τηλέφου, Ἀσκληπιάδης δὲ ἐξ Ἰφιγενείας [V E Vb3: other mss.
abbreviate])

239

ΤΗΛΕΦΟΣ

ἁπλῆ <γὰρ> οἶμος εἰς Ἅιδου φέρει

Plato, *Phaedo* 107e–108a (ὁ Αἰσχύλου Τήλεφος . . . ἁπλῆν
οἶμόν φησιν εἰς Ἅιδου φέρειν)

Poetic text restored as above by E. A. J. Ahrens.

ΤΟΞΟΤΙΔΕΣ

*It is evident from frr. 241 and 244 that the central figure of
this play was Actaeon (son of Aristaeus and of Autonoe,
daughter of Cadmus), who was torn to pieces by his own
hunting dogs when Artemis turned him into a stag for an
offence against her (or in some versions, against Zeus—see
below). Since women archers were not a feature either of
ancient Greek society or (except in the case of Amazons) of
the ancient Greek imagination, the chorus is likely to have
consisted of nymphs accompanying Artemis.*

*It is possible that the play was part of a tetralogy whose
other plays dealt with Actaeon's aunt Semele, her son Dionysus, and her other nephew Pentheus; see introductory*

238

Son of Atreus, great and glorious ruler of the Achaeans,
learn from me.

*Addressed to Agamemnon, probably by the chorus (the metre is
dactylic).*

239

TELEPHUS

For the route that leads to Hades is a simple one.[1]

---

[1] Implying "the difficulty is to get back again": cf. *Seven* 613;
Virgil, *Aeneid* 6.126–9.

ARCHERESSES

note to Wool-Carders. *According to Stesichorus* (PMG
236) *Artemis brought about Actaeon's death "to prevent
him marrying Semele", and the early mythographer Acusi-
laus (fr. 33 Fowler) similarly says that (though without
mention of Artemis) that Zeus was angry with Actaeon because he had courted Semele. It is tempting to suppose that
Aeschylus used this version of the story (and that in frr. 242
and 243 it is of Semele that Actaeon is primarily thinking);
in this case the male person who is said in fr. 221 (from
Semele) to have been killed by Zeus might well be Actaeon
(the alternative would be to identify him as the unborn
child of Semele, believed to have perished along with his*

241

οὔπω τις Ἀκταίων᾽ ἄθηρος ἡμέρα
κενόν, πόνου πλουτοῦντ᾽, ἔπεμψεν εἰς δόμους

Photius α470; *Anecdota Bekkeri* 1.351.9–10

242

†ἅδων ταῖς† ἁγναῖς παρθένοις γαμηλίων
λέκτρων ταπεινὴ βλεμμάτων ῥέπει βολή

Antigonus of Carystus, *Collection of Oddities* 115.2

1 ἅδων ταῖς cod.: αἰδοῖ <μὲν> Schwenck, αἰδοῖ <γὰρ>
Bothe   2 ταπεινὴ Emperius: αστειμη cod.   ῥέπει βολή
Salmasius: ῥεπιβουλη cod.

243

νέας γυναικὸς οὔ με μὴ λάθῃ φλέγων
ὀφθαλμός, ἥτις ἀνδρὸς ᾖ γεγευμένη·
ἔχω δὲ τούτων θυμὸν ἱππογνώμονα

Antigonus loc. cit. (who, after quoting fr. 242, continues καὶ
διαλιπὼν προσέθηκε "νέας γυναικὸς . . . "); Plutarch, *Moralia*
81d (from φλέγων to end of line 2) and 767b (lines 1–2); several
lexicographers also cite the phrase θυμὸν ἱππογνώμονα without
naming the author

3 ἔχω δὲ Grotius: ἔχων δὲ codd.

mother). Another possibility is that the Aeschylean Actaeon conceived a passion for Artemis herself (cf. Diodorus Siculus 4.81.3–5), perhaps mistaking the virginal goddess for a seduceable mortal. The story made famous by Ovid (Metamorphoses 3.138–252) *that Artemis was angry with Actaeon because he had seen her bathing is not attested before Callimachus* (Bath of Pallas 108–116); *in Euripides* (Bacchae 337–340) *he had boasted that he was a better hunter than the goddess.*

241

Never yet has a barren day's hunting sent Actaeon home with abundance of toil but with empty hands.

Very likely spoken by Actaeon himself, perhaps in the prologue as he looks forward to a successful day of hunting.

242

In maidens who are pure of the bed of wedlock, the glance of their eyes inclines low from modesty (?).

Probably Actaeon priding himself (cf. next fragment) on being able, as he supposes, to tell at sight whether a woman is a virgin or not.

243

I never fail to take note of the glittering eye of a young woman who has tasted man's company: my senses are good judges of that kind of horseflesh.[1]

Slightly later in the same speech.

[1] lit. "I have a spirit that is a judge of horses in these things". Cf. Anacreon *PMG* 417 (a love-poem in which the girl is addressed as a "Thracian filly" who does not have a "skilful, experienced horseman" to ride her) and Alcman *PMG* 1.45–59.

244

κύνες διημάθυνον ἄνδρα δεσπότην

Scholia to *Iliad* 9.593 (Αἰσχύλος . . . περὶ τοῦ Ἀκταίωνος λέγων)

ΤΡΟΦΟΙ

The first Hypothesis to Euripides' Medea reports that Aeschylus in this play told how Medea "rejuvenated the nurses of Dionysus, together with their husbands, by boiling them"—as in other accounts she had done to Jason and/or his father Aeson, and as she had pretended she would do to his uncle Pelias. A reference to this story by Ovid (Metamorphoses 7.294–6) suggests that Medea did this at the request of Dionysus. Rejuvenation—at any rate successful rejuvenation—is a theme for satyr-drama, not tragedy; the role of Dionysus in the story points the same way, and there is virtually no doubt that this play was indeed satyric. A vase-painting of about 460 BC (Ancona, Mus. Naz. 3198; see e.g. KPS pl. 23a,b) shows on one side a female leading an elderly satyr towards a cauldron (exactly as in several images in which the woman is Medea and the old man Pelias) and on the other side a family scene consisting of what seems like the same satyr, now black-haired and vigorous, with his wife and a small satyr-child; it could very well have been inspired by this play.

The "nurses of Dionysus" are in most accounts the nymphs of Mount Nysa in Thrace; as Germar and

244

The dogs were tearing my [*or* their] master to shreds.

Doubtless from a messenger-speech; a slave of Actaeon, accompanying him on the hunt, would be an appropriate speaker.

THE NURSES OF DIONYSUS

Krumeich (below) point out, nymphs ought to be immortal and not need rejuvenation, but perhaps one should not apply such logic to a satyr-play. Nor is it clear what Medea is doing in this region; perhaps it is after her plot against Theseus and her flight from Athens.

This play certainly has some abnormal features, not least the fact that the satyrs, creatures whose sexual desires are always intense and nearly always frustrated, are to all appearances happily married. It is also rare for a satyr-drama to have a secondary chorus, which the "nurses" must have been (unless they were silent throughout). And in order for the rejuvenation to take effect, both the satyrs and the nymphs must at some point have left the scene and presently returned with new masks. It is particularly sad, therefore, that we have no quotation from the play more than three words long, and no papyrus fragments identified.

This may well have been the fourth play of a Dionysiac tetralogy; see introductory note to Wool-Carders.

Recent discussions: R. Germar and R. Krumeich in KPS 197–202; Podlecki 14–15.

ΥΨΙΠΥΛΗ

Hypsipyle, daughter of Thoas, was the leader of the women of Lemnos when they killed all the men on the island (see introductory note to Lemnian Women). *Our only information about the play, apart from two single-word quotations, comes from a scholium to Apollonius Rhodius,* Argonautica *1.769–773. In Aeschylus' play, according to this scholium, when the Argonauts were caught in a storm off Lemnos and hoping to come in and land there, the Lemnian women "came against them in arms" and refused to let them put in unless they swore to have intercourse with the*

ΦΙΛΟΚΤΗΤΗΣ

Aeschylus, Euripides and Sophocles (in that chronological order) all dramatized the story of how Philoctetes, who had been abandoned on the island of Lemnos by the Greeks on their way to Troy, was persuaded, tricked or forced, nine years later, into rejoining the expedition, because the Greeks had learned that his presence, or at least that of the bow and arrows of Heracles which he possessed, was essential if Troy was to be captured. Only Sophocles' play survives complete, but we are provided with much information about the other two by Dio Chrysostom, whose 52nd Oration is a comparison of the three plays. Dio notes that in comparison with his successors, Aeschylus is sometimes a little insouciant about questions of realistic probability. For example, whereas in Euripides' play Odysseus was transformed by Athena so as not to be recognized by Philoctetes, and in Sophocles he keeps out of Philoctetes'

HYPSIPYLE

women as soon as they landed. Such an episode, taking place at sea, is not suitable for direct dramatic treatment in tragedy, and must therefore have been narrated retrospectively, perhaps in a prologue.

Hypsipyle *was probably part of an Argonautic tetralogy, following* Lemnian Women *and preceding* Cabeiri *and* The Argo *(qq.v.)*

Recent discussions: B. Deforge, "Eschyle et la légende des Argonautes", *REG* 100 (1987) 30–44, at 36–38.

PHILOCTETES

way until the bow is safely in the hands of his confederate Neoptolemus, Aeschylus simply did not allow the issue to be raised of whether Philoctetes would have recognized his old enemy (§§5–6). Likewise, Aeschylus brought on a chorus of Lemnians without raising the issue of why they had done nothing for nine years to help Philoctetes (§§6–7); in Euripides the chorus apologize for their neglect, while Sophocles cuts the knot by making Lemnos an uninhabited island. Philoctetes gave a full narrative of his abandonment and subsequent experiences to the chorus (§9), doubtless before meeting Odysseus. Odysseus had come to Lemnos alone (§14), whereas in Euripides he was accompanied by Diomedes, in Sophocles by Neoptolemus; he "tried to win Philoctetes over" by spinning a tale of a series of disasters that had befallen the army—Agamemnon dead, Odysseus apparently executed for "an utterly dis-

*graceful crime" (§10)—doubtless, like Neoptolemus in
Sophocles' play, building a superstructure of falsehood on
the truthful foundation of the death of Achilles and the suicide of Ajax. Despite this, the Aeschylean Odysseus still
strikes Dio as less dishonest and unheroic than his Euripidean and Sophoclean counterparts (§§5, 9), even though,
like them, he used deception to deprive Philoctetes of the
bow which was his only means of procuring food (cf. §2);
on the evidence Dio has provided, Odysseus in Aeschylus
took far fewer precautions than in Euripides or Sophocles
to minimize the danger in which he would be placing himself so long as Philoctetes had the bow, and perhaps this is
what Dio is responding to.*

*We also learn from Aspasius' commentary on Aristotle's
Nicomachean Ethics (p.133.6–10 Heylbut) that in Aeschylus, as in Sophocles, Philoctetes at first tried to conceal the
pain he was in, but was eventually unable to do so (cf. Fr.
255, also the brief fr. 254 in which Philoctetes apostro-*

249

ΦΙΛΟΚΤΗΤΗΣ

Σπερχειὲ ποταμὲ βούνομοί τ' ἐπιστροφαί

Aristophanes, *Frogs* 1383, with scholia

*phizes his foot and asks it "shall I get rid of you?"). It may
have been this acute attack of Philoctetes' malady that provided Odysseus (as it provided Neoptolemus in Sophocles'
play) with an opportunity to take possession of the bow;
perhaps (as Müller [see below] argues [pp.60–61], citing
some later artistic evidence) he grabbed the weapon when
Philoctetes had hung it up (cf. fr. 251) in order to attend
to his wound (if so, this is likely to have happened offstage, and been narrated subsequently by an indignant
Philoctetes). We cannot tell how the action then proceeded;
at the end, of course, Philoctetes will have left the island in
Odysseus' company, but we do not know whether he con-
sented to do so willingly or reluctantly, nor whether he was
still to any extent influenced by Odysseus' lies about the
plight of the army.*

Recent discussions: C. W. Müller, *Euripides: Philoktet* (Berlin,
2000) 38–64; F. Jouan [and H. van Looy], *Euripide: Fragments* iii
(Paris, 2002) 272–7.

249

PHILOCTETES

O river Spercheius, and you haunts where cattle graze!

*Apostrophizing his homeland of Malis; very probably the first line
he speaks, and quite possibly the first line of the play.[1]*

[1] In the Aristophanic scene in which the line is quoted, Euripides and Aeschylus are having their verses "weighed" in the bal-
ance, each speaking one line at a time; Euripides has just recited
the opening line of *Medea*.

ATTRIBUTED FRAGMENTS

250

ἔνθ᾽ οὔτε μίμνειν ἄνεμος οὔτ᾽ ἐκπλεῖν ἐᾷ

Plutarch, *Moralia* 476b; Photius ε935; *Suda* ε1368; Apostolius 7.22; Diogenianus 4.88; Gregory of Cyprus 2.47 (2.13 in Leiden codex, 3.20 in Moscow codex); Arsenius, *Garden of Violets* p.230.6 Walz; only the *Suda*, Apostolius and Arsenius name the author (and Philoctetes as the speaker); in addition Aristaenetus, *Letters* 1.27, quotes the line with an altered and unmetrical word-order

οὔτ᾽ ἐκπλεῖν Photius, *Suda*, cett.: οὔτ᾽ ἐπλεῖν Aristaenetus: οὔτε πλεῖν Plutarch, Gregory (Leid., Mosc.)

251

κρεμάσας <∪> τόξον πίτυος ἐκ μελανδρύου

Scholia, and Eustathius, on *Odyssey* 14.12

κρεμάσας Eustathius: κρεμάσασα schol.   <τὸ> Bothe: <δὲ> Nauck

252

οὐ γὰρ δράκων ἀνῆκεν, ἀλλ᾽ ἐνῴκισεν
δεινὴν †στομάτων† ἔμφυσιν, ποδὸς βλάβην

Plutarch, *Moralia* 1087f

1 δράκων Heath: ὁ δράκων codd.   2 στομάτων codd.: ὀδόντων Reiske, Heath: χαλινῶν De Stefani (*Eikasmos* 7 [1996] 97)   βλάβην Schneidewin: λαβεῖν codd.

250

PHILOCTETES

Where the wind allows one neither to remain nor to sail out.[1]

[1] The *Suda* and the paroemiographers make it clear that the expression is being used metaphorically "of those who have fallen into circumstances hard to cope with". Doubtless Philoctetes is speaking of himself: his present condition is intolerable, but he has no way to escape from it.

251

Hanging the bow on a dark-leaved pine tree.

Perhaps Philoctetes' explanation of what he habitually does when he feels an attack of his malady coming on.

252

PHILOCTETES

For the serpent did not let go, but fearsomely fixed and embedded its fangs in me,[1] so as to maim my foot.

Describing, probably to the chorus, how he sustained his injury.

[1] The language is very similar to that used in speaking of snake-bites by Herodotus (3.109.1) and Nicander (*Theriaca* 233–4).

253

ΦΙΛΟΚΤΗΤΗΣ

φαγέδαιναν, ἥ μου σάρκας ἐσθίει ποδός

Aristotle, *Poetics* 1458b23

φαγέδαιναν Butler: φαγέδαινα recc.: φαγάδαινα[ ] B: φαγάδενα A: φαγέδαινά γ᾽ Barnes: φαγέδαιν᾽ (ἀεί μου) Boissonade

255

ΦΙΛΟΚΤΗΤΗΣ

ὦ θάνατε παιών, μή μ᾽ ἀτιμάσῃς μολεῖν·
μόνος γὰρ εἶ σὺ τῶν ἀνηκέστων κακῶν
ἰατρός, ἄλγος δ᾽ οὐδὲν ἅπτεται νεκροῦ

Stobaeus 4.52.32 (Αἰσχύλου); the first three words are cited by Maximus of Tyre, *Discourses* 7.5e (as if a continuation of fr. 254, for which he had named Philoctetes as the speaker), and line 3 (from ἄλγος) by [Plutarch], *Moralia* 109f, neither giving a source

2 γὰρ Parisinus 1985, conj. Canter: om. cett.

ΦΙΝΕΥΣ

Phineus, the blind prophet of Thrace, was persecuted by the Harpies, who persistently snatched his food from the table or even from his mouth (fr. 258), until they were driven away, and in some accounts killed, by Zetes and Calaïs, sons of the North Wind (Boreas) and of the Athenian princess Oreithyia, when Phineus' land was visited by

253

PHILOCTETES

The malignancy that is eating the flesh of my foot.[1]

---

[1] The line was reused by Euripides (fr. 792), but for ἐσθίει "is eating" he substituted the more poetic θοινᾶται "is feasting on".

255

PHILOCTETES

O Death the Healer, do not disregard my prayer that you come! For you are the only physician for ills that are beyond remedy: pain cannot touch a dead man.

Spoken during one of his attacks of pain.

PHINEUS

the Argonauts. From a passage of Philodemus, On Piety (pp. 16.14–18.7 Gomperz), it appears that Aeschylus' version of the story was one of those that ended with the death of the Harpies; there is little more that we can say about its content (but see below).

Phineus *was the first play in Aeschylus' production of 472 BC, the other three being* Persians, Glaucus of Potniae *(q.v.) and* Prometheus the Fire-Bearer *(q.v.). I have suggested in the Introduction to* Persians *(vol. i), and more fully in the article cited below, that just as Aeschylus may have created a connection between the story of Glaucus of Potniae and the Syracusan victory at Himera in 480 (cf. fr. 25a), so he may have created one between the story of how the sons of the North Wind saved Phineus and the story of how their divine father—or so Athenians believed—helped to save Athens and Greece by wrecking*

258

καὶ ψευδόδειπνα πολλὰ μαργώσης γνάθου
ἐρρυσίαζον στόματος ἐν πρώτῃ χαρᾷ

Athenaeus 10.421f

2 ἐρρυσίαζον Lobeck: ερρυσιας οἷον cod.: ἐρρυσιάσθη Kaibel   πρώτῃ χαρᾷ Musurus: πρωτιοχαραι cod.

258a

<×–> ἄνηστις δ᾽ οὐκ ἀποστατεῖ γόος

Etymologicum Genuinum s.v. ἄνηστις (Αἰσχύλος ἐν φωνεῖ [sic: Φινεῖ Reitzenstein])

259

πέλλυτρ᾽ ἔχουσιν εὐθέτοις ἐν ἀρβύλαις

Pollux 7.91

*a large part of Xerxes' fleet off Cape Sepias in Thessaly
(Herodotus 7.188–191; see also introductory note to* Oreithyia*): Phineus' prophetic powers would provide an obvious mechanism for this.*

Recent discussion: A. H. Sommerstein, "La tetralogia di Eschilo
sulla guerra persiana", forthcoming in *Dioniso* n.s. 7 (2008) (English version forthcoming in J. Davidson and D. Rosenbloom ed.
Greek Drama IV [London]).

258

And there have been many meals that proved not to be
meals,[1] which they pillaged from my [*or* his] ravenous jaws
just when my [*or* his] mouth was taking its first delight in
them.

*A description of the Harpies' depredations, probably but not cer-
tainly by Phineus himself.*

　[1] lit. "many false meals".

258a

There is no lack of wailing over my [*or* his] getting no food.

Perhaps from the same speech.

259

They have ankle-supports[1] inside their well-fitting shoes.

Probably from a description of the swift-footed sons of Boreas.

　[1] πέλλυτρα were bandages (of felt, according to Pollux)
"which were wrapped around the ankles and heels of runners to
reduce the risk of dislocations" (Hesychius π1357 Schmidt).

ΦΟΡΚΙΔΕΣ

The Phorcides (daughters of Phorcys), or Graeae ("old women"), were significant secondary figures in the story of Perseus and the Gorgon's head; their most famous characteristic was that they had only one eye and one tooth between the three of them, so that Perseus by stealing the eye and tooth was able to render them helpless. In one common version of the myth, presented for example by Aeschylus' contemporary Pherecydes (fr. 11 Fowler), he thereby forced them to tell him how to find the nymphs (water-nymphs [naiads] according to the inscription on one sixth-century vase painting [LIMC Perseus 88]) who possessed the winged sandals and cap of invisibility that he needed in order to get near the Gorgon Medusa, and the bag (kibisis) in which to put her head. In this account there is a wide gap in space and time between the Graeae and the Gorgons themselves; Aeschylus, as we learn from [Eratosthenes], Catasterisms 22 (= Aeschylus fr. 262), closed this gap—doubtless for dramatic convenience—by making the Graeae "sentinels" to the Gorgons. Perseus seized their eye while one of them was handing it to another, threw it into

PHORCIDES

Lake Tritonis (this detail tells us the geographical setting of the play), and so was able to get past them, find the Gorgons asleep, and cut off Medusa's head. These exploits were apparently reported by a third party in what must have been a long and elaborate messenger-speech (cf. fr. 261), presumably to the chorus (which perhaps consisted of nymphs of the lake, friendly to Perseus—cf. above).

This play is assigned by Aristotle, Poetics *1456a2–3, to the same subcategory of tragedy as* Prometheus *and "all those plays set in Hades"; unfortunately textual corruption has left it uncertain how he defined this category. It may have been produced together with* Polydectes *and the satyr-play* Net-Haulers *(qq.v.), though no other related play can be identified that would complete a tetralogy. There are some slight indications that this production came rather late in Aeschylus' career.*

Recent discussions: J. H. Oakley, "Perseus, the Graiai, and Aeschylus' *Phorkides*", *AJA* 92 (1988) 383–391; Gantz 304–6; S. E. Goins, "The date of Aeschylus' Perseus tetralogy", *RhM* 140 (1997) 193–210.

261

$$<\cup-> \ \text{ἔδυ δ' ἐς ἄντρον ἀσχέδωρος ὥς}$$

Athenaeus 9.402b; Eustathius on *Odyssey* 19.439.

ΦΡΥΓΕΣ ἢ ΕΚΤΟΡΟΣ ΛΥΤΡΑ

This was the third play of the Achilles trilogy (following Myrmidons *and* Nereids, *qq.v.), and corresponded closely to the final book of the* Iliad. *As in* Myrmidons, *the scene was Achilles' hut. The Phrygians of the title had come there with Priam (Aristophanes fr. 696), and as a chorus they performed some highly distinctive dances (ibid.); they were perhaps servants rather than Trojan citizens. Before their arrival Achilles had had a short dialogue with Hermes (who may have been assigned the role which in* Iliad *24.120–142 is played by Thetis) and then, again as in* Myrmidons, *sat silent and veiled for a long time (scholia to Aristophanes,* Frogs *911; Life of Aeschylus 6). In the* Iliad *(22.346–354) Achilles had vowed that he would not return Hector's body for burial even if Priam were to offer Hector's weight in gold as a ransom; in Aeschylus, precisely this ransom was offered and accepted, being apparently literally weighed in scales against Hector's corpse (scholia to* Iliad *22.351;* Lycophron, Alexandra *269–270 with scholia). In addition to Achilles, Priam and Hermes, fr. 267 suggests (though it does not prove) that there was a fourth*

261

He plunged into the cave like a wild boar.[1]

*The subject is Perseus (so Athenaeus), and the cave is doubtless
that of the Gorgons; the line evidently comes from a messenger-
speech.*

 picked it up on one of his visits to Sicily; on this, however, see M.
Griffith in R. D. Dawe ed. *Dionysiaca: Nine Studies . . . presented
to Sir Denys Page* (Cambridge, 1978) 104–6.

PHRYGIANS *or*
THE RANSOMING OF HECTOR

*individual dramatis persona, a woman; the scholiast who
quotes the fragment identifies her as Andromache, Hector's
widow, but the text of the fragment itself, stressing as it
does the fact that this person comes from the same city as
Andromache, suggests rather that it is someone else, most
likely Briseis. Did she, Achilles' heterosexual partner, give
crucial help to Priam in mollifying Achilles, as Achilles' ho-
mosexual partner had mollified him in* Myrmidons *(and as
Tecmessa tries in vain to mollify Ajax in Sophocles'* Ajax*)?
The play will doubtless have included laments over Hector
by Priam and the chorus, replacing the laments of the
women in* Troy *(Iliad 24.718–776) which the structure of
Aeschylus' play did not allow him to include.*

The medieval catalogue of Aeschylus' plays lists Φρύγες *and* Φρύγιοι *as two separate dramas. This is the only
mention of an Aeschylean title* Φρύγιοι, *and such a title
would be contrary to fifth-century usage (*Φρύγιος *being
then in use only as an adjective). Either, therefore, the title*
Φρύγιοι *is a mere doublet of* Φρύγες, *or else, as Bothe first*

263

263

ἀλλὰ ναυβάτην
φορτηγόν, ὅστις ῥῶπον ἐξάγει χθονός

Pollux 7.131

264

suggested, it is a corruption of Φρύγιαι *and this was the title of another play, perhaps one with a chorus of captive women from Troy or the surrounding territory.*

Recent studies: M. Staltmayr, "Aischylos und die Phryger", *Hermes* 119 (1991) 367–374; A. Garzya, "Sui frammenti dei *Frigî* di Eschilo", *Cuadernos de Filología Clásica: estudios griegos y indoeuropeos* 5 (1995) 41–52; A. Moreau, "Eschyle et les tranches des repas d'Homère: la trilogie d'Achille", *CGITA* 9 (1996) 3–29; Sommerstein, *Aeschylean Tragedy* 344–7; M. L. West, "*Iliad* and *Aethiopis* on stage: Aeschylus and son", *CQ* 50 (2000) 338–352, esp. 341–2; P. Michelakis, *Achilles in Greek Tragedy* (Cambridge, 2002) 54–56.

263

. . . but a seafaring merchant who is exporting low-value goods from the country.[1]

Evidently describing the appearance of Priam; very likely the lost first half of the first line meant something like "He does not resemble a king . . . "

[1] This comparison is probably inspired by *Iliad* 24.381–2, where the disguised Hermes, meeting Priam on his way to Achilles with the ransom, asks him whether he is "sending many fine goods away to foreigners" for safety, or whether Hector's death has panicked the Trojans into abandoning their city altogether. The speaker here is likely to be Hermes too: in view of all we are told about Achilles' long silence, *he* is not likely to have spoken at the time when Priam first came into his presence, and before that point he would not have been in a position to make a comment like this.

264

ἀνὴρ δ' ἐκεῖνος ἦν πεπαίτερος μόρων

Athenaeus 2.51c; Eustathius on *Iliad* 2.235

266

καὶ τοὺς θανόντας εἰ θέλεις εὐεργετεῖν
εἴτ' οὖν κακουργεῖν, ἀμφιδεξίως ἔχει·
<   >
καὶ μήτε χαίρειν μήτε λυπεῖσθαι βροτούς.
ἡμῶν γε μέντοι νέμεσίς ἐσθ' ὑπερτέρα,
5 καὶ τοῦ θανόντος ἡ Δίκη πράσσει κότον

Stobaeus 4.57.6

2 εἴτ' οὖν Hermann: ὁ γοῦν vel sim. codd.   2/3 lacuna
posited by Radt, e.g. <τεθνηκότας γὰρ ἀσθενεῖν τε μοῖρ' ἔχει>

264

That man was softer than a ripe blackberry.

Describing Hector[1] (so Athenaeus).

 [1] But what is being said about Hector, and by whom? The past verb ἦν makes it almost certain that the living, not the dead, Hector is being spoken of, which rules out the suggestion of K. J. Dover (*CR* 14 [1964] 12) that it is "a grisly joke . . . spun out of the mockery of the dead Hector . . . in *Il.* xxii 373f" and therefore spoken by a Greek, presumably Achilles; rather we must revert to the older view that this is Priam recalling the gentleness of Hector's character (cf. *Iliad* 24.771–2).

266

And if you want to do good to the dead, or again to do them harm, it makes no difference; for ‹the lot of› mortals ‹when they die is to have no sensation›[1] and feel neither pleasure nor pain. *Our* indignation,[2] on the other hand, is more powerful, and Justice exacts the penalty for the wrath of the dead.

Hermes warning Achilles that his maltreatment of Hector's body is futile and dangerous.[3]

 [1] This is only an approximate restoration of the sense of the lost line.   [2] The contrast with βροτούς shows that the first person plural refers to the gods.   [3] Cf. *Iliad* 24.53–54 (Apollo speaking).

ATTRIBUTED FRAGMENTS

267

Ἀνδραίμονος γένεθλον <–> Λυρνησσίου,
ὅθεν περ Ἕκτωρ ἄλοχον ἤγαγεν φίλην

Scholia to Euripides, *Andromache* 1

1 <ὦ> Hermann: <ὸν> Wagner

ΨΥΧΑΓΩΓΟΙ

*This play, as fr. 275 shows, dramatized the Homeric
Nekyia (Odyssey 11), and, like it, included a prophecy of
Odysseus' death, presumably made by Teiresias; we do not
know how many of the other characters who appear in the
Homeric episode (the main ones are the sailor Elpenor,
Odysseus' mother Anticleia, Agamemnon, Achilles and a
silent Ajax) figured in Aeschylus' play. The scene was a lake
with a connection to the underworld (frr. 273, 273a); it
has been identified as Lake Avernus in Campania (cf. Maximus of Tyre, Discourses 8.2b), as the Acherusian lake
in Thesprotia (cf. Herodotus 5.92η.2), and even as Lake
Stymphalus in Arcadia (so the medieval scholar Thomas
Magister, on Aristophanes, Frogs 1266—but Odysseus, in
a ship, could never have got there), and the chorus consisted of devotees of Hermes living beside the lake and
operating a necromantic sanctuary there (this perhaps
slightly favours the Thesprotian location; cf. Alexis fr. 93,*

267

Child of Andraemon of Lyrnessus, the place from which
Hector brought his dear wife.[1]

[1] In the *Iliad* Andromache comes not from Lyrnessus but from
Thebe, and her father's name is Eëtion (*Iliad* 6.395–7). Briseis
does come from Lyrnessus (*Iliad* 2.689–690, 19.60), but her father's name is Briseus (*Iliad* 1.392 etc.). Achilles had sacked both
cities in the same campaign (2.690–3), killing Eëtion and his seven
sons (*Iliad* 6.416–424); thus there was already in Homer a link between the fates of Briseis and Andromache, and Aeschylus makes
this link closer by making them natives of the same city. We cannot
tell whether Briseis is here being addressed or only spoken about
(for example in a speech by Achilles explaining to Priam the chain
of events that led to Hector's death).

GHOST-RAISERS

from a comedy called The Thesprotians). *The play probably stood first in an Odyssean tetralogy, being followed
by* Penelope, Bone-Gatherers *and the satyr-drama* Circe
(qq.v.)

Recent discussions: A. Henrichs, "Namenlosigkeit und Euphe-
mismus: Zur Ambivalenz der chthonischen Mächte im attischen
Drama", in H. Hofmann and A. M. Harder, *Fragmenta Dramatica*
(Göttingen, 1991) 161–201, at 187–192; Sommerstein, *Aeschylean Tragedy* 349–350; M. Librán Moreno, "*TrGF* 2 Adesp. fr. 370
K.-Sn.: Aeschylus' *Psychagogoi*?", *Exemplaria Classica* 8 (2004)
7–29; R. Bardel, "Spectral traces: ghosts in tragic fragments", in F.
McHardy et al. ed. *Lost Dramas of Classical Athens* (Exeter,
2005) 83–112, at 85–92; C. Cousin, "La *Nékyia* homérique et
les fragments des Évocateurs d'âmes d'Eschyle", *Gaia* 9 (2005)
137–152.

273

ΧΟΡΟΣ

Ἑρμᾶν μέν πρόγονον τίομεν γένος οἱ περὶ λίμναν

Aristophanes, *Frogs* 1266 with scholia

273a

ΧΟΡΟΣ

ἄγε νυν, ὦ ξεῖν', ἐπὶ ποιοφύτων
ἵϲτω ϲηκῶν φοβερᾶϲ λίμνηϲ,
ὑπό τ' αὐχένιον λαιμὸν ἀμήϲαϲ
τοῦδε ϲφαγίου ποτὸν ἀψύχοιϲ
5 αἷμα μεθίει
δονάκων εἰϲ βένθοϲ ἀμαυρόν·
Χθόνα δ' ὠγυγίαν ἐπικεκλόμενοϲ
χθόνιόν θ' Ἑρμῆν πομπὸν φθιμένων
[αἰ]τοῦ χθόνιον Δία νυκτιπόλων
10 ἑϲμὸν ἀνεῖναι ποταμοῦ ϲτομάτων,
οὗ τόδ' ἀπορρὼξ ἀμέγαρτον ὕδωρ

Köln Papyrus 125 col. II; attributed to *The Ghost-Raisers* by Kramer

Corrections and supplements are by Kramer unless otherwise stated

1 ξιν Π   2 φοβερα Π   6 ἀμαυρόν Kramer:
εμ . υρον Π: ἐρεμνόν Lloyd-Jones   8 ερμηϲ πομπομ Π
9]του χθνιων Π: corr./suppl. Gronewald   -πόλων Merkelbach: -παλων Π   10 ἑϲμὸν Merkelbach: θεϲμον Π
11 τοτε αποροξ Π   ἀμέγαρτον Gronewald: τομεγαρτο Π: τὸ
μέγαρτὸν Merkelbach

273

CHORUS

We, the folk that dwell around the lake, honour Hermes as our ancestor.

A dactylic hexameter; very probably the opening line of the choral parodos, and quite likely of the whole play.

273a

CHORUS

Come now, stranger, take your stand
on the grass-grown borders of the fearsome lake,
slit the windpipe in the neck
of this sacrificial beast, and let the blood run
for the dead to drink,
down into the dim, reedy depths.
Call upon the age-old Earth
and Hermes of the Underworld, escort of the departed,
and ask the Zeus of the Underworld[1] to send up
the swarm of souls[2] from the night-shrouded mouth of
 the river—
the river whose offshoot is this body of water,[3] gloomy

---

[1] i.e. Hades-Pluto; cf. *Supp.* 156–7, 230–1, *Ag.* 1386–7.

[2] "Of souls" is not in the Greek but has been added for clarity.

[3] Cf. *Odyssey* 10.513–529, where Odysseus is instructed to make his sacrifices and prayers to the dead at the junction of three rivers one of which is "Cocytus, which is an offshoot of the water of Styx" (514).

κἀχέρνιπτον
Στυγίοις νᾳ[ς]μοῖςιν ἀνεῖται.

274

καὶ σκευοθηκῶν ναυτικῶν τ᾽ ἐρειπίων

Pollux 10.10

275

ΤΕΙΡΕΣΙΑΣ

ἐρῳδιὸς γὰρ ὑψόθεν ποτώμενος
ὄνθῳ σε πλήξει, νηδύος χαλώμασιν·
ἐκ τοῦδ᾽ ἄκανθα ποντίου βοσκήματος
σήψει παλαιὸν δέρμα καὶ τριχορρυές

Scholia to *Odyssey* 11.134

2 ὄνθῳ σε πλήξει νηδύος Heath: ὅν θ᾽ ὡς ἔπληξεν ἡ δ᾽ υἱὸς
vel sim. codd.   χαλώμασιν Diels: χειλώμασιν codd.: κενώ-
μασιν Nauck

---

[1] A sting-ray, according to schol. *Odyssey* 11.134 and Oppian,
On Fishing 2.497–505. The usual story (almost certainly derived
from the sixth-century epic known as the *Telegony* or *Thesprotis*)
was that the barb was given by Circe to Telegonus, her son by
Odysseus, to use as a spear-point, and he killed Odysseus with it
not knowing him to be his father; but the version we find here is
given as an alternative by Sextus Empiricus, *Against the Teachers*
1.267 (though the bird is a seagull rather than a heron). Both are
ultimately based on Teiresias' prophecy (*Odyssey* 11.134–6) that

and not fit for the washing of hands,[4]
rising up from the streams of Styx.

*Instructions (in chanted anapaests) to Odysseus to perform the
rites required in order to call up the ghosts.*[5]

[4] sc. before a sacrifice (because polluted by its connection with
the dead). In the semi-parody of this play in Aristophanes, *Birds*
1553–64, the chorus sing of a "lake of the unwashed" (λίμνη . . .
ἄλουτος) where necromantic rites are performed by Socrates.
[5] In the *Odyssey* comparable instructions had been given by Circe
before Odysseus left her (10.504–540).

274

And sea-chests and pieces of wreckage

*Perhaps from a prophecy by Teiresias about Odysseus' coming
tribulations.*[1]

[1] Cf. *Odyssey* 11.112–4; also *Ag.* 659–660.

275

TEIRESIAS

For a heron in flight will strike you from above with its
dung when it opens its bowels; and from this the barb of a
sea-creature[1] will rot your aged, hairless skin.[2]

death would come to Odysseus in old age ἐξ ἁλός . . . ἀβληχρός;
these words were probably intended to mean that Odysseus'
death would be a gentle one, far from the sea, but they were capable of being taken to mean almost exactly the opposite. Aeschylus'
version, which may be his own invention, is evidently designed to
save Odysseus from the disgrace of being killed, even unwittingly,
by his own son, while retaining the sting-ray (which was apparently already so firmly established in the myth that it could not
be discarded).   [2] Clearly the skin referred to is that of the
scalp.

ΨΥΧΟΣΤΑΣΙΑ

This play must have been a sequel to Memnon *(q.v.) In it, as we learn from Plutarch* (Moralia 17a) *and from scholia to* Iliad *8.70 and 22.210, Zeus weighed the souls of Achilles and Memnon in the scales as they fought each other, and the mothers of the two heroes, Thetis and Eos, pleaded each on behalf of her son. This weighing of the souls (or fates) of Achilles and Memnon appears in art from the sixth century onwards (though it is usually Hermes who holds the scales), and it doubtless featured in the cyclic epic, the* Aethiopis; *it is parodied by Aristophanes in* Frogs 1365– 1410. *A reference by Pollux (4.130) to the weighing scene is directly followed by mention of the use of the* mēchanē *(here called γέρανος "crane") by "Eos snatching up the body of Memnon", and it is likely that he is still thinking of the same play (certainly there is no other we know of to which he could be referring).*

ΩΡΕΙΘΥΙΑ

Oreithyia, daughter of the Athenian king Erechtheus, was abducted by Boreas (the North Wind) and became the mother of Zetes and Calaïs (see introductory note to Phineus). *We only know of the existence of Aeschylus' play about her from a single reference by the rhetorician John of Sicily* (Commentary on Hermogenes On Types of Style *p.225.24–26 Walz) who paraphrases a passage about Boreas "puffing with both his cheeks and stirring up the sea"; this seems to come from the same speech by Boreas*

THE WEIGHING OF SOULS

This is the only known tragedy in which Zeus was definitely present on stage, though it is possible that he appeared in Prometheus Unbound.

West (see below) has argued that The Weighing of Souls, *like the* Prometheus *plays with which it shares a fondness for divine characters and extravagant spectacle, was not written by Aeschylus but by his son Euphorion, to complete a sequence of plays which Aeschylus had left unfinished; see also introductory note to* Carians.

The only surviving fragments attributed to this play are three single words cited by lexicographers.

Recent discussions: M. L. West, "*Iliad* and *Aethiopis* on stage: Aeschylus and son", *CQ* 50 (2000) 338–352, esp. 345–7; M. Farioli, "Due parodie comiche della 'psychostasia': Ar. *Ran*. 1364–1413 e fr. 504 K.-A.", *Lexis* 22 (2004) 251–267.

OREITHYIA

from which "Longinus" quoted fr. 281. "Longinus" describes that passage, and other expressions such as "vomiting towards heaven"[1] and Boreas being described as a "piper", as "not tragic but paratragic . . . descending from

---

1 Sidgwick ingeniously combined this phrase with that quoted by John of Sicily into a plausible couplet: σιαγόσιν δισσαῖσιν ἐκφυσῶν ἐγὼ | κυκῶ θάλασσαν ἐξεμεῖν πρὸς οὐρανόν ("Puffing with both my cheeks, I stir the sea to vomit itself up towards heaven").

281

ΒΟΡΕΑΣ

†καὶ† καμίνου σχῶσι μάκιστον σέλας·
εἰ γάρ τιν' ἑστιοῦχον ὄψομαι †μόνον†,
μίαν παρείρας πλεκτάνην χειμάρροον
στέγην πυρώσω καὶ κατανθρακώσομαι·
5   νῦν δ' οὐ κέκραγά πω τὸ γενναῖον μέλος

"Longinus", *On the Sublime* 3.1; the surviving text does not
identify the author or play, but does mention Boreas, and the
overblown style is similar to that of the passage from *Oreithyia*
paraphrased by John of Sicily (see introductory note)

1 καὶ cod. (the first word after a lacuna of four lost pages): εἰ
καὶ Musgrave, ἦν καὶ Lebègue   2 μόνον cod.: σποδόν
Jacobs: perh. <φλόγα> vel sim.?

"THE DIKE PLAY"

*The play from which come the forty-seven lines, or frag-
ments of lines, that survive as frr. 281a and 281b is known
to be Aeschylean by the appearance in 281a.28 of a phrase
cited elsewhere as by Aeschylus. The main speaker identifies herself as Dike (Justice) in 281a.15, and explains how
she administers the justice of Zeus; by way of example, she
then speaks of an insane, shameless child of Zeus and Hera,
who must be Ares the god of war and violence, and whom
she has presumably encouraged or forced to direct his hos-
tility only against unrighteous communities. She is ad-*

the awe-inspiring towards the contemptible", and it is not surprising that Oreithyia *has sometimes been thought to have been a satyr-drama; certainly there is nothing in what we know of the myth to suggest how Aeschylus could have used it to excite tragic emotion, let alone to generate a tragic outcome.*

281

BOREAS

... even if (?) they stop the high-flying flame of the furnace; for if I see a ‹spark of fire (?)› on the hearth, I'll weave it into one great coil like a torrent, set the house ablaze and reduce it to ashes. But at present I am not yet sounding out my highest-quality[1] tune.

Threatening to destroy the house of Erechtheus if his demand for Oreithyia's hand is rejected?

[1] lit. "noble, thoroughbred". Boreas means that he is not yet putting forth his full power.

"THE DIKE PLAY"

dressing a group of males (281a.14) whom one would naturally suppose to be the chorus of the play.

It is very hard to identify the play from which this fragment comes, or even to determine whether it is a tragedy or a satyr-drama. Some details of language (ὁτιή, 281a.9; ἐρρύθμιξα, 281b.4) suggest satyr-drama; but the words of the chorus (if chorus they are) contain no trace of the amorality we expect from satyrs. Fraenkel, and many others after him, have suggested that the play is Women of

Aetna, which according to the Life of Aeschylus (§9) was written to "augur a good life for those who were joining in settling the city [of Aetna]", and for which, therefore, a scene promising peace (and no doubt prosperity) to a city that upheld justice would be highly appropriate; and certainly a play first produced away from Athens, on a unique occasion, and known to have other highly unusual features (e.g. its many changes of scene), might be slightly loose in its application of linguistic genre conventions. However, the identification might well seem to be ruled out by the masculine gender of the chorus—unless, indeed, the speaker of the even-numbered lines from 281a.14 to 22 (possibly also 24) is not after all the chorus-leader but a

281a

ΔΙΚΗ

[Remains of four lines including μακάρων (1) and αυτη θεων (2).]

5 ἵζει δ᾿ ἐν αὐτῶι . [] .. [.] .. [.] . [
    δίκη κρατήςας τῶιδε . [
    πατὴρ γὰρ ἦρξεν ἀνταμ[
    ἐκ τοῦ δέ τοί με Ζεὺς ἐτίμ[ηςεν

Oxyrhynchus Papyrus 2256 fr. 9(a); scholia, and Eustathius, on Iliad 6.239 (οὔτε δῆμος οὔτ᾿ ἔτης ἀνήρ [28] ascribed to Aeschylus)

7 ἀνταμ[εύψασθαι] Görschen, then [κακοῖς] Garabo: ἀνταμ[υν-] Mette   8 suppl. Lobel, then [μέγα] Fraenkel, Page

*male representative of the people (cf. στρατῷ, 281a.24) of
"this land" (281a.12)—say, a mythical king of Syracuse?*

*It is more than possible that fr. 451n, in praise of peace,
also comes from this play, perhaps from the same speech.*

Recent discussions: M. L. Garabo, "Eschilo, fr. 281A, 5–13 Radt",
Giornale Filologico Ferrarese 9 (1986) 51–57; J. M. Bremer,
"Poets and their patrons", in H. Hofmann and A. M. Harder ed.
Fragmenta Dramatica (Göttingen, 1991) 39–60, esp. 39–41; C.
Corbato, "Le 'Etnee' di Eschilo", in B. Gentili ed. Catania antica
(Pisa, 1996) 61–72; A. Wessels in KPS 98–106; P. Patrito, "Sul
'frammento di Dike' (= Aesch. fr. 281a-b Radt)", in Quaderni
del Dipartimento di Filologia A. Rostagni (2001) 77–95; Podlecki
15–16.

281A
JUSTICE

[*Remains of four lines including* of the blessed ones *(1) and* myself
(?) *of the gods (2).*]

And he took his seat on it[1] . . . [. . .] having justly
triumphed[2] by this (?) [. . .] For the Father began to

---

[1] Probably referring to the throne of Olympus. [2] Presumably over Cronus and the older generation of gods. This is
here presented as just requital for a wrong done to Zeus; cf.
Hesiod, Theogony 466–491, where Zeus's mother Rhea, ag-
grieved that Cronus is swallowing their children as soon as she
gives birth to them, consults her parents, Uranus and Gaea, as to
how she can conceal the birth of her latest child, Zeus, so that
Cronus "might suffer requital from the avenging spirits of his
father [Uranus, whom Cronus had castrated] and of his children,
whom [he] had swallowed": Cronus is given a stone wrapped in
swaddling clothes, which he swallows thinking it is the infant
Zeus.

ὁτιὴ παθὼν ἠμ[είψατ'

10 ἴζω Διὸς θρόνοιϲιν [… (.)]ϊϲμένῃ·
πέμπει δέ μ' αὐτὸς οἷϲιν εὐμεν[ὴϲ
Ζ[ε]ύϲ, ὅϲπερ εἰϲ γῆν τήνδ' ἔπεμψέ μ' ευ[
δ[. (.)]εϲθε δ' ὑμεῖϲ εἴ τι μὴ μά[την] λέγω.

<   >

τ̣[ί ϲ'] οὖ[ν προ]ϲ̣εν̣ν̣έποντεϲ εὖ κ̣[υ]ρήϲομε[ν;

ΔΙΚΗ

15 Δίκην μ̣ . [… (.)]ο̣ν πρέϲβος ἧϲ ε … ρο̣ . [

<   >

ποίαϲ δὲ τ[ιμ]ῆϲ ἀρχι̣. ε̣ …. ειϲ λ̣[

ΔΙΚΗ

το]ῖϲ μὲν δ[ι]καίοιϲ ἔνδικον τείνω βίο[ν.

<   >

……. (.)] . (.)ϲα θέ[ϲ]μ̣[ι]ο̣ν̣ τόδ' ἐν βρ[ο]τ̣ο̣[ιϲ.

ΔΙΚΗ

τοῖϲ δ' αὖ μα]ταίοιϲ . [.] . [.] …. [..] …. φ[

9 suppl. Vysoký, then [ἔνδικον τίϲιν] id.   10 [ἠγλα]ϊϲμένη
(doubtfully) Lobel   11 suppl. Lobel, then [πέλει] id.
12 εὔ[φρονα] or εὖ [φρονῶν] Lobel   13 δ[έξ]εϲθε Fraenkel
(perh. rather δ[έχ]εϲθε)   μά[την] Lobel   14 suppl.
Lobel   15 μέ[γιϲτ]ον πρέϲβος ἧϲ ἐν οὐραν[ῷ] Lobel
16 τ[ιμ]ῆϲ Lobel   ἀρχιτεκτονεῖϲ; λ[έγε] Page
18 [καλόν γε θ]εῖϲα Fraenkel   19 (beginning) suppl. Lobel

re[quite evil with evil (?).] As a result of this, you see, Zeus hon[oured] me [greatly (?)], because, having suffered wrong, he re[quited it with just punishment (?).] I sit [glori]fied (?) on the throne of Zeus, and Zeus himself sends me to anyone towards whom he [is] friend[ly]— Zeus, who has sent me to this land [in] good [will]. Please [r]eceive me,[3] if what I say is not em[pty].

⟨?⟩

W[hat] shall we [c]all [you], if we are to h[it the mark (?)]?

JUSTICE

Justice, who has the gr[eates]t primacy in heaven (?)

⟨?⟩

And over what h[onou]rable function do you pre[side (?)], t[ell us (?)]?

JUSTICE

For the righteous I prolong their righteous life.

⟨?⟩

That is a [fine (?)] law that you are [lay]ing [down] for humanity.

JUSTICE

For the wicked, on the other hand, [I cause them to change their ways (?)]

---

[3] Fraenkel's restoration gives the sense "You will receive me"; but cf. *Eum.* 236, 893, fr. 220c.5.

< >

20   ἐ]πῳδαῖς ἢ κατ' ἰςχύος τρόπο[ν;

ΔΙΚΗ

γράφουσα] τὰ<μ>πλακήματ' ἐν δέλτῳ Διό[ς.

< >

ποίῳ χρό]νωι δὲ πίνακ' ἀναπτύςςει[ς] κακ[ῶν;

ΔΙΚΗ

]ηι ςφιν ἡμέρα τὸ κύριον.

< >

]εκτέα ςτρατῷ

ΔΙΚΗ

25   ]έχοιτό μ' εὔφρ[όν]ως.

[*Remains of two lines; the second (27) may include*
ἐπιςπές̣θ̣α[ι].]

28 πό]λις τις οὔτε δῆμος οὔτ' ἔτης ἀνὴρ
τοιάνδε μοῖραν π[αρ]ὰ θεῶν καρπουμένη[ι.
30 τέκμαρ δὲ λέξω τῶι τόδ' εὐδερκὲ[ς] φέρε[

20 [πειθοῦς ἐ]πῳδαῖς Pohlenz   21 (beginning) suppl. Lobel
τἀμπλακήματ' Lloyd-Jones: τᾱπ̣λακήματ' Π   22 suppl.
Lobel (but preferring κακ[οῖς] at end)   23 [εὖτ' ἂν φέρ]ῃ
Lobel   24 [οὐκοῦν (οὔκουν . . . ; Lloyd-Jones) προθύμως εἶ
σὺ δ]εκτέα ςτρατῷ e.g. Lobel   25 [καὶ κάρτ' ὄναιτ' ἄν, εἰ
δ]έχοιτό e.g. Lobel   29 (end) suppl. Fraenkel   30 φέρε[ις]
or φέρε[ι] or φέρε[ιν] Lobel

"THE DIKE PLAY"

<?>

By the charms [of persuasion (?)], or by the method of force?

JUSTICE
[By writing down] their transgressions on the tablet of Zeus.

<?>

And [at what ti]me do you unfold the tablet [of] their crimes?

JUSTICE
[When] a day [comes that brings] them their ordained fate.

<?>

[Then] should [you not be enthusiastically (?) re]ceived by the people?

JUSTICE
[They will indeed benefit greatly (?), if they re]ceive me with good [w]ill.

[The next two lines are lost except for a few letters. The following, partly restored sentence will have begun in the second of these lines (27).]

Neither a [c]ity, nor a village, nor an individual [would refuse to (?)] follow [a goddess (?)] who enjoys such a portion f[ro]m the gods. And I will give you a proof that will

ἔθρε[ψ .] παῖδα μάργον ὃν τίκτει [ποτὲ
Ἥρα μιγεῖςα Ζηνὶ θυμοιδ[
δ]ύςαρκτ[ο]ν, αἰδὼς δ' οὐκ ἐνῆ[ν] φρ[ον]ήματι·
  ] . υκτα τῶν ὁδοιπόρων βέλη
35   ] . δως ἀγκύλαιςιν ἀρταμῶν,
      ]ῶν ἔχ[αι]ρε κἀγέλα κακὸν
       ]ν ςτάζοι φόνος·
       ]μουμένη
     ] . ιπρ[.....]γον χέρα
40   ]οῦν ἐνδίκως κικλήςκεται
     ]νιν ἔνδικ[.....] . οc.

  31 ἔθρε[ψε] or ἔθρε[ψα] Lobel (he preferred the former,
Mette the latter) [ποτὲ] Görschen 32 θυμοιδ[ὲς
τέκνον] Mette: θυμοίδ[η θεόν] Lloyd-Jones 34 [πολλοῖς
δ' ἄ]φυκτα Mette 35 [ἀνα]ιδῶς Lobel, before which
[ἐφείς,] Mette (perh. [ἴαπτ'], cf. Ag. 510) 36 [καὶ τοῦτο
δρ]ῶν Diggle 37 ςτά(ζοι) γρΠ in margin: ἄζοι or ὄζοι Π
perh. [ἐκ χεροῖ]ν? 38 perh. e.g. [ἐνθυ]μουμένη?
39 [κ]αὶ πρ[οσήγαγ]ον Fraenkel 40 perh. [Ἄρης] οὖν?

make this plain to see. I reared[4] the savage son[5] whom
Hera [once] bore in union with Zeus, an unruly [child (?)]
of swollen spirit, in whose mentality there was no shame;
[he shot many (?)] wayfarers with arrows [from which] one
could [not escape (?), shameles]sly (?) slaughtering them
with the bowstring, [and] he laughed and rejoiced [in doing these (?)] evil deeds [whenever (?)] the blood [of his
victims (?)] dripped[6] [from his hand]s (?). [I . . .] taking
[this to heart (?) . . . an]d e[xtend]ed (?) my hand [to him (?)
 . . . ;] therefore he is rightly[7] called [Ares (?), because . . .]
him righteous [. . .] . . .

[4] Reading ἔθρε[ψα]; the meaning is that she acted as nurse
and tutor to the young god. The alternative restoration, ἔθρε[ψε],
is clearly inferior: (i) after Dike's statement of her great power to
do humans good, we expect to hear of something that *she* has
done; (ii) if the third-person verb has Hera as its subject (and
there is no room for any other), her name ought to have been
placed early in the sentence, not tucked away in a relative clause.
[5] This must be Ares, the only universally recognized son of Zeus
and Hera (Hesiod, *Theogony* 921–3); the other son sometimes
credited to them, Hephaestus (e.g. *Iliad* 1.577–9, but cf. Hesiod,
Theogony 927–9), obviously does not fit the description given
here.   [6] The papyrus's marginal variant is surely right:
φόνος is not a suitable subject either for ἄζοι "dried up (something else)" or for ὄζοι "smelt (of something)".   [7] The name
"Ares" was probably explained through a pun on one of the nu-
merous similar words in the tragic lexicon, e.g. ἄρος "benefit" (cf.
Supp. 885) or ἀρείων "better". Dike will have gone on to explain
that she taught Ares to end his acts of random violence (34–37)
and instead attack only those who did not respect justice, leaving
others in peace (cf. fr. 451n, if it belongs to this play).

ATTRIBUTED FRAGMENTS

281b

[*Remains of six lines including*]ἐρρύθμιξα *(4)*,]παιca *(5)*, παίεcθαί *(6)*.]

Oxyrhynchus Papyrus 2256 fr. 9(b)

281b

[*Remains of six lines including* I arranged *(4)*, I struck *(5)*, to be struck *(6)*.]

UNATTRIBUTED FRAGMENTS

UNATTRIBUTED FRAGMENTS

281c (198)

ἀλλ' ἱππάκης βρωτῆρες εὔνομοι Σκύθαι

Strabo 7.3.7; attributed to *Prometheus Unbound* by Schütz

282

κυρεῖν παρασχὼν ἰταμαῖς κυσὶν ἀεροφοίτοις

Aristophanes, *Frogs* 1291 with scholia, which wrongly attribute it to *Agamemnon*; attributed to *Memnon* by Bergk (cf. frr. 128, 129, 130), but many other attributions have been suggested

284

Βούράν θ' ἱερὰν καὶ Κερύνειαν,
Ῥύπας, Δύμην, Ἑλίκην, Αἴγιον
ἠδ' Αἴγειραν τήν τ' αἰπεινὴν
ζαθέαν Ὤλενον

Strabo 8.7.5 (from Δύμην to end is preserved in cod. V only); Stephanus of Byzantium, *Ethnica* p.707.13 Meineke (τὴν αἰπεινὴν ζαθέαν Ὤλενον)

1 Κερύνειαν Bölte: Κεραννίαν V: κεραννίας cett.
2 Αἴγιον Aly: Αιγειρον V   3 Αἴγειραν Wilamowitz:
Αγειραν Vᵖᶜ: Εγειραν Vᵃᶜ

281c (198)

But the law-abiding Scythians who feed on mares'-milk cheese[1] . . .

[1] Cf. fr. 197 and *Iliad* 13.5–6.

282

Leaving him/them[1] as prey to the brutal air-roaming hounds.

[1] Probably a dead warrior or warriors; the "hounds" are vultures or other carrion birds. The line is lyric, the metre identical to that of (e.g.) *Ag.* 108–9.

284

Sacred Bura and Ceryneia,
Rhypes, Dyme, Helice, Aegium,
and Aegeira and steep,
holy Olenus.

A catalogue of towns in Achaea.

UNATTRIBUTED FRAGMENTS

288

δέδοικα μῶρον κάρτα πυραύστου μόρον

Aelian, *On the Nature of Animals* 12.8; *Suda* π3194; Apostolius 18.18; Zenobius 5.79; attributed by Hermann to the satyr-play *Prometheus the Fire-Kindler*

289

βοᾷς τοιοῦδε πράγματος θέωρος ὤν

Ammonius, *On Differences between Related Words* 226

291

θρηνεῖ δὲ γόον τὸν ἀηδόνιον

Anecdota Bekkeri i 349.7; Photius α442

293

ἄκουε < –◡ > τὰς ἐμὰς ἐπιστολάς

Anecdota Bekkeri i 372.8; Photius α812

<τοίνυν> Blaydes; perh. <δὴ νῦν>.

297

πέπλοισι βαιοῖς καὶ μανοστήμοις ἰδεῖν

Lexicon Ambrosianum in cod. Ambrosianus B12 sup., folio 108r (s.v. μανώτερος); see N. Pace, *Acme* 54.i (2001) 185–8; the *Etymologica* (s.v. μανόν), Zonaras *Lexicon* 1332.4, and *Anecdota Oxoniensia* i 288.22, cite ἐν μανοστήμοις πέπλοις vel sim.

288

I fear I may suffer the very stupid death of a moth.[1]

[1] Which flies into flames; the line has been linked with fr. 207 where Prometheus warns a satyr against trying to kiss a flame.

289

You cry out, though only a spectator of such a deed.

291

(S)he laments like the wailing nightingale.[1]

[1] Cf. Aristophanes, *Frogs* 683. The metre here is anapaestic, but it is not clear whether the anapaests are chanted or (as in the Aristophanic passage) lyric.

293

Listen to my instructions.

297

In garments poor and threadbare to behold.

UNATTRIBUTED FRAGMENTS

298

ἐτονθόρυζε ταῦρος ὡς νεοσφαγής

Anecdota Oxoniensia ii 414.13

ἐτονθόρυζε Cramer: ἐτονθώρυζε cod.   ὡς Cramer: om. cod.

299

οὗτοι μ᾽ ἄπειρον τῆσδε τῆς προσῳδίας

Scholia to Dionysius Thrax (p.474.25–26 Hilgard)

301

ἀπάτης δικαίας οὐκ ἀποστατεῖ θεός

Double Arguments 3.12; scholia, and Eustathius, on *Iliad* 2.114

οὗτοι Dindorf, Hermann: οὗτι codd.

302

ψευδῶν δὲ καιρὸν ἔσθ᾽ ὅπου τιμᾷ θεός

Double Arguments 3.12

ὅπου Hermann, τιμᾷ de Varis: ὅποι τιμῆ (τημῆα Y1, τομη Y2) codd.

298
He gurgled like a bull that has just had its throat cut.

299
. . . me, experienced as I am in being appealed to in this way.

301
God does not reject deception in a just cause.

302
In some circumstances god respects an appropriate time for falsehood.

UNATTRIBUTED FRAGMENTS

303

μὴ παρασπιστὴς ἐμοὶ
μήτ᾽ ἐγγὺς εἴη

Aelius Aristides, *Oration* 3.607 (the full sentence is μὴ μὲν
οὖν ἔμοιγε κατ᾽ Αἰσχύλον μήτε [UR²: μή μοι O] παρασπιστὴς
μήτ᾽ ἐγγὺς εἴη ὅστις μὴ φίλος τῷ ἀνδρὶ τούτῳ μηδὲ τιμᾷ τὰ
πρέποντα: possibly Aristides has skipped over half a line after
εἴη—e.g. <δαΐαισιν ἐν μάχαις>—and the Aeschylean passage
then continued e.g. ὃς τἀνδρὶ τῷδε μή φίλος)

305

τὸ συγγενὲς γὰρ καὶ φθονεῖν ἐπίσταται

Aristotle, *Rhetoric* 1388a8, with an anonymous commentary
(*CAG* xxi.2 p.114.26–27)

307

σφύρας δέχεσθαι κἀπιχαλκεύειν μύδρος,
ὡς ἀστενακτὶ θύννος ὣς ἠνείχετο
ἄναυδος

Athenaeus 7.303c

1 μύδρος Dobree: μύδρους cod.   2 ἠνείχετο Hermann:
ἠνιχετο cod.   3 ἄναυδος Ald.: ἂν λυδός cod.

303

May he not carry a shield next to me, nor be close to me[1] . . .

[1] This metrical fragment is extracted from a sentence of Aristides' which reads in full: "On the contrary, may he not—in the words of Aeschylus—either carry a shield next to me or be close to me, *who is not a friend to this man* and does not honour what it is appropriate to honour." The italicized clause is somewhat poetic in expression (ἐστι "is" is omitted) and can easily be modified so as to be metrical; it cannot, however, have directly followed "be close to me" in Aeschylus' text, and Aristides may have passed over some words that did not suit his own purposes, e.g. δαΐαισιν ἐν μάχαις "in deadly battles". If the clause "who is not a friend to this man" does derive from Aeschylus, "this man" may have meant "me" as e.g. in *Ag.* 1438 (where it is "this woman") and Sophocles, *Oedipus the King* 534.

305

For kindred also knows how to envy.

307

He was like a lump of metal receiving hammer-blows as the smith works on it, so completely without a groan, like a voiceless tunny-fish, did he endure the battering.[1]

[1] See on *Pers.* 424–6.

UNATTRIBUTED FRAGMENTS

308

τὸ σκαιὸν ὄμμα παραβαλὼν θύννου δίκην

Plutarch, *Moralia* 979e; Athenaeus 7.303c; Aelian, *On the Nature of Animals* 9.42; Eustathius on *Iliad* 14.398 (last four words only); Apostolius 8.96; scholia to Oppian, *Halieutica* 4.504, 511 and 525

309

ἐγὼ δὲ χοῖρον καὶ μάλ᾽ εὐθηλούμενον
τόνδ᾽ ἐν νοτοῦντι κριβάνῳ θήσω. τί γὰρ
ὄψον γένοιτ᾽ ἂν ἀνδρὶ τοῦδε βέλτιον;

Athenaeus 9.375e

310

λευκός – τί δ᾽ οὐχί; – καὶ καλῶς ἠφευμένος
ὁ χοῖρος. ἕψου, μηδὲ λυπηθῇς πυρί

Athenaeus 9.375e

311

θύσας δὲ χοῖρον τόνδε τῆς αὐτῆς ὑός,
ἢ πολλά γ᾽ ἐν δόμοισιν εἴργασται κακά,
δονοῦσα καὶ τρέπουσα τύρβ᾽ ἄνω κάτω

Athenaeus 9.375e

308

Looking sideways with his left eye, like a tunny-fish.[1]

[1] The authors who quote this line (probably from a satyr-drama) all agree that tunnies had some abnormality or defect in their visual physiology, but not on what this was. Without their dubious aid, one would take the line to imply merely that the fish had the power to direct its eyes independently of one another; the gruesome process of killing them (see on *Pers.* 424–6) would give plenty of opportunity for observing this.

309

I am going to put this piglet—a very well suckled one— into a moistened pot. What could be a better dish for a man than that?[1]

[1] This and the next two fragments, which Athenaeus quotes together with it, are probably from the same scene (evidently of a satyr-drama). The speaker of this fragment (who seems to envisage eating the whole piglet himself) may well be the notoriously gluttonous Heracles, in which case this group of fragments would probably come from *Heralds* (so Droysen) or *The Lion.*

310

The piglet is white—it certainly is!—and well singed. [*Addressing the piglet in the pot*] Stew away, and don't let the fire make you sore!

311

And sacrificing this piglet, born of the same sow—a sow that's done a great deal of harm in the house, disturbing things and turning them over higgledy-piggledy.[1]

[1] And therefore is being justly punished by losing two of her offspring in one day?

UNATTRIBUTED FRAGMENTS

312

αἱ δ' ἔπτ' Ἄτλαντος παῖδες ὠνομασμέναι
πατρὸς μέγιστον ἆθλον οὐρανοστεγῆ
κλαίεσκον, ἔνθεν νυκτέρων φαντασμάτων
ἔχουσι μορφὰς ἄπτεροι Πελειάδες

Athenaeus 11.491a, citing Asclepiades of Myrlea; ascribed by
Butler and Hermann to *Daughters of the Sun*.

3 ἔνθεν van Herwerden: ἔνθα cod.

313

χλιδῶν τε πλόκαμος, ὥστε παρθένου γ' ἁβρᾶς·
ὅθεν καλεῖν Κουρῆτα λαὸν ᾔνεσαν

Athenaeus 12.528c, citing Phylarchus; cf. Eustathius on *Iliad*
23.141

1 παρθένου γ' ἁβρᾶς Sommerstein: παρθένου ἁβρᾶς
Athenaeus^CE, Eustathius: παρθένοις ἁβραῖς Athenaeus^A

312

And the seven maidens who bore the name of Atlas[1] wept for their father's great task[2] of upholding the roof of heaven; as a result of which they now have the form of things that appear in the night,[3] the wingless Doves.

[1] sc. as that of their father.   [2] Imposed on him as a punishment by Zeus; cf. *Prom.* 347–350 and Hesiod, *Theogony* 517–520.   [3] i.e. stars (the P[e]leiades, cf. πέλεια or πελειάς "dove"). It is possible that the mourning of the Atlantides/Pleiades for their father's humiliation is being compared to the mourning of the Daughters of the Sun for the death of their brother Phaëthon.

313

. . . and luxuriant hair, like that of a delicate maiden; whence they agreed to call the people Curetes.[1]

[1] The ethnonym Κουρῆτες, which in antiquity was etymologized in many different ways, is here taken to be derived from κούρη (Attic κόρη) "maiden". It was the name borne in the heroic age by the people of Pleuron in Aetolia, and is mentioned mainly in connection with Pleuron's neighbour Calydon, the hero Meleager, and the story of the Calydonian Boar (e.g. *Iliad* 9.529–599; Hesiod fr. 25.9–13; Bacchylides 5.124–6). If our fragment came from a play on this subject, that play is almost bound to have been *Atalanta* (q.v.)

314

εἴτ᾽ οὖν σοφιστὴς †καλὰ† παραπαίων χέλυν

Athenaeus 14.632c

καλὰ cod.: Ἰάδα Wilamowitz: σκαιὰ Ellis

315

τῷ πονοῦντι δ᾽ ἐκ θεῶν
ὀφείλεται τέκνωμα τοῦ πόνου κλέος

Clement of Alexandria, *Stromateis* 4.7.49.2; Arsenius 17.46e;
ascribed by West to *Prometheus Unbound*

316

ἀλλ᾽ ἔστι κἀμοὶ κλῂς ἐπὶ γλώσσῃ φύλαξ

Clement of Alexandria, *Stromateis* 5.5.27.6

317

οἴκοι μένειν χρὴ τὸν καλῶς εὐδαίμονα

Clement of Alexandria, *Stromateis* 6.2.7.6; Stobaeus 3.39.14
(attributed to Sophocles); Diogenianus 7.35 and Apostolius 12.45
(unattributed)

1 χρὴ Clement: δεῖ cett.   {2} Clement adds καὶ τὸν
κακῶς πράσσοντα, καὶ τοῦτον μένειν: del. Nauck (attributing it
to a comic poet satirizing the passage [*com. adesp.* 140 Kassel-
Austin])

---

1 Implying that anyone who has to travel abroad (like the
speaker?) is thereby shown not to be truly happy (cf. Euripides fr.
789a Kannicht, spoken by Odysseus when on a dangerous mission

314

. . . or whether, again, it is an expert player striking false
notes on the lyre[1] (?)

[1] lit. "tortoise-shell" (from which the lyre's sound-box was
made). Possible restorations of the corrupt text are "clumsily
striking false notes . . ." (Ellis) or ". . . on the Ionian lyre"
(Wilamowitz). The fragment is in any case likely to be satyric; the
speaker seems to be trying to identify a semi-musical noise that
has struck his/her ears.

315

To him who labours, the gods owe Glory, which is the offspring of Toil.

316

But I too have a key on my tongue to guard it.[1]

[1] Cf. *Ag.* 36–37.

317

He who is truly happy ought to stay at home.[1]

to Lemnos). The second line quoted by Clement appears to be a
satirical addition by a comic dramatist: a second character asks
"And what about someone who's *un*happy?" and the first replies
"He should stay at home as well!" It is impossible to tell whether
the first line is by Aeschylus (so Clement) or by Sophocles (so
Stobaeus; it is Sophocles fr. 934 in *TrGF*); they cannot both have
used it, otherwise Clement, who is discussing plagiarism by Greek
poets, would certainly have mentioned the fact. This line too has
sometimes been judged spurious, either the work of a comic dramatist or a late forger (most recently by A. Colonna, *Sileno* 17
[1991] 239–241); but it appears to have been parodied by Euripides (fr. 894, doubtless from a satyr-play: "he who is truly happy
eats other people's food").

UNATTRIBUTED FRAGMENTS

318

τοσαῦτα, κῆρυξ, ἐξ ἐμοῦ διάρτασον

Etymologicum Genuinum and *Etymologicum Magnum* s.v. ἄρταμος

διάρτασον *Et.Mag.*: διάρ . . . ον *Et.Gen.*[B]: διάρπασον *Et.Gen.*[A]

319

εἶτ᾽ οὖν ἀσαλὴς θεόθεν μανία

Etymologicum Genuinum (cod. A) and *Etymologicum Magnum* s.v. ἀσαλής (*Et.Mag.* gives only ἀσαλὴς μανία, as do *Anecdota Bekkeri* i 450.28, Photius α2941, and a second citation in *Et.Gen.* [codd. AB])

εἶτ᾽ οὖν Nauck: τουν *Et.Gen.*

322

<×–> κάπηλα προσφέρων τεχνήματα

Etymologicum Genuinum, *Etymologicum Gudianum*, *Etymologicum Magnum* s.v. κάπηλος; *Anecdota Oxoniensia* ii 456.6; *Suda* κ337

προσφέρων *Et.Gud.*[l]: προσφέρονται *Et.Gud.*[w], *Anecdota*: προσφέροντες *Et.Gud.*[z]: προφέρων cett.

327

πρὶν ἂν παλαγμοῖς αἵματος χοιροκτόνου
αὐτός σε χράνῃ Ζεὺς καταστάξας χεροῖν

Eustathius on *Iliad* 19.251; ascribed to *Ixion* by Pauw, to *The Perrhaebian Women* by Hermann

2 χράνῃ Porson: χράναι cod.

318

Report this much in detail, herald, from me.

319

. . . or, again, reckless madness sent by a god.[1]

[1] The metre is anapaestic.

322

. . . applying huckster-like trickery.

327

. . . until Zeus himself has purified you by the stain of a slaughtered young pig's blood,[1] sprinkling it on your hands.

Spoken to Ixion.

[1] Cf. *Eum.* 281–3, 448–452; and, on the purification of Ixion, *ibid.* 441, 717–8.

329

πότερα γυνή τις Αἰθίοψ φανήσεται;

Eustathius on *Odyssey* 4.84

330

λεοντόχορτον βούβαλιν νεαίρετον

Eustathius on *Odyssey* 9.222

λεοντόχορτον L. Dindorf, Bergk: λεοντοχόρταν codd.
νεαίρετον W. Dindorf: νεαίτερον codd.

332

ἔλα, δίωκε μή τι μαλκίων ποδί

Harpocration μ3

ἔλα, δίωκε μή τι Wagner: ἐλαδίω (AQ: ἐλλαδίῳ cett.)
κεκμῆτι codd.

332a

τὸ λαμπρὸν [.....] †δοθερμοναθ᾽ † ἥλιον
θάλποντα κἀκχέο[ν]τα βλάστιμον θέροϲ

Herodian, *General Prosody* fr. 15 Hunger

1 λαμπρον [.....] δοθερμοναθ᾽ cod.: λαμπρὸν [δ᾽ ὄμμα,]
θερμὸν G. M. Lee   2 βλάστημον cf. schol. *Seven* 12 and
Nicander, *Theriaca* 548: βλαστημὸν iHerodian θέρος Zuntz:
θορϙα (but θερϙϲ also possible) cod.

337

ἄπτηνα, τυτθόν, ἄρτι γυμνὸν ὀστράκων

Hesychius o1464

ἀπτῆνα, τυτθόν Scaliger: ἀπτὴν ἄτυτθον cod.

329

Is it an Ethiopian woman that's going to appear?

Probably from a satyr-drama.[1]

1 So Taplin, *Stagecraft* 423 n.1. The woman might perhaps be Circe (daughter of the Sun) or her niece Medea (in *The Nurses of Dionysus*; cf. Herodotus 2.104 on the alleged resemblance of Colchians to black Africans).

330

A newly-caught antelope[1] that would make a meal for a lion.

1 Since the βούβαλις was an African animal (Herodotus 4.192.1), this fragment is probably from a play set in Africa; perhaps therefore *Phorcides* (q.v.), whose scene was near the African lake Tritonis. Was Perseus required to sacrifice the antelope?

332

Drive on, pursue, don't let your feet get numb at all![1]

1 Or possibly "don't get cramp in your legs".

332a

The brilliant [. . .], the hot (?) sun, which spreads warmth and pours out heat that fosters growth.

337

Wingless, tiny, only just divested of the eggshell.

UNATTRIBUTED FRAGMENTS

339a
ἀκμὴν δ' ὅσα
τὰ κύμβαλ' ἠχεῖ

Lexicon Vaticanum 3 (p.4 Reitzenstein)

2 ἤχει Radt

342
δέσποινα νύμφη, δυσχίμων ὀρῶν ἄναξ

Orion, *Etymologicum* p.26.5–6 Sturz

δυσχίμων Schütz, ὀρῶν Sturz: δυσχείμων ὀρῶν cod.

348
ἄτεγκτος ἄνθρωπος παρηγορήμασιν

Phrynichus, *Praeparatio Sophistica* p.7.7 de Borries (om. ἄνθρωπος); Photius α3064 (om. παρηγορήμασιν); *Anecdota Bekkeri* i 458.18; Suda α4329; Apostolius 4.16; only Phrynichus ascribes the phrase to Aeschylus

350

ΘΕΤΙΣ
< ὁ δ' > ἐνδατεῖται τὰς ἐμὰς εὐπαιδίας

Plato, *Republic* 383b (τοῦτο οὐκ ἐπαινεσόμεθα . . . Αἰσχύλου, ὅταν φῇ ἡ Θέτις τὸν Ἀπόλλω ἐν τοῖς αὐτῆς γάμοις ᾄδοντα ἐνδατεῖσθαι τὰς ἑὰς εὐπαιδίας κτλ.); Eusebius, *Praeparatio Evangelica* 13.3.35; Athenagoras, *For the Christians* 21.6 (lines 5–9); Plutarch, *Moralia* 16e (lines 7–8); Phoebammon, On Figures of Speech 2.4 (lines 7–8); ascribed to *The Weighing of Souls* by Stanley, to *The Award of the Arms* by Lachmann

339a

And all the cymbals that are even now resounding[1] . . . .

[1] Or (with the accentuation ἤχει) "that were resounding just now". Perhaps from *Edonians* (cf. fr. 57), or another Dionysiac play such as *Wool-Carders* or *Pentheus*.

342

My lady nymph, queen of the wintry mountains . . .

348

A man who cannot be softened by persuasion.

350

THETIS

⟨And⟩ he[1] dwelt on the excellent offspring I would have,[2]

[1] Apollo, "singing at her wedding [to Peleus, which all the gods attended]" (Plato). [2] Achilles. Apollo spoke truly when he said that Achilles would never experience sickness, and Thetis may later have discovered that the other part of his prophecy was also true, if Aeschylus adopted the version of the myth according to which Achilles was granted immortality (cf. Euripides, *Andromache* 1259–61)—or she may even have made it come true herself (according to the cyclic epic, the *Aethiopis* [Arg. §4 West], she snatched her son from his funeral pyre and conveyed him to the "White Island"). Apollo's words were, however, extremely misleading by omission and ambiguity: apart from the failure to refer to Achilles' early death, one may note that εὐπαιδία, especially in the plural, would hardly suggest a one-child family.

---

1 ⟨ὁ δ'⟩ ἐνδατεῖται Hermann, τὰς ἐμὰς Grotius: ἐνδατεῖσθαι (ἐνδυντ- codd. Aᵃᶜ M D² of Plato, ἐνδαιτ- Eusebius) τὰς ἑὰς Plato, Eusebius

νόσων τ' ἀπείρους καὶ μακραίωνας βίου,
ξύμπαντά τ' εἰπὼν θεοφιλεῖς ἐμὰς τύχας
παιών' ἐπηυφήμησεν, εὐθυμῶν ἐμέ.
5 κἀγὼ τὸ Φοίβου θεῖον ἤλπιζον στόμα
ἀψευδὲς εἶναι, μαντικῇ βρύον τέχνῃ·
ὁ δ' αὐτὸς ὑμνῶν, αὐτὸς ἐν θοίνῃ παρών,
αὐτὸς τάδ' εἰπών, αὐτός ἐστιν ὁ κτανὼν
τὸν παῖδα τὸν ἐμόν

2 μακραίωνας βίου Stephanus: μακραίωνας βίους Plato: μα-
κραίωνος βίου Eusebius   5–6 ἤλπιζον . . . ἀψευδὲς
Degani: ἀψευδὲς . . . ἤλπιζον codd.

352
θάρσει· πόνου γὰρ ἄκρον οὐκ ἔχει χρόνον

Plutarch, Moralia 36b

353
ὡς οὐ δικαίως θάνατον ἔχθουσιν βροτοί,
ὅσπερ μέγιστον ῥῦμα τῶν πολλῶν κακῶν

[Plutarch], Moralia 106c

which would have length of life and never know sickness, and after completing these words he struck up a holy paean-song about my good fortune in being loved by the gods, which delighted my heart. And I supposed that the divine voice of Phoebus, pregnant with prophetic skill, was incapable of falsehood. But he who himself sang that song, who himself attended that feast, who himself spoke those words, he himself it is who has killed my son![3]

[3] Achilles was killed by "Paris and Phoebus Apollo . . . at the Scaean Gate" (*Iliad* 22.359–360, cf. *Aethiopis* Arg. §3 West), and this would most naturally be taken to mean that he was killed by Paris' arrow which Apollo directed to its mark (first made explicit by Virgil, *Aeneid* 6.56–58); but in Pindar (*Paean* 6.75–86) Apollo himself is said to have taken the shape of Paris to do the deed. Thetis' words could fit either version.

352

Take courage! Suffering, when it reaches its peak, does not stay there long.[1]

[1] lit. "the peak of suffering does not have ‹extension in› time".

353

For mortals are wrong to hate death; it is the greatest defence against life's many ills.

UNATTRIBUTED FRAGMENTS

353a

βριθὺς ὁπλιτοπάλας, δάιος ἀντιπάλοισι

Plutarch, *Moralia* 317e, 334d; *ib.* 640a (first two words only); Plutarch, *Comparison of Demosthenes and Cicero* 2.1; Eustathius on *Iliad* 5.2

ἀντιπάλοισι Plut. 334d: ἀντιπάλοις Plut. *Comp.*:[1] in Plut. 317e codd. are divided (and the majority omit the fragment entirely): ἀντιμάχοισι Eustathius

[1] This reading would make the fragment an elegiac pentameter (which would lead us to ascribe it to an epigram rather than to a drama); the reading adopted here (cf. Fraenkel, *Agamemnon* iii 830, who points especially to the non-Ionic form of ὁπλιτοπάλας) makes it a lyric verse of similar form to *Eum.* 963–4.

354

ἀποπτύσαι δεῖ καὶ καθήρασθαι στόμα

Plutarch, *Moralia* 358e

στόμα Stanley: τὸ στόμα codd.

355

μειξοβόαν πρέπει
διθύραμβον ὁμαρτεῖν
σύγκωμον Διονύσῳ

Plutarch, *Moralia* 389a-b; ascribed by Hermann to *The Youths*

3 σύγκωμον Tyrwhitt: σύγκοινον (σύγκονον A, σύγγονον E) codd.

353a

A formidable wielder of hoplite arms, deadly to his adversaries.

354

One must spit and so purify one's mouth.[1]

[1] The context in Plutarch is that reference has just been made to gruesome tales about the gods ("the dismemberment of Horus and the decapitation of Isis") which are presented as blasphemous and false; the context in Aeschylus may for all we know have been entirely different. For "spitting as a form of apotropaic magic" see Hunter on Theocritus 6.39; related is the practice, mentioned in *Laius* (fr. 122a) and *Perrhaebian Women* (fr. 186a), of tasting and spitting out the blood of a person one has murdered.

355

It is proper that the dithyramb,
song mingled with shout, should attend
upon Dionysus as his fellow-reveller.

Part of a choral song, in aeolic metre.

356

λαβὼν γὰρ αὐτόθηκτον Εὐβοικὸν ξίφος

Plutarch, *Moralia* 434a

357

ὑψηλὸν ἡβήσασα τεκτόνων πόνον

Plutarch, *Moralia* 454e (speaking of a fire [φλόξ]); the next word may have been ἔφθειρε (ταχὺ διέφθειρε καὶ συνεῖλεν Plutarch)

358

†οὐδὲ† ἄπω[θεν] αὐτόν· οὐ γὰρ ἐγγύθεν
[× –]· γέρων δὲ γραμματεὺς γενοῦ σαφής

Plutarch, *Moralia* 625d

1 οὐδὲ cod.: σὺ δέξ' Radt: δέχου δ' Kamerbeek   ἄπω[θεν] Dindorf: ἀπὸ [. . .] cod.   2 [. . . . . .] cod.: [βαλεῖς] Radt: [τεύξῃ] Degani: [γνώσῃ] Mette

359

σύ τοι μ' ἔφυσας, σύ με †καταίθειν† δοκεῖς

Plutarch, *Demetrius* 35.4 (i) and *Moralia* 827c (ii)

μ' ἔφυσας codd. K L¹ R¹ of (i), cod. U¹ of (ii): με φυσᾷς cett. καταίθειν (μοι add. codd. K L² R of (i)) codd.: καταίθειν αὖ Mette: καταιθαλοῦν Conington: καταφθίσειν Dindorf: καθαιρήσειν Salmasius

---

¹ Or "and now you think you will".   ² Not his/her mother (otherwise we would have had ἔτικτες, not ἔφυσας); so the attributions to Pentheus in *Wool-Carders* (Stanley) or Meleager in

356

For, taking a self-sharpened[1] Euboean sword . . .

[1] It is not clear what this adjective (αὐτόθηκτον) is meant to signify, but none of the many proposed emendations is convincing. Possibly the point is that Euboean bronze swords (made from a celebrated local ore, a mention of which gives Plutarch occasion to cite this line) were of such high quality that they hardly ever needed sharpening.

357

⟨The fire,⟩ gaining full vigour, ⟨destroyed (?)⟩ the lofty product of builders' toil.

358

Face (?) him at a distance, because at close range you won't [hit (?)] him; be like a man who reads clearly in old age.[1]

Apparently advice to a warrior about to enter single combat with an opponent who is deadly at close quarters.

[1] Alluding to the already well-known tendency (presbyopia) of close-up vision, especially for reading, to deteriorate with advancing age (cf. Sophocles fr. 858).

359

It was you who begot me, and now it looks as though you will[1] destroy (?) me.

Spoken by a character who sees him/herself as betrayed by his/her own father.[2]

Atalanta (Bothe) are wrong. The speaker is more likely to be Iphigeneia in her name-play, or Teucer speaking to Telamon in *Women of Salamis*, or a son of Zeus (e.g. Tantalus in *Niobe*—suggested by Hartung, though he took Tantalus to be addressing Τύχη as, according to Plutarch, Demetrius Poliorcetes did when he quoted this line at a low point in his fortunes).

UNATTRIBUTED FRAGMENTS

361

ἐξ ὀσφυαλγοῦς κωδυνοσπάδος λυγροῦ
γέροντος

Plutarch, *Moralia* 1057f (speaking of rejuvenation); ascribed
by Hartung to *The Nurses of Dionysus*

362

ἀλλ᾽ οὔτε πολλὰ τραύματ᾽ ἐν στέρνοις λαβὼν
θνῄσκει τις, εἰ μὴ τέρμα συντρέχοι βίου,
οὔτ᾽ ἐν στέγῃ τις ἥμενος παρ᾽ ἑστίᾳ
φεύγει τι μᾶλλον τὸν πεπρωμένον μόρον

Pseudo-Plutarch, *On Homer II* 157

363

ὀξυγλύκειάν τἄρα κοκκιεῖς ῥόαν

Pollux 6.80

361

From a wretched old man with a sore back, racked by pain
. . .

*Perhaps Medea describing her rejuvenation of Jason's father
Aeson?*[1]

[1] Cf. *The Returns* fr. 6 West; Hartung thought rather of Pelias,
who, however, was not rejuvenated by Medea but, through her
deception, murdered by his daughters.

362

But a man will not die, even though he has been wounded
repeatedly in the chest, should the appointed end of his
life not have caught up with him; nor can one who sits beside his hearth at home escape his destined death any the
more.[1]

[1] Cf. Euripides fr. 10; Demosthenes 18.97.

363

Then you'll be stoning a pomegranate that's not fully ripe.[1]

[1] i.e., probably, deflowering an immature girl (cf. Aristophanes, *Acharnians* 275); the line evidently comes from a satyr-play.
It is quoted by Pollux not from Aeschylus but from Aristophanes
(fr. 623); he says, however, that "Aristophanes used this iambic
line not as one of his own, but as one of Aeschylus", i.e., presumably, he introduced it with κατὰ τὸν Αἰσχύλον or the like (cf.
Birds 807–8).

UNATTRIBUTED FRAGMENTS

364

Λιβυρνικῆς μίμημα μανδύης χιτών

Pollux 7.60; ascribed by Hartung to *The Edonians*

365

σὺ δὲ σπαθητοῖς τριμιτίνοις ὑφάσμασιν

Pollux 7.78 (cf. 7.36)

σὺ δὲ A: οὐδὲ F S

366

λοῦταί γε μὲν δὴ λουτρὸν οὐ τὸ δεύτερον,
ἀλλ᾽ ἐκ μεγίστων εὐμαρῶς λουτήριον

Pollux 7.167

2 λουτήριον A: λουτηρίων F S

372

ἀφρὸς
βορᾶς βροτείας ἐρρύη κατὰ στόμα

Scholia to Aristophanes, *Lysistrata* 1257; ascribed to *Glaucus of Potniae* by Kausche and Hartung (but *Archeresses* is another possibility)

2 ἐρρύη κατὰ Porson: ἐρρυηκότα cod.

364

A tunic that resembles a Liburnian *mandye*.[1]

[1] This is the earliest reference to a garment of this name. The only other appearances of the word, before Roman times, are in the Septuagint (*Judges* 3.16; *1 Kings* [= *1 Samuel*] 17.38, 39; *2 Kings* [= *2 Samuel*] 10.4, 20.8) where it denotes the robe of a king, prince, or general. The Liburnians were a people of the north-east Adriatic coast (the later Dalmatia). The line may be part of a description of the garb of Dionysus or his followers (cf. fr. 59).

365

But you ⟨are dressed (?)⟩ in closely-woven, triple-threaded garments.

366

But anyway, he is being bathed in no second-class bath, but in a bath that's easily one of the biggest.

Clearly from a satyr-drama.

372

Foam from their human food flowed over their jaws.

Describing either the horses of Glaucus, or the hounds of Actaeon, when they devoured their master.

373

δεινοὶ πλέκειν τοι μηχανὰς Αἰγύπτιοι

Scholia to Theocritus 15.48 (the only source to name Aeschylus as author); Stephanus of Byzantium, *Ethnica* p.44.15–16 Meineke; Herodian, *On Derivatives* p.877.3–4 Lentz; Photius δ126; *Suda* δ352; Diogenianus 4.35, and many other collections of proverbs; Eustathius on *Odyssey* 4.231; Eustathius, *Commentary on Dionysius Periegetes* 232; ascribed to *Danaids* by Hermann (but *Proteus* is another possibility)

τοι most sources: τὰς Photius: many of the paroemiographers omit τοι or substitute γε or δὲ

374

ἥνικ' ἔκειρ' ἀνθεα λειμώνια

Scholia to Aristophanes, *Clouds* 1364

ἥνίκ' Holwerda: οὕνεκ' codd.   ἔκειρ' Degani (ἔκειραν Holwerda): ἐκεῖ (ἔχει R) codd.

[375 = *Cho.* 983a]

379

ὑμεῖς δὲ βωμὸν τόνδε καὶ πυρὸς σέλας
κύκλῳ περίστητ' ἐν λόχῳ τ' ἀπείρονι
εὔξασθε

Scholia to *Iliad* 14.200 and *Odyssey* 1.98 (indicating that the addressees are female)

373

Egyptians, you know, are clever at weaving crafty schemes.

374

When she[1] was plucking flowers in the meadows . . .

From a choral song; the metre is choriambic.

[1] Persephone? The quotation bears, on the face of it, no relation to the Aristophanic passage in illustration of which it is cited by the scholiast, in which a father asks his son to recite a passage of Aeschylus holding a myrtle-branch in his hand. Presumably the scholium has been garbled by abbreviation; for an attempt at reconstructing it, see D. Holwerda, *Mnemosyne* 21 (1968) 71–72.

[375 = *Libation-Bearers* 983a]

379

But do you, please, stand all round this altar and its blazing fire, form an endless[1] band, and pray.

Addressed to a chorus of women.

[1] i.e. circular.

381

ὅπου γὰρ ἰσχὺς συζυγοῦσι καὶ δίκη,
ποία ξυνωρὶς τῶνδε καρτερωτέρα;

Scholia to *Iliad* 16.542

382

πάτερ Θέοινε, μαινάδων ζευκτήριε

Scholia to Lycophron, *Alexandra* 1247; Tzetzes on same passage; cf. Harpocration θ7

383

Ἥρα τελεία, Ζηνὸς εὐναία δάμαρ

Scholia to Pindar, *Nemean* 10.[17] 31

384

ἐναγώνιε Μαίας καὶ Διὸς Ἑρμᾶ

Scholia to Pindar, *Pythian* 2.[10] 18

385

οἵ τοι στεναγμοὶ τῶν πόνων ῥαΐσματα

Scholia to Sophocles, *Electra* 286 and to *Iliad* 23.10

οἵ τοι Σ *Il.*: οἵ τε (L), οἱ δὲ (GRM), οἱ γὰρ (S) Σ Soph.
ῥαΐσματα M. Schmidt (cf. explanation in Σ Soph., ἐπικουφίζεται
τοῖς δακρύοις ἡ συμφορά): ἐρίσματα (Lᵃᶜ), ἐρείσματα (Lᵖᶜ
cett.) Σ Soph.: ἰάματα Σ *Il.*

381

For where might and right are yoked together, what team can be stronger than they?

382

Father Theoenus[1] who unites the maenad band![2]

[1] A title of Dionysus.   [2] lit. "yoker of the maenads".

383

Hera, goddess of marriage, wife and bedfellow of Zeus.

384

Hermes, god of competitions,[1] son of Maia and Zeus!

From a choral song; the metre is probably dactylic.

[1] A regular title of Hermes: cf. *Cho.* 729; Simonides *PMG* 555.1; Pindar, *Olympian* 6.79, *Pythian* 2.10, *Isthmian* 1.60; *IG* i³ 5.3; Aristophanes, *Wealth* 1161–3.

385

Sighing and groaning, you know, give relief from suffering.

386

λαμπραῖσιν ἀστραπαῖσι, λαμπάδων σθένει

Scholia to Sophocles, *Oedipus at Colonus* 1048 (which say that Aeschylus was speaking of "the mystic flame and the sacred torches" at Eleusis); ascribed to *The Eleusinians* by Pauw

λαμπάδων codd.: καὶ δᾴδων Burges

387

ἔφριξ' ἔρωτι τοῦδε μυστικοῦ τέλους

Scholia to Sophocles, *Oedipus at Colonus* 1049; ascribed to *The Eleusinians* by Pauw

ἔρωτι Brunck (cf. Sophocles, *Ajax* 693): ἔρως δὲ cod.: ἐρῶ δὲ Dindorf

387a

ἐπῆμεν τῆς ὁδοῦ τροχήλατον
σχιστῆς κελεύθου τρίοδον, ἔνθα συμβολὰς
τριῶν κελεύθων Ποτνιάδας ἠμείβομεν

Scholia to Sophocles, *Oedipus the King* 733 (discussing the location, in Aeschylus' treatment, of the road-junction where Oedipus met and killed Laius); ascribed to *Oedipus* by Valckenaer, to *Laius* (tentatively) by Schneidewin, (firmly) by Hartung

1 ἐπῆμεν Scaliger: επειημεν L: ἐπήειμεν cett.   2 ἔνθα LGM: om. R: perh. εἶτα?   3 Ποτνιάδας Bruhn: ποτνιάδων codd.

UNATTRIBUTED FRAGMENTS

386

With brilliant lightning-flashes, with the power of torches.

Describing the celebration of the Mysteries at Eleusis.

387

I shudder with passionate delight at this mystic rite.

Again cited by the scholiast in connection with a Sophoclean passage about Eleusis.[1]

[1] This, or at least the context from which it comes, may well have been one of the passages which gave rise to the story (Aristotle, *Nicomachean Ethics* 1111a8–10, with the anonymous commentary in *CAG* xx 145.23–146.3) that Aeschylus had been accused of divulging secrets of the Mysteries in his plays. The commentator names five plays—*Archeresses, Priestesses, Sisyphus the Stone-Roller, Iphigeneia,* and *Oedipus*—none of which is otherwise known to have had any Eleusinian connection; without that information, or misinformation, one would certainly have thought rather of *Eleusinians* or *Cercyon,* the only plays known to have been set at Eleusis.

387a

On our journey we were approaching the junction of three wagon-tracks where the road forks, where[1] we were passing the meeting of the three ways at Potniae.[2]

From an account by a survivor of Laius' last journey.

[1] Or perhaps "and then".   [2] A town just south of Thebes (see introductory note to *Glaucus of Potniae*): wherever Laius was going, it was not Delphi, his destination in Sophocles.

UNATTRIBUTED FRAGMENTS

388

ΧΟΡΟΣ

δέσποιν' Ἑκάτη,
τῶν βασιλείων πρόδομος μελάθρων

Scholia to Theocritus 2.35–36; Aelius Aristeides, *Oration*
37.29 (line 2 only)

2 πρόδομος cod. Bodleianus Canonicianus gr. 86 of Σ
Theocr.: πρόδρομος Σ Theocr.[cett.], Aristeides

389

κοινὸν τύχη, γνώμη δὲ τῶν κεκτημένων

Stobaeus 2.8.10; authenticity doubted by Sidgwick

390

ὁ χρήσιμ' εἰδώς, οὐχ ὁ πόλλ' εἰδὼς σοφός

Stobaeus 3.3.11; Apostolius 13.82a = Arsenius, *Garden of Violets* p.400.1 Walz (not naming the author); authenticity doubted
by Hartung

391

ἁμαρτάνει τοι χὠ σοφοῦ σοφώτερος

Stobaeus 3.3.14; authenticity doubted by Hartung

χὠ Crusius: καὶ codd.

392

ἦ βαρὺ φόρημ' ἄνθρωπος εὐτυχῶν ἄφρων

Stobaeus 3.4.18; Apostolius 8.41d = Arsenius, *Garden of Violets* p.271.12 Walz (not naming the author)

388
CHORUS

Lady Hecate,
you who dwell in front of the royal palace[1] . . .

[1] Shrines of Hecate were frequently placed outside house doors: cf. Aristophanes, *Wasps* 804, and Theopompus, *FGrH* 115 F 344. That the chorus can address Hecate at such a shrine shows that this passage (in chanted anapaests) is from a latish play, produced after the *skene* came into use.

389

Good luck can belong to anyone, but good judgement belongs to those who possess it.

390

The wise man is not he who has much knowledge, but he who has useful knowledge.

391

Even one who is wiser than wise, you know, can make mistakes.

392

A foolish man enjoying good fortune is a hard thing to bear.[1]

[1] Cf. fr. 398 and *Prom.* 979 (with 977).

UNATTRIBUTED FRAGMENTS

393

κάτοπτρον εἴδους χαλκός ἐστ᾽, οἶνος δὲ νοῦ

Stobaeus 3.18.12; Apostolius 9.59c = Arsenius, *Garden of Violets* p.317.17 Walz (attributing the line to Euripides); Maximus Confessor, *Serm.* 30 Combefis (attributing it to Aeschines [!]); Athenaeus 10.427f (apparently crediting the saying to Pittacus of Mytilene [ca. 600 BC]); authenticity doubted by Kaibel and Wilamowitz

394

οὐκ ἀνδρὸς ὅρκοι πίστις, ἀλλ᾽ ὅρκων ἀνήρ

Stobaeus 3.27.2; Apostolius 13.21a (who, misled by a corrupt text of Stobaeus, attributes the line to the comic poet Alexis)

395

φιλεῖ δέ τοι,
δαιμόνιε, τῷ κάμνοντι συσπεύδειν θεός

Stobaeus 3.29.21; Apostolius 17.86c (attributing the line to Euripides, again owing to a corruption in his text of Stobaeus)

1–2 τοι δαιμόνιε StobaeusM: om. Stobaeuscett., Apostolius

396

καλὸν δὲ καὶ γέροντι μανθάνειν σοφά

Stobaeus 3.29.24; [Menander], *Monosticha* 416

γέροντι [Menander]: γέροντα Stobaeus

397

πρὸ τῶν τοιούτων χρὴ λόγων δάκνειν στόμα

Stobaeus 3.34.5

393

Bronze makes a mirror for the face, wine for the mind.

394

Oaths do not give credibility to men, but men to oaths.[1]

[1] i.e. one cannot know whether a sworn assertion or promise is worthy of belief unless one knows the character of the person who has made it.

395

You know, my good fellow, when a man strives hard, a god tends to lend him aid.[1]

[1] If this longer form of the text is correct (see textual note), the fragment will have come from a satyr-drama, since the address-form δαιμόνιε is not found in tragedy.

396

It is good, even in old age, to enlarge one's understanding.[1]

[1] Cf. *Ag.* 584.

397

One should bite one's lips before uttering words like those.

UNATTRIBUTED FRAGMENTS

398

κακοὶ γὰρ εὖ πράσσοντες οὐκ ἀνασχετοί

Stobaeus 4.4.14

399

τὸ γὰρ βρότειον σπέρμ᾽ ἐφημέρια φρονεῖ,
καὶ πιστὸν οὐδὲν μᾶλλον ἢ καπνοῦ σκιά

Stobaeus 4.34.44; Apostolius 16.98

1 ἐφημέρια Stobaeus[S], Apostolius (cf. *Odyssey* 21.85): ἐφήμερα Stobaeus[MA]

400

γῆρας γὰρ ἥβης ἐστὶν ἐνδικώτερον

Stobaeus 4.50.7

402

<× -> , ἀφ᾽ οὗ δὴ Ῥήγιον κικλήσκεται

Strabo 6.1.6 (after paraphrasing what preceded this in Aeschylus' text: ἀπορραγῆναι . . . ἀπὸ τῆς ἠπείρου τὴν Σικελίαν ὑπὸ σεισμῶν . . . εἴρηκεν); ascribed to *Prometheus Unbound* by Schütz (cf. [Apollodorus], *Library* 2.5.10), to *Glaucus the Sea-god* by Hermann (comparing fr. 40a—which its source, Hesychius, actually cites from *Glaucus of Potniae*!)

κικλήσκεται codd.: κεκλήσεται Thomson

402a

Κύπρου Πάφου τ᾽ ἔχουσα πάντα κλῆρον

Strabo 8.3.8; Eustathius on *Iliad* 2.615

398

Base men enjoying prosperity are unendurable.[1]

[1] Cf. fr. 392.

399

For the race of mortals has thought only for the day, and is no more to be relied on than the shadow of smoke.[1]

[1] For the idiom "the shadow of smoke" (= "something utterly insubstantial") cf. Sophocles, *Antigone* 1170–1, *Philoctetes* 946–7.

400

For old age respects justice more than youth does.

402

... whence it is called Rhegium.[1]

[1] Rhegium (Reggio di Calabria) was said to have been so named after Sicily *broke off* (ἀπορραγῆναι or ἀπορρήγνυσθαι) from the mainland as a result of earthquakes. Since the god responsible for earthquakes was Poseidon, it is very tempting to ascribe this fragment to *Glaucus of Potniae*, in which Poseidon is likely to have been prominent and there were probably at least two other references to the western Greek lands (frr. 25a, 40a); see Introduction to *Persians* (vol. 1) and my forthcoming article cited on p. 23.

402a

You who possess the whole domain of Cyprus and Paphos.

Addressed to Aphrodite; probably from a choral song.[1]

[1] For the metre (a catalectic iambic trimeter) cf. e.g. *Ag.* 369 = 387.

PROBABLY AESCHYLEAN
PAPYRUS FRAGMENTS

The great majority of surviving Aeschylean papyri were written in the second century AD by one single scribe; many of these have been printed above under the plays to which they belong, but there are a considerable number of other fragments in the same hand (frr. 451c–m Radt) whose style either points to or at any rate does not exclude an attribution to Aeschylus, but which cannot be confidently associated with a specific play. There also survive many further fragments (frr. 451n–s Radt), likewise Aeschylean in style so far as can be judged, in the hand of the scribe who wrote the fragments of the "Dike play" (frr. 281a–b), and one or two in other hands (frr. 451t–u Radt) which are generally ascribed to Aeschylus on reasonable grounds.

Two of these fragments (frr. 451l and 451k Radt) have been ascribed in this edition to specific plays; they appear above as frr. 78a (from Chamber-Makers*) and 180a (from* Palamedes*) respectively. Three more (frr. 451h, 451n and 451q), which meet the criteria for inclusion in this edition (preservation of one complete line or two connected half-lines), are printed below.*

Of most of the remainder there is little that can be said with assurance. Fr. 451c comprises 37 lines, most if not all of them lyric, whose content appears to have to do largely with warfare; at the end (33–37) it seems to be predicted that someone who may or may not be described as courageous will flee on horseback from an attack and (but?) that a for[eign] soil will receive him. Fr. 451e refers to someone or something Asian *and several times to musical and other sounds; it may well therefore come from a play with strong Dionysiac connections, such as one from the Lycurgus or the Semele/Pentheus tetralogies. Fr. 451f, which probably contains the end of one speech and the beginning of another, mentions a* bed *or sexual relationship (14) and, just previously, that* Hera . . . has come *(12–13); it is very tempting to associate this with frr. 220a–c and ascribe the fragment to Semele. In fr. 451g a chorus greets a king, beginning with the same words that are used by the Argive elders when they greet Agamemnon (Ag. 783). Fr. 451m consists of nearly forty scraps, which are unlikely all to come from the same play; one of them mentions* Peleus *(1.7), but we do not know in what connection. Fr. 451o twice mentions* the people of Tenedos *(53.3 and 7), and a character asks* how is this friendly to (or approved by) the [Ar]gives?; *the only known story which this fits is that of the sacking of Tenedos, and the killing of its king Tennes, by the Greek expedition on its way to Troy, a story which is told only in later sources (e.g.* [Apollodorus], Epitome *3.23–26) but which was the subject of a fifth-century play variously ascribed to Euripides and to Critias; this papyrus has thus been taken by Mette and others as evidence for an other-*

wise unattested Tennes *of Aeschylus. Fr. 451s consists of more than seventy small pieces of papyrus, again probably belonging to several different plays; one (55) has been thought to coincide with a book-fragment of* Myrmidons *(see on fr. 136).*

451h

ΧΟΡΟΣ

χειρ.[

ἰδὲ γάρ, ὦ Ζ[εῦ] ξέ[νιε] ν[. .] . [

τ]ὸν ξενοδόκον κατασκ[

. . .]ςτιν χάρις ἐν θ[εο]ῖς

5   ἀν]δρ[ά]ςι τοῖς δικαίοις(;)

        τοίγαρ κ[ατα]πρίςςομ[

        κόμας [ἀ]φειδεῖ χερ[

        τόδ' ἄνα[υ]λον βρέγμαπ . [. .] . [

        δυρομ[έν]α ςὸν πότμον γό[οιςιν.]

[*Remains of four more lines—vertically aligned with lines 2–5—followed by a horizontal stroke (παράγραφος).*]

Oxyrhynchus Papyrus 2251

3 κατασκ[αφέντα] Snell   4 ἆρ' ἐ]στιν Page
5 suppl. Webster   6 καταπρισσομ[ένα] Snell
7 χερ[ὶ] Snell: χερ[ῶν ἀκμᾷ] e.g. Radt   8 βρέγμα πα[τάσ-
σω] Snell: βρέγμα πλ[ήσσω] Bindzus   9 γό[οισιν] Snell

---

1 Or "fingers", if χερ[ῶν ἀκμᾷ] or the like is to be restored.
2 lit. "without pipe-music", i.e. "without rejoicing, with nothing to be happy about".

451h

CHORUS

hand [. . .]
See this, Z[eus god of] hos[pitality . . .]
the hospitable [house (?)] overt[hrown]!
Is [there any] favour from the g[o]ds
for righteous [m]e[n]?
This is why, tear[ing]
my hair with merciless hands,[1]
[I beat (?)] this miserable[2] skull of mine,
griev[in]g over your fate with lament[s].
[*Remains of four more lines.*]

A chorus of women lament the ruin of a man who had been noted for his hospitality and justice, and had apparently suffered as a result of these qualities. (It is clear that at least one death has occurred, but we cannot tell whether the victim is the hospitable man himself, or one or more members of his family, or both.) Perhaps the play was Cretan Women, *and the hospitable man was Minos who had lost his young son Glaucus (on Minos' reputation for justice, cf.* Odyssey *11.568–571 and Plato,* Apology *41a). Polyidus, the seer who discovered Glaucus' body and later restored him to life, was a stranger in Crete (he was a Corinthian: see* Iliad *13.663 and Pindar,* Olympian *13.74–75), and in the play he may well have arrived there only shortly before the disappearance of Glaucus—and been blamed for it, and then for the boy's death. Such a scenario would help to explain Minos' demand—which looks as though it were designed to be an impossible one—that he should bring Glaucus back to life (or else forfeit his own?)*

451n

]. ϲ ... ` ννῦϲα μὴ ϲπείρειν κακ[
]ντ.ʹτʹ ἐϲτιν εἰρήνη βροτοῖϲ
]. αἰνω τήνδε· τι[μ]ᾷ γὰρ πόλιν
ἐν ἡϲύ[χοιϲ]ι πράγμαϲιν καθημένην,
5 δόμων τ᾽ ἀέξει κάλλοϲ ἐκπαγλού[μ]ενον
ἅ]μιλλαν ὥϲτε γειτόνων ὄλβῳ κρατεῖν·
οἱ] δ᾽ αὖ φυτεύειν, οἱ δ[ὲ] γῆϲ ἐπεμβολὰϲ
θυ]μῷ λέληνται, δαΐαϲ πεπαυμέ[νοι
ϲάλ]πιγγοϲ, οὐδὲ φρουρίων ἐξ ...´ [.] . [
[*Remains of two further lines.*]

Oxyrhynchus Papyrus 2256 fr. 8

1 κακ[ά] Lobel   3 [θεὸν δ᾽ ἐ]παινῶ Lloyd-Jones:
[μάλιϲτ᾽ ἐ]παινῶ Vysoký   5 ἐκπαγλού[μ]ενον Π:
ἐκπαγλουμένη Lloyd-Jones   7 [οἱ] Radt   οιδ[Πpc: ηδ[
Πac   επεμβολαϲ Πac: ἐπεμπολαϲ Πpc   8, 9 suppl. Lobel

451q

ΧΟΡΟΣ

[*Remains of five lines*]
ϲτρ. τὸν δὴ περιρρυ[τ] .. [
7   ὤλ[εϲ]αν ῥυϲίπτολ[ιν
π[οι]μανδρίδαι [

Oxyrhynchus Papyrus 2256 fr. 71; supplements by Lobel unless
otherwise stated

6 περιρρύ[τ]αϲ [χθονὸϲ ϲτραταγὸν] e.g. Lloyd-Jones

451n

. . . not to disseminate evils (?). It is Peace who [. . .] to mortals. I praise (?) her [greatly (?)]; for she hon[ou]rs a city that sits at rest in a state of quie[tud]e, and increases the splendour of its houses, which is magnified so that they surpass their neighbours and [r]ivals in prosperity; and then [some] desire in [their hearts (?)] to plant trees and others to penetrate the soil,[1] having got rid of the martial [tru]mpet, and not [having to worry about (?)] spells of guard-duty [at] un[godly hours (?) . . .]

This fragment is in the same hand as those of the "Dike play" (q.v.) (frr. 281a-b) and would fit very well into it; cf. Dike's account of her taming of Ares in fr. 281a.31–41. If so, the speaker here is probably still Dike.

[1] sc. with the plough.

451q

CHORUS

[*Remains of five lines*]
The [commander (?)] from the sea-girt [land (?)],
the defender of the cit[y], was des[tro]yed
by the s[he]pherds of men[1] [. . .]

[1] i.e. kings (cf. the Homeric formula ποιμένα λαῶν), probably meaning Agamemnon and Menelaus.

ὄρχαμ[οί] τ᾽ ἐπίϲκο[ποι
10 τευχ[έ]ων [ἀ]πε[λ]πίϲαντ[

ἀντ. δίκᾳ δ᾽ Ὀδυϲϲῆϊ ξυνῆϲαν [
    ο]ὐκ ἰϲο[ρ]ρ[όπ]ῳ φρενί·
      ] ϲφιν εὐθύν[...] .. [
    μελ]αγχίτων[
15 . [..] .. αιϲ ξιφοκτον[οιϲ

    ὥϲπερ καὶ Τελαμω[ν
    αὐ]τοκτόνος ὤλετο [
    [Remains of one further line.]

9 (end) suppl. Snell   10 [ἀ]πε[λ]πισ- Kakridis:
[ἐ]πε[λ]πίσ- Snell; then e.g. -σαντ[α θείων] or -σαντ['
Ἀχιλλέως]   11 (end) [ἀρχοὶ] Lloyd-Jones   14 (beginning) [φρὴν] Snell   16 Τελαμῶ[νος ἐσθλὸς υἱὸς] e.g.
Lloyd-Jones; or perh. e.g. Τελαμω[νιάδας ὁ μείζων]

and the control[ling] ruler[s]
when he [lost] the hope of gaining the [divine (?)]
     armour.

In the dispute [the rulers (?)] sided with Odysseus –
their minds were [n]ot evenly [b]al[anc]ed.
[*In the next three lines the only intelligible words are*
     steer for them (?) *(13)*, [bla]ck-garbed *(14)*, *and*
     slaying with the sword *(15)*.]

Just as [the greater (?) son of] Telamon[2]
perished by his [ow]n hand [. . .]

*As Snell and others have noted, this summary of the events leading
to the death of Ajax almost certainly does* not *come from a play
about those events themselves; lines 16–17 seem to be comparing
the fate of Ajax to the actual or prospective fate of someone else. It
could well, however, as Mette proposed, come from* Women of
Salamis, *if the comparison is taken to be between Ajax and Teucer.
In principle it might also come from another play set in Salamis or
Attica (since "defender of the city" could refer to Ajax's posthumous role as a hero protecting Athens) at some time after the Trojan war; but other than* Women of Salamis *and* Eumenides, *no
Aeschylean play we know of fits that description.*

[2] This restoration is based on the Homeric formulae μέγας
Τελαμώνιος Αἴας *and* Αἴαντος . . . Τελαμωνιάδαο.

DOUBTFULLY ASCRIBED
FRAGMENTS

This section includes: (i) one fragment (fr. 452a = 61a Radt) assigned by Radt, without direct evidence, to a specific play of Aeschylus, and which I would regard as only possibly, not probably, of Aeschylean authorship;[1] (ii) the fragments of one line or more, other than papyrus fragments, printed by Radt in his "Fragmenta dubia" section, excluding those for which I see no good reason to regard Aeschylean authorship as a substantial possibility;[2] (iii) four fragments (here numbered 489a–d) which in TrGF are printed among the Adespota *but for which there is a substantial possibility of Aeschylus being the author.*

---

[1] I have excluded altogether fr. 164 Radt, of whose existence there is no trace before the sixteenth century; see R. de Lucia, *Atti dell'Accademia Pontaniana* 38 (1989) 113–120.   [2] The excluded fragments are frr. 453, 456, 458, 467, and 471–4 Radt; also omitted from this section is fr. 469 Radt (= *Eum.* {286}).

452

οὐ χρὴ λέοντος σκύμνον ἐν πόλει τρέφειν

Aristophanes, *Frogs* 1431a (Aeschylus speaking); attributed to Aeschylus by Grotius

Most mss. (but not V A E[ac] K[ac] M[ac] Np1 Vb3) add another verse (1431b) μάλιστα μὲν λέοντα μὴ ʼν πόλει τρέφειν, which Zielinski diagnosed as a doublet of 1431a[1]

[1] B. B. Rogers in his edition (London, 1902) argued that Aristophanes substituted 1431b for 1431a when *Frogs* was restaged; K. J. Dover (Oxford, 1993) argued the reverse.

452a (61a)

τί δʼ ἀσπίδι ξύνθημα καὶ καρχησίῳ;

Anonymous collection of proverbs (*CPG* Suppl. i p.41); attributed to Aeschylus by Kaibel, to *The Edonians* by Kassel (cf. fr. 61)

καρχησίῳ Cohn: καρχησίων cod.

465

ὃς εἶχε πώλους τέσσαρας ζυγηφόρους
φιμοῖσιν αὐλωτοῖσιν ἐστομωμένας

Eustathius on *Iliad* 18.495, citing Pausanias the Atticist (α169 Erbse); attributed to Aeschylus by Soping and Stanley (misled by Eustathius' reference, just previously, to Pausanias α168 which cites Aesch. fr. 419); attribution doubted by Erbse, but can still be supported on stylistic grounds

452

One ought not to rear a lion's whelp in a city.[1]

[1] Cf. *Ag.* 717–736, on how a man reared a lion-cub *in his house* with disastrous results.

452a

What connection has a shield with a drinking-cup?

Possibly from Lycurgus' taunting interrogation of Dionysus (cf. Aristophanes, Thesmophoriazusae *140, cited above on fr. 61).*[1]

[1] I suspect, however, with Kaibel, that the verse may rather come from a comic parody, for example in Eupolis' *Taxiarchs* (cf. Eupolis frr. 272, 276), where Dionysus is represented as attempting incompetently to function as a soldier or sailor, or Eubulus' *Dionysius* (cf. Eubulus fr. 24)

465

. . . who had four young mares under the yoke, equipped with muzzles with pipes.[1]

From a description of a warrior in a chariot (Memnon has been suggested).

[1] Cf. *Seven* 463–4: "his horses . . . are snorting in their harness, eager to fall upon the gate; their muzzles, filled with the breath of their proud nostrils, are whistling [n.b.] a barbarian music".

DOUBTFULLY ASCRIBED FRAGMENTS

466

ζόης πονηρᾶς θάνατος αἱρετώτερος·
τὸ μὴ γενέσθαι δ' ἐστὶν ἢ πεφυκέναι
κρεῖσσον κακῶς πάσχοντα

Stobaeus 4.53.17 (Αἰσχύλου); [Menander], *Monosticha* 276
(line 1 only); authenticity doubted by Butler, denied by Dindorf

1 αἱρετώτερος [Menander] (cf. Aristophanes, *Knights* 84;
Xenophon, *Lacedaemonian Constitution* 9.1; Isocrates 4.95):
εὐπορώτερος Stobaeus   2 ἐστὶν Grotius: ἐστὶ μᾶλλον
codd.   3 πάσχοντα A (S omits the line): πράσσοντα
Grotius: πράσσοντι Blaydes

468

καὶ μὴ (?) πρὸς ὀργὴν σπλάγχνα θερμήνῃς κότῳ

Aristophanes, *Frogs* 844 (Dionysus addressing Aeschylus); attributed to Aeschylus by Hermann

καὶ μὴ may be an adjustment by Aristophanes to fit his context
(so Radt): Aeschylus could have written e.g. μή τοι

470

γύναι (?), γυναιξὶ κόσμον ἡ σιγὴ φέρει

Sophocles, *Ajax* 293: the scholia say that the line is by
"Aeschines the orator"; Peppink suggested they meant Aeschylus

γύναι may be a modification by Sophocles (so Radt); Aeschylus could have written e.g. αἰεὶ or χρησταῖς

466

Death is preferable to a wretched life;[1] and it is better not
to be born than to be born and suffer misery.

[1] Cf. fr. 90; Radt suggests that this line is nothing but a variant
form of fr. 90 (and lines 2–3 an entirely separate quotation by
Stobaeus from a different author), but the repeated appearance
of αἱρετώτερος in expressions of the same sentiment in the fifth
and fourth century (see apparatus) is a phenomenon requiring explanation.

468

And (?) do not heat up your inward parts with angry
wrath.[1]

[1] Neatly parodied by Euripides, *Cyclops* 424, who for κότῳ
"wrath" substitutes ποτῷ "drink".

470

Woman (?), it is silence that gives women dignity.

DOUBTFULLY ASCRIBED FRAGMENTS

489a (adesp. 208)

ἐμπεδὴς δὲ γάμορος
ἔμαρψεν Ἅιδης

Hesychius ε2425; Photius ε738 (ἐμπεδὴς γάμορος only); attributed to Aeschylus by West

1–2 δὲ γάμορος ἔμαρψεν West: γάμορος μάρψεν Hesychius (which could be right, if the verse is lyric)

489b (adesp. 291)

λακιστὸν ἐν πέτραισιν εὑρέσθαι μόρον

Lucian, *The Fisherman* 2 (speaking of the death of "some Pentheus or Orpheus"); attributed to Aeschylus by West (who assigns it to *Bassarids*; but *Wool-Carders* or *Pentheus* are also possible)

489c (adesp. 375)

ἀλλ' εἴ σ' ἔνυπνον φάντασμα φοβεῖ
χθονίας θ' Ἑκάτης κῶμον ἐδέξω

Plutarch, *Moralia* 166a; attributed to Aeschylus by Porson

1 εἴ σ' Wilamowitz: εἴτ' codd.

489a (adesp. 208)

Hades, the relentless Owner of the Soil,[1] laid hold on him/
her.

---

[1] The noun γάμορος, which in ordinary usage means "land-
owner", appears here to be re-etymologized as "he who received
the soil (i.e. everything below ground level) for his portion", sc. in
the sharing out of the universe between Hades and his brothers
Zeus and Poseidon (*Iliad* 15.187–191).

489b (adesp. 291)

. . . to find his death by being torn apart among the rocks.

*Referring either to the death of Orpheus on Mount Pangaeum, or
to that of Pentheus on Mount Cithaeron.*

489c (adesp. 375)

But if you are terrified by a vision seen in sleep
and have been visited by the revel-band of Hecate[1] from
    the underworld . . .

*Anapaests; probably a chorus reassuring an apprehensive
hero(ine).*

---

[1] Cf. Euripides, *Helen* 569–570 where Menelaus, thinking he
is beholding a phantom in Helen's shape, begs Hecate to send
instead "friendly apparitions", and Helen assures him that the
woman he sees is not "an attendant of Enodia [= Hecate] appear-
ing in a vision of the night".

DOUBTFULLY ASCRIBED FRAGMENTS

489d (adesp. 391)

θύννος βολαῖος πέλαγος ὡς διαστροβεῖ

Plutarch, *Lucullus* 1.5 and *Moralia* 554f; attributed to Aeschylus by Stark (who assigned it to *Net-Haulers*; but *Glaucus the Sea-god* is also possible)

διαστροβεῖ *Mor*.: διεστρόβει *Luc*. (the tense in each case is that required by the context in Plutarch)

489d (adesp. 391)

He/it is/was[1] stirring up the sea like a netted tunny.

Clearly from a satyr-drama; probably referring either to the floating chest containing Danaë and Perseus (in Net-Haulers)[2] *or to Glaucus when first seen in the waters (in* Glaucus the Sea-god).[3]

[1] Plutarch quotes the line once in the present tense and once in the imperfect, each time using the tense that fits his own context; we cannot tell which of the two quotations has been altered for this purpose and which has not. [2] In this case the line might come either from the prologue (before fr. 46a; the speaker would probably be the Fisherman) or from the later scene in which the satyrs hauled the chest ashore (the speaker would then probably be Silenus). Either way, the tense of the verb would probably be present. [3] In this case the line might come from the speech of the Oxherd of which fr. 25e is part, and since the Oxherd is describing what he *has seen* (κατεῖδον, fr. 25e.12), the tense of the verb would doubtless be imperfect.

CONCORDANCE

Except as shown here, all fragments in this edition are numbered as in *TrGF*.

TrGF	This edition
23	23.1+23a.1
23a	23b
61a	452a
78a	78c.1–36, 61–72
78c	78c.37–52, 73–end
168	220a
168a	220b
168b	220c
187a	206
198	281c
296	150a
300	126a
341	23a.2
369	207b
375	(*LB* 983a)
404	215a
451k	180a
451l	78a
adesp. 144	23.2
adesp. 208	489a
adesp. 291	489b
adesp. 375	489c
adesp. 391	489d

INDEX

This index includes all mentions of personal or place names in the (Greek) text of the fragments, but only the more significant references in the introductions and annotations. References are to fragment numbers. In general, entries for countries, regions or cities (e.g. Phocis, Argos) include references to their peoples (e.g. Phocians, Argives). Reference to names mentioned in the text are in boldface; those to names mentioned in an annotation only are in regular type. References to play introductions are included only for names that do not appear in the fragments of, or annotations to, the play in question. They are made by quoting the number of the first fragment of the play that is printed in this edition, *preceded* by an asterisk; e.g. references to the introduction to *Athamas* appear as *1. Where the play has no fragment long enough to be printed in this edition, its introduction is referred to by quoting the number of the last preceding fragment, *followed* by an asterisk; thus a reference to the introduction to *Laius* would appear as 116*.

INDEX

INDEX

INDEX

INDEX